PENGUIN REFERENCE

The Penguin Dictionary of Accounting

Dr Christopher Nobes is PricewaterhouseCoopers Professor of Accounting at the University of Reading. He has held temporary posts at universities in San Diego, New York, Sydney, Hobart and Auckland. He was a visiting professor at the University of Nyenrode (Netherlands) from 1994 to 2001 and is now a visiting professor at the University of Venice.

He is author or co-author of fourteen books, including *The Economics of Taxation* (seventh edition, 2001), *An International Introduction to Financial Accounting* (2001), *Comparative International Accounting* (sixth edition, 2000), *Pocket Accounting* (fourth edition, 2001), *International Guide to Interpreting Company Accounts* (second edition, 1999) and *The Convergence Handbook* (2000).

He was a member of the Accounting Standards Committee of the UK and Ireland from 1987 to 1990, and one of the two UK representatives on the Board of the International Accounting Standards Committee from 1993 to 2001. He is now a member of the ICAEW Financial Reporting Committee and is vice-chairman of the accounting working group of the Fédération des Experts Comptables Européens, a body which advises the EC Commission.

The Penguin Dictionary of

Accounting

Christopher Nobes

PENGUIN BOOKS

PENGUIN BOOKS

Published by the Penguin Group
Penguin Books Ltd, 80 Strand, London WC2R 0RL, England
Penguin Putnam Inc., 375 Hudson Street, New York, New York 10014, USA
Penguin Books Australia Ltd, 250 Camberwell Road, Camberwell, Victoria 3124, Australia
Penguin Books Canada Ltd, 10 Alcorn Avenue, Toronto, Ontario, Canada M4V 3B2
Penguin Books India (P) Ltd, 11 Community Centre, Panchsheel Park, New Delhi – 110 017, India
Penguin Books (NZ) Ltd, Cnr Rosedale and Airborne Roads, Albany, Auckland, New Zealand
Penguin Books (South Africa) (Pty) Ltd, 24 Sturdee Avenue, Rosebank 2196, South Africa

Penguin Books Ltd, Registered Offices: 80 Strand, London WC2R 0RL, England

www.penguin.com

First published 2002

6

Copyright © Christopher Nobes, 2002

The moral right of the author has been asserted

Set in 7.75/10.25 pt ITC Stone Serif
Typeset by Rowland Phototypesetting Ltd, Bury St Edmunds, Suffolk
Printed in England by Clays Ltd, St Ives plc

Coventry University

Contents

List of Figures   vi
List of Tables   vii
Introduction   ix

Dictionary of Accounting   1

List of Figures

Figure 1   An account form balance sheet (USA)   35
Figure 2   A statement form balance sheet (UK)   36
Figure 3   Some types of taxes   284

List of Tables

Table 1   Abbreviated company names   69
Table 2   Professional accountancy bodies in the UK
            and Ireland   75

Introduction

A theory is gaining ground among historians that the origins of both writing and numbering systems are closely connected to the need to keep account. Today, as 5,000 years ago, civilization is not possible without tax, and tax is not possible without some accounting. So, for us, there is nothing as certain as death and taxes and accounting. At the Last Judgment, we shall all be called to account.

This dictionary is designed for those who read, write or speak accounting terms; for preparers of financial statements, auditors, managers, investors, students, and so on. The book's scope is set by the territory of accountants: financial accounting (including bookkeeping and financial reporting), management accounting and control, auditing and taxation, with forays across the borders into economics, finance and law.

Increasingly, the language of accounting is English. However, the UK and US versions of many accounting terms are different. There is also the English of the International Accounting Standards Committee (IASC). The standards of that body are already used in many countries, and may soon become compulsory for the consolidated statements of listed companies throughout the EU. This dictionary is based on UK and IASC terms (which are often the same), with frequent inclusion of, and contrast to, US terms.

As is common in a dictionary, certain terms in the definitions are highlighted (in SMALL CAPITALS) to show that readers can find those terms defined, in their turn, elsewhere. This technique could, in principle, be used in at least three ways:

(a) in all cases where a word is defined elsewhere;
(b) in cases where it might sometimes be helpful to cross-refer, depending on the expertise of the reader; and
(c) only when no reader could properly understand the word without cross-referring.

The first option would lead to vast usage of small capitals. The third would lead to very sparse use. Given a wide variety of potential readers, this only leaves the second. Consequently, a word in small capitals does not denote the *need* to refer elsewhere, but only the *ability* to do so when necessary. It may often be helpful for beginners, but perhaps seldom necessary for advanced readers.

In writing this dictionary, I have benefited greatly from hundreds of suggestions for improvement from my colleagues, Bob Parker and Alan Roberts. Again, as usual, Carol Wright has cheerfully processed all the words. I also thank my Penguin editor, Martin Toseland, for encouragement and support.

Christopher Nobes
University of Reading
March 2001

AAA Abbreviation for the AMERICAN ACCOUNTING ASSOCIATION.

AARF Abbreviation for the AUSTRALIAN ACCOUNTING RESEARCH FOUNDATION.

AAS Abbreviation for an Australian Accounting Standard.

AASB Abbreviation for the Australian Accounting Standards Board.

AAT Abbreviation for the ASSOCIATION OF ACCOUNTING TECHNICIANS (of the UK).

abacus An instrument for arithmetical calculation, involving the sliding of beads along rods. It has an ancient lineage and is still used in parts of the world. The word is also used as the title of Australia's oldest academic accounting journal, based at the University of Sydney.

abatement A reduction (perhaps leading to cancellation) of a payment. For example, an insufficiency of funds might lead to a pro rata reduction in payments to settle competing claims on those funds.

ABB Abbreviation for ACTIVITY-BASED BUDGETING.

abbreviated accounts Abbreviated FINANCIAL STATEMENTS filed in the UK by SMALL and MEDIUM COMPANIES with the REGISTRAR OF COMPANIES. Permission is granted by the COMPANIES ACT to file such statements under certain conditions, such as that the auditors confirm that the legal provisions are satisfied.

ABC Abbreviation for ACTIVITY-BASED COSTING.

ability-to-pay In the context of taxation, a taxpayer's taxable capacity, bearing in mind both the item to be taxed (e.g. income or wealth) and any inevitable calls on the item. For example, when calculating taxable income, the income tax system might take account of allowances for subsistence or for the support of children.

abnormal gain An excess of manufacturing output over that anticipated after taking the NORMAL LOSS into account.

abnormal loss A deficit of manufacturing output below that anticipated after taking the NORMAL LOSS into account.

abnormal shrinkage Part of an ABNORMAL LOSS of output caused by unexpected SHRINKAGE.

abnormal spoilage Part of an ABNORMAL LOSS of output caused by unexpected SPOILAGE.

abnormal waste Part of an ABNORMAL LOSS of output caused by unexpected WASTE.

above par In excess of the PAR VALUE or NOMINAL VALUE of a FINANCIAL INSTRUMENT.

above the line An expression relating to the INCOME STATEMENT or PROFIT AND LOSS ACCOUNT. The 'line' in question is the NET PROFIT of such statements. A 'below the line' amount would include an appropriation such as dividends. Thus, an 'above the line' amount is an EXPENSE or REVENUE of the business. EARNINGS PER SHARE figures are calculated excluding below the line amounts.

abridged accounts FINANCIAL STATEMENTS published outside of the general requirements of the COMPANIES ACT; also called 'non-statutory accounts'. Such accounts might include extracts published in newspapers.

absorb To attach an OVERHEAD COST to another account heading, as in ABSORPTION COSTING.

absorbed overhead The amount of the OVERHEAD costs of an enterprise that has been included in PRODUCT COSTS as part of a mechanism of ABSORPTION COSTING.

absorption costing The allocation of all FIXED and VARIABLE COSTS of production in the calculation of the cost of goods or services produced. This can be compared to MARGINAL COSTING.

absorption rate A ratio, calculated in advance of a production period, by which the OVERHEAD COSTS are included in PRODUCT COST. Absorption rates can be calculated by reference to the amount of labour used, the units of output produced, and so on.

ACA Abbreviation for an Associate of the INSTITUTE OF CHARTERED ACCOUNT- ANTS IN ENGLAND AND WALES.

Academy of Accounting Historians A body, based in the USA, which promotes the study of accounting history.

ACCA Abbreviation for the ASSOCIATION OF CHARTERED CERTIFIED ACCOUNT- ANTS, or an Associate of that body.

accelerated cost recovery system A method, used in the USA, whereby DEPRECIATION is allowed at a faster rate than might be thought to be commercially realistic. This is allowed for tax purposes and is designed to encourage investment.

accelerated depreciation DEPRECIATION at a faster rate than would be sug- gested by normal economic criteria. This is most commonly found in the context of tax concessions designed to encourage investment. For the calculation of taxable income in such cases, businesses would be allowed to depreciate certain assets (such as energy-saving devices or assets in depressed regions) more quickly than accountants otherwise would. This occurs in many countries; for the UK system, *see* CAPITAL ALLOWANCES.

acceleration The speeding up of the repayment of debts.

acceptance credit A line of credit at a bank which is granted to a foreign importer of goods against which a domestic company (the exporter) can draw.

accommodation bill A BILL OF EXCHANGE which is guaranteed by someone.

account In a BOOKKEEPING system, a record of all the transactions relating to a particular person or item.

accountability *See* STEWARDSHIP.

accountancy The profession or activities of accountants. Sometimes, the word ACCOUNTING is used to refer to the technical or academic subject matter, whereas 'accountancy' relates to the professional practice, and might be taken to include AUDIT. The word is also used as the title of the journal of the INSTITUTE OF CHARTERED ACCOUNTANTS IN ENGLAND AND WALES.

accountancy bodies Institutes and associations of accountants. *See* ACCOUNT- ANCY PROFESSION.

accountancy profession The representative bodies of accountants. The oldest professional bodies of accountants in the private sector were formed in the 1850s in Edinburgh and Glasgow. Shortly afterwards, there was similar activity throughout the English-speaking world, and eventually elsewhere. (For more detail on the UK bodies, *see* CONSULTATIVE COMMITTEE OF ACCOUNTANCY BODIES.)

The professional bodies set standards of entry for training; they operate training and examination systems; they make ethical and technical rules.

The profession is also organized at an international level (*see* GROUPE D'ETUDES DES EXPERTS COMPTABLES DE LA CEE, INTERNATIONAL FEDERATION OF ACCOUNTANTS).

accountant A person engaged in the work of ACCOUNTING. The term is not defined in law, so it can be used rather loosely. Sometimes it refers to an accountant who has qualifications and belongs to an ACCOUNTANCY BODY.

Accountants' International Study Group (AISG) A body founded in 1966, comprising members from professional accountancy bodies in the UK, the USA and Canada. Its purpose was to study and report on accounting practices in the three countries. Twenty studies were issued, mainly on financial reporting matters, e.g. on INVENTORIES (1968), CONSOLIDATED FINANCIAL STATEMENTS (1972) and INTERIM REPORTS (1975). The AISG was wound up in 1977 when the INTERNATIONAL FEDERATION OF ACCOUNTANTS was formed.

accountants' report As a technical term, this refers to a report included as part of a PROSPECTUS of a company that is seeking a listing on a stock exchange.

account code A number allocated to a particular account within an organized numerical system of accounts, such as a CHART OF ACCOUNTS.

accounting The various technical activities performed by accountants, including FINANCIAL ACCOUNTING, BOOKKEEPING and MANAGEMENT ACCOUNTING.

accounting bases A similar term to ACCOUNTING POLICIES.

accounting concepts A similar term to ACCOUNTING CONVENTIONS.

accounting conventions The assumptions on which accounting practice is based or ought to be based. Lists of such assumptions might include PRUDENCE and CONSISTENCY. They can be linked together in a CONCEPTUAL FRAMEWORK.

accounting entity The unit for which FINANCIAL STATEMENTS are prepared. *See*, also, REPORTING ENTITY.

accounting equation (balance sheet equation) An algebraic representation of a summary of what happens in the DOUBLE-ENTRY BOOKKEEPING system. The BALANCE SHEET might be expressed as $A_0 = L_0 + C_0$ (Eq. 1) i.e. TOTAL ASSETS at time zero = total LIABILITIES and TOTAL CAPITAL at time zero. The capital figure grows from time zero to time one by the earning of profit for the period; i.e. $C_0 + P_1 = C_1$ (Eq. 2). The profit (P_1) is made up of the total REVENUES less the total EXPENSES of the period: i.e. $P_1 = R_1 - E_1$ (Eq. 3). It is, of course, also the case that $A_1 = C_1 - L_1$ (Eq. 4).

Thus, inserting (Eq. 3) in (Eq. 2), we get:

$C_1 = C_0 + R_1 - E_1$

Inserting this in (Eq. 4), we get:

$A_1 = L_1 + C_0 + R_1 - E_1$

Rearranging this, we get:

$A_1 + E_1 = L_1 + C_0 + R_1$

That is, the items on the left (assets and expenses) are all the debits, which are seen to equal the items on the right (liabilities, capital and revenues) which are all the credits. This is a basic principle of double-entry bookkeeping.

accounting event A transaction or other change that is recorded in the BOOKS OF ACCOUNT of an enterprise.

accounting exposure The risk that a loss would be recorded due to adverse foreign currency movements. For example, depending on the method of CURRENCY TRANSLATION used, an enterprise might have accounting exposure if it had an excess of ASSETS over LIABILITIES denominated in a foreign currency. It might then be exposed to a loss if the foreign currency fell. *See*, also, ECONOMIC EXPOSURE.

Accounting Hall of Fame A means of honouring eminent accountants, organized by the Ohio State University in the USA.

accounting identity *See* ACCOUNTING EQUATION.

accounting manual An organized written description of an enterprise's accounting procedures. Most large companies would be expected to maintain such a manual, particularly for the training of staff and use by AUDITORS.

accounting period *See* FINANCIAL YEAR.

accounting plans Detailed rules for the maintenance of BOOKKEEPING records and the preparation of annual financial reports. In some countries, the plans are issued by government-controlled committees. Several European countries, including France and Spain, use such plans. The plans generally include CHARTS OF ACCOUNTS.

accounting policies The detailed methods of RECOGNITION and MEASUREMENT which a particular company has chosen from those generally accepted by law, ACCOUNTING STANDARDS or commercial practice. These policies must be used consistently, and must be disclosed (this is required in the UK, for example, by FINANCIAL REPORTING STANDARD 18 and by COMPANY LAW). A company's ANNUAL REPORT will include a 'statement of accounting policies' that have been applied in the FINANCIAL STATEMENTS.

Examples of DISCLOSURE of policies would include whether a company was using STRAIGHT-LINE or REDUCING BALANCE DEPRECIATION; whether it was using FIFO or average cost for the valuation of inventory STOCKS; and how it was treating provisions for future pension payments.

accounting principles The word 'principles' is a slight problem in accounting. In the USA it tends to mean conventions of practice, whereas in the UK it means something more fundamental and theoretical. Thus, the American 'GENERALLY ACCEPTED ACCOUNTING PRINCIPLES' encompasses a wide range of broad and detailed accounting rules of practice. In the UK, the detailed rules are often called 'practices', 'policies' or 'bases'; and broader matters like ACCRUALS or CONSERVATISM were traditionally referred to as 'concepts' or 'conventions'.

However, perhaps because lawyers (and including those in Brussels) were involved in the drafting of the EC FOURTH DIRECTIVE which led to the Companies Act 1981 in the UK, British usage is now more confused. The 1981 Act referred to five broad 'principles' of accounting: GOING CONCERN, CONSISTENCY, PRUDENCE, the ACCRUAL BASIS (including matching) and separate valuation. The first four were all to be found in the UK's STATEMENT OF STANDARD ACCOUNTING PRACTICE 2, described as 'concepts'.

The problem with these broad principles, in any country, is that there is potential for conflict. For example, in a going concern, the matching concept suggests that development costs ought to be carried forward and matched against the future revenues that they are designed to create (*see* RESEARCH AND DEVELOPMENT COSTS). However, prudence suggests that because it is *possible* that no benefits will arise, all research and development (R & D) costs should be immediately charged as expenses. This would also lead to greater consistency. Similar remarks would apply to advertising expenditure.

In the USA, conservatism and consistency win, as can be seen in STATEMENT OF FINANCIAL ACCOUNTING STANDARDS 2, which does not allow the capitalization of R & D costs. In the UK, the initial Exposure Draft 14 followed that precedent, but after complaints from heavy R & D spenders, Exposure Draft 17 and the subsequent STATEMENT OF STANDARD ACCOUNTING PRACTICE 13 allowed capitalization of development expenditure under prudent conditions.

It is clear that trade-offs between the principles are necessary. It is fortunate, then, that these mandatory principles are vague and may be broken in (disclosed) special circumstances or in order to allow a TRUE AND FAIR VIEW.

There are many other accounting conventions, such as MATERIALITY and via the MONEY MEASUREMENT CONVENTION.

Accounting Principles Board (APB) Set up in the USA in 1959 by the AMERICAN INSTITUTE OF CERTIFIED PUBLIC ACCOUNTANTS (AICPA). It replaced the AICPA's Committee on Accounting Procedure which, between 1939 and 1959 had issued fifty-one ACCOUNTING RESEARCH BULLETINS. The APB lasted until it, too, was replaced in 1973 by the FINANCIAL ACCOUNTING STANDARDS BOARD (FASB).

The APB issued thirty-one 'Opinions' and four 'Statements'. In many cases these have not been replaced by subsequent standards, and thus remain part of GENERALLY ACCEPTED ACCOUNTING PRINCIPLES.

The demise of the APB followed the setting up of two committees by the AICPA to investigate deficiencies in the rule-making procedures. One source of dissatisfaction was alleged dominance by large accountancy firms. The WHEAT REPORT of 1972 led to the FASB. Another problem was seen to be the lack of a CONCEPTUAL FRAMEWORK. The TRUEBLOOD REPORT led to the FASB's major project designed to discover or invent such a framework.

accounting rate of return *See* RATE OF RETURN.

accounting records *See* BOOKS OF ACCOUNT.

accounting reference date The last day of a company's ACCOUNTING REFERENCE PERIOD.

accounting reference period A legal term in the UK for a company's accounting year. The time limits for holding an ANNUAL GENERAL MEETING and for FILING OF ACCOUNTS are set in terms of lengths of time after the last day of the period (the ACCOUNTING REFERENCE DATE).

Accounting Regulatory Committee A body of the European Commission that considers whether INTERNATIONAL FINANCIAL REPORTING STANDARDS are suitable for adoption in the European Union. It is advised by the EUROPEAN FINANCIAL REPORTING ADVISORY GROUP.

Accounting Research Bulletins Documents produced between 1939 and 1959 by the Committee on Accounting Procedure of the AMERICAN INSTITUTE OF CERTIFIED PUBLIC ACCOUNTANTS. There were fifty-one such bulletins, some of which have not been superseded by the publications of the ACCOUNTING PRINCIPLES BOARD or the FINANCIAL ACCOUNTING STANDARDS BOARD.

Accounting Research Studies Publications of the AMERICAN INSTITUTE OF CERTIFIED PUBLIC ACCOUNTANTS in which particular technical issues in financial reporting were investigated, with recommendations for setting ACCOUNTING STANDARDS.

Accounting Series Releases Pronouncements from the SECURITIES AND EXCHANGE COMMISSION on issues relating to financial reporting. This series has been ended and new pronouncements are called FINANCIAL REPORTING RELEASES.

accounting standards Technical accounting rules of RECOGNITION, MEASUREMENT and DISCLOSURE. The exact title of accounting standards varies from country to country. The practical use of the term seems to have originated officially with the ACCOUNTING STANDARDS STEERING COMMITTEE (later the ACCOUNTING STANDARDS COMMITTEE) in the UK in 1970. Standards in the UK are called STATEMENTS OF STANDARD ACCOUNTING PRACTICE ('SSAPs') and (from those after 1990) FINANCIAL REPORTING STANDARDS ('FRSs'). In the USA, STATEMENTS OF FINANCIAL ACCOUNTING STANDARDS ('SFASs') have been issued by the FINANCIAL ACCOUNTING STANDARDS BOARD (FASB) since its foundation in 1973.

In the UK, the standards are designed to be used in the preparation of all FINANCIAL STATEMENTS intended to give a TRUE AND FAIR VIEW, and the latter is required by COMPANY LAW for all companies. Directors of large companies are required to disclose departures from standards. One sanction for a company whose directors break standards is generally a qualification of the AUDIT REPORT. Also, the standards would be persuasive in a court of law that was determining whether a set of financial statements gave a true and fair view.

In the USA, the standards of the FASB form part of GENERALLY ACCEPTED ACCOUNTING PRINCIPLES, which are insisted upon by the SECURITIES AND EXCHANGE COMMISSION. In Canada, the professionally set standards are incorporated into law.

Standards were often criticized for being inconsistent with each other and for not being based on a CONCEPTUAL FRAMEWORK. They may be criticized by practical accountants for reducing the room to manoeuvre or to give a fair view.

Accounting Standards Board (ASB) UK body which has set ACCOUNTING STANDARDS since 1990. Like the FINANCIAL ACCOUNTING STANDARDS BOARD in the USA, the ASB is independent of (though influenced by) the accountancy profession and the government.

The ASB has two full-time and eight part-time members, who are appointed by the FINANCIAL REPORTING COUNCIL. A subsidiary committee is the URGENT ISSUES TASK FORCE.

Accounting Standards Committee (ASC) UK body that set ACCOUNTING STANDARDS until 1990. The ASB was set up in 1970 (known, until 1976, as the ACCOUNTING STANDARDS STEERING COMMITTEE) by the INSTITUTE OF CHARTERED ACCOUNTANTS IN ENGLAND AND WALES (ICAEW) soon joined by the five other major UK and Irish accountancy bodies: the INSTITUTE OF CHARTERED ACCOUNTANTS OF SCOTLAND, the INSTITUTE OF CHARTERED ACCOUNTANTS IN IRELAND, the CHARTERED ASSOCIATION OF CERTIFIED ACCOUNTANTS, the CHARTERED INSTITUTE OF MANAGEMENT ACCOUNTANTS and the CHARTERED INSTITUTE OF PUBLIC FINANCE AND ACCOUNTANCY.

The cause of the setting up of the Committee was a gradual loss of confidence in the profession's technical rules. This was partly the result of several scandals and catastrophes. For example, in October 1967, during a contested takeover by the General Electric Company, Associated Electrical Industries Ltd (AEI) forecast a profit of £10 m for 1967. In July 1968 a loss of £4.5 m was reported instead. Accounting for the difference, the former joint auditors of AEI attributed 'roughly £5 m to adverse differences which are matters substantially of fact rather than judgement and the balance of some £9.5 m to adjustments which remain substantially matters of judgement'. Other disquieting events were the collapse of Rolls Razor and the bid by Leasco Data Processing Equipment Corporation for Pergamon Press Ltd.

At the end of 1969, the ICAEW published a 'Statement of Intent on Accounting Standards in the 1970s', which led to the formation of what was to become the ASC.

The ASC was replaced by the ACCOUNTING STANDARDS BOARD in 1990 after a review of its operations.

Accounting Standards Steering Committee A committee of the UK and Irish accountancy profession, which became the ACCOUNTING STANDARDS COMMITTEE in 1976.

accounting system The records and procedures used within an enterprise to collect accounting data, process them and report them. The term may also be used, in an international comparative context, to mean the accounting features shared by all of (or a set of) the enterprises within a country.

accounting technician A skilled worker in such fields as BOOKKEEPING, generally less highly qualified than a member of one of the main ACCOUNTANCY BODIES.

accounts The accounting records of an enterprise. In the UK, the term is also used to mean the FINANCIAL STATEMENTS of an enterprise.

accounts payable US expression for CREDITORS, particularly unpaid suppliers.

accounts receivable US expression for DEBTORS, particularly amounts due from customers.

accretion The increase in an asset caused by physical growth. For example, BIOLOGICAL ASSETS such as forests grow in size and value even if prices stay at the same level.

accrual *See* ACCRUED EXPENSE.

accrual basis of accounting One of the underlying assumptions of financial reporting, whereby transactions and other events are reported in the periods to which they relate, rather than when CASH is received or paid. Part of the accrual basis is the MATCHING of EXPENSES and REVENUES. The accrual basis is not used in CASH FLOW STATEMENTS.

accruals concept *See* ACCRUAL BASIS OF ACCOUNTING.

accrued benefits Benefits due to a member of a PENSION SCHEME relating to the service performed up to date.

accrued benefits method An ACTUARIAL VALUATION METHOD which does not take account of prospective service that current employees might be expected to give.

accrued charge *See* ACCRUED EXPENSES.

accrued expenses Those expenses which relate to an ACCOUNTING PERIOD but will not be paid until later. They result from the need regularly to draw up FINANCIAL STATEMENTS at a fixed time, e.g. at the end of a company's year.
   During a year, electricity will be used or properties will be rented, yet at the year end the related bills may not have been paid. Thus, at the year end, 'accrued' expenses are charged against income by accountants even though cash has not been paid or perhaps the bills even received. The DOUBLE-ENTRY BOOKKEEPING for this is the creation of a CURRENT LIABILITY on the BALANCE SHEET, which is the credit corresponding to the debit 'ACCRUED EXPENSES'. This practice may apply also to wages and salaries, taxes, and so on. An allocation of amounts to 'this year' and 'next year' may be necessary where a supplier's account straddles two accounting years. The practice is an example of the use of the ACCRUAL BASIS OF ACCOUNTING.

accrued income Those revenues which relate to an accounting period but will not be received until later. For example, interest income may relate to a particular year but be received in cash shortly after the year end. According to the ACCRUAL BASIS OF ACCOUNTING, the income should be recognized before its receipt in this case.

accrued liability A LIABILITY recognized on a BALANCE SHEET as a result of an ACCRUED EXPENSE.

accrued revenue *See* ACCRUED INCOME.

accumulated depreciation The total amount by which the CARRYING VALUE of a FIXED ASSET has so far been reduced to take account of the fact that it is wearing out or becoming obsolete (*see* DEPRECIATION).

accumulated dividend A dividend that has not been paid on a company's CUMULATIVE PREFERENCE SHARES.

accumulated earnings *See* RETAINED PROFITS.

accumulated fund The total of the members' financial interests in a NON-PROFIT organization such as a charity. It is equivalent to the EQUITY of a profit-making enterprise.

accumulated profits *See* RETAINED PROFITS.

accumulating compensated absences COMPENSATED ABSENCES that can be carried forward and used in future. In the context of accounting for EMPLOYEE BENEFITS, the employees in some companies are entitled to a particular number of days of paid sickness or other absence in a year. In some cases, those benefits unused can be carried forward by the employee. This creates a LIABILITY for the employer.

accumulating shares Shares issued to existing shareholders in exchange for forgoing dividends.

acid test *See* QUICK RATIO.

ACIS Abbreviation for an Associate of the INSTITUTE OF CHARTERED SECRETARIES AND ADMINISTRATORS (of the UK).

ACMA Abbreviation for an Associate of the CHARTERED INSTITUTE OF MANAGEMENT ACCOUNTANTS (of the UK).

acquired surplus A US term generally meaning the RETAINED PROFITS of an enterprise at the date on which it was purchased by another.

acquiree An enterprise that is purchased in a BUSINESS COMBINATION accounted for as an ACQUISITION.

acquirer An enterprise that purchases another in a BUSINESS COMBINATION accounted for as an ACQUISITION.

acquisition A BUSINESS COMBINATION in which one of the enterprises obtains control over another enterprise in exchange for the transfer of ASSETS, incurrence of a LIABILITY or issue of EQUITY. In the USA, this is called a 'purchase'. An acquisition (purchase) is accounted for by bringing all the components of the NET ASSETS of the acquiree at FAIR VALUES. Any excess of acquisition cost over the fair value of the net assets is GOODWILL. The alternative method of accounting for certain business combinations is called MERGER ACCOUNTING (UK), POOLING OF INTERESTS (USA) or UNITING OF INTERESTS (INTERNATIONAL ACCOUNTING STANDARDS).

acquisition accounting *See* ACQUISITION.

AcSB Abbreviation for the Accounting Standards Board of the CANADIAN INSTI-
TUTE OF CHARTERED ACCOUNTANTS.

ACT Abbreviation for ADVANCE CORPORATION TAX.

active market In the context of INTERNATIONAL ACCOUNTING STANDARDS,
a market where *all* the following exist:

(a) the items traded are homogeneous;
(b) willing buyers and sellers can normally be found; and
(c) prices are available to the public.

   This definition is used, for example, in the context of accounting for INTAN-
GIBLE ASSETS. Intangible assets are only allowed to be revalued if there is an
active market in which to assess their FAIR VALUE.

active stocks Shares in a company whose shares are traded frequently on a
stock exchange.

activity-based budgeting The process of allocating resources on the basis of
separately identifiable functions or activities within a business. A BUDGETING
system on this basis would also include monitoring how the planned allocations
relate to the outcomes.

activity-based costing A modern system of COST ACCOUNTING whereby costs
are collected on the basis of functions or activities, and then allocated to products
on the basis of their use of those activities.

activity-based management The control of an organization by the use of
ACTIVITY-BASED COSTING.

activity ratio The level of production for a period as a proportion of that
regarded as reasonably achievable.

actual cost The cost incurred, as opposed to the planned standard or budgeted
cost, of particular activities.

actuals (physicals) Commodities themselves, as opposed to FUTURES CON-
TRACTS related to them.

actuarial assumptions An enterprise's best estimates of the demographic and
financial variables that will determine the ultimate cost of providing POST-
EMPLOYMENT BENEFITS such as pensions. Such assumptions include those concerning mortality rates, future salary levels and DISCOUNT RATES.

actuarial gains and losses Gains and losses which result from:

(a) experience adjustments (the effects of differences between the previous ACTU-ARIAL ASSUMPTIONS and what has actually occurred); and

(b) the effects of changes in actuarial assumptions.

The context is accounting for pensions and other forms of POST-EMPLOYMENT BENEFITS. The actuarial gains and losses are taken to income or postponed, depending on their size and nature.

actuarial valuation method The techniques used to measure the size of defined benefit employee obligation. The method generally required is the PROJECTED UNIT CREDIT METHOD. The term 'actuarial method' can also be used, in LEASE ACCOUNTING, to refer to the apportionment of rentals on a compound interest basis.

actuary A professional expert in probability theory and statistics related to mortality, particularly concerned with calculations in the insurance industry.

added-value statement *See* VALUE ADDED STATEMENTS.

additional paid-in capital US term for SHARE PREMIUM, the excess paid in by purchasers of a company's shares in excess of PAR VALUE. An equivalent term is 'CAPITAL SURPLUS'.

additional voluntary contributions Extra voluntary payments made by employees into PENSION SCHEMES. These enhance subsequent pension benefits. Up to a point, such contributions are tax-deductible.

adjudication A decision of a court on the subject, e.g. of BANKRUPTCY arrangements or taxes.

adjusted trial balance A list (TRIAL BALANCE) of the balances in a BOOKKEEPING system after they have been adjusted at a period end for various items such as the closing inventory/STOCKS.

adjusting entries Entries in a BOOKKEEPING system designed to take account of items that are measured at a period end, such as DEPRECIATION or closing inventory/STOCKS.

adjusting events (post balance sheet events) Events after the BALANCE SHEET date that lead to a change to the ASSETS and LIABILITIES recognized in the balance sheet (*see* POST BALANCE SHEET EVENTS).

administration Generally, the management of an organization, but also used as a specific legal term to mean the running of a potentially insolvent company under a court order designed to allow reorganization and recovery.

administration cost variance The difference between the budgeted ADMINIS-TRATIVE EXPENSES for a period and those actually incurred.

administration order An order of court which places a potentially insolvent company into the hands of a professional administrator who is required to try to reorganize and rescue the company. It gives certain temporary protections from CREDITORS.

administration overheads Those INDIRECT COSTS of an organization that are caused by general management activities that cannot be related to such functions as manufacturing or distribution.

administrative expenses Expenses related to the management of an enterprise, but not including cost of sales, selling costs, financial expenses and tax.

administrative receiver A person appointed by the holder of a FLOATING CHARGE on a company's ASSETS in order to recover money from the company.

administrator Generally, a manager of an organization, but also used as a specific legal term to mean a person appointed by a court to look after the affairs of an intestate deceased person or a company under an ADMINISTRATION ORDER.

ADR Abbreviation for an AMERICAN DEPOSITARY RECEIPT.

ad valorem duty A tax based on the value of an item rather than on its size or other features.

advance A payment in excess of, or earlier than, the amounts originally agreed.

Advance Corporation Tax Part of the UK corporation tax system until 1999. As its name suggests, it was an advance payment of part of the CORPORATION TAX liability of a company. The tax was triggered by the payment of a DIVIDEND, and its size was proportionate to the size of the dividend.

advancement A payment made to a child, during a parent's lifetime, out of what would be received by the child as heir.

adverse opinion In a UK context, a statement by an AUDITOR as part of the AUDIT REPORT that a company's FINANCIAL STATEMENTS do not give a TRUE AND FAIR VIEW or in some other way do not comply with the COMPANIES ACT.

adverse variance An unfavourable difference between a budgeted amount and the actual outcome, e.g. if a cost exceeds the budget for it, that is an adverse variance.

advice note A notification from a supplier to a customer that goods have been despatched.

AFA Abbreviation for the ASEAN FEDERATION OF ACCOUNTANTS.

affiliate A US term with no precise meaning, referring to an enterprise linked to another in some way.

AG *Aktiengesellschaft*, an Austrian, German or Swiss equivalent to a UK PUBLIC LIMITED COMPANY. Not all such companies are listed on a stock exchange.

age allowance As part of the UK income tax system, a personal allowance for taxpayers aged 65 and over that is taken into account in the calculation of taxable income.

age analysis The categorization of amounts of DEBTORS on the basis of how old the balances are. The purpose is to enable attention to be focused on the collection of overdue amounts.

agency costs Costs that arise when the owners of companies are separate persons from the managers. Such costs may include monitoring the agents and suffering inefficiencies of various kinds. *See* AGENCY THEORY.

agency fee As a technical term, an amount paid to an AGENT for managing a loan.

agency theory An application in accounting research of theories from economics and the behavioural sciences. It is suggested that directors and other managers (the agents), particularly those of a large company, have many aims other than that of maximizing the long-run wealth of the owners of the company, the shareholders (the principals). Thus, the behaviour of managers with respect, for example, to dividend policy or the choice of accounting policies, will only be predictable by assuming self-interest and studying what that would lead to.

When it comes to choosing accounting policies or to lobbying for or against particular changes in ACCOUNTING STANDARDS, managers may consider the effects of the change on declared profit figures. This may involve them in considerations of the effects on their compensation schemes or their reputations as managers if profits seem too large or small.

This problem of the inefficiencies that may result from the separation of management from ownership is also important in more general considerations of the theory of the behaviour of companies.

agent A person appointed to act on behalf of another person (the PRINCIPAL). In companies, the directors act as agents for the shareholders.

aggregate depreciation Synonym for ACCUMULATED DEPRECIATION.

agio The difference between two rates. In Dutch, the equivalent to SHARE PREMIUM.

AGM Abbreviation for an ANNUAL GENERAL MEETING.

agreed bid An offer to buy out the shareholders of a company which is supported by the majority of the company's shareholders.

agricultural produce The harvested product coming from BIOLOGICAL ASSETS. If the biological asset is a sheep, then the agricultural produce might include wool or a carcass to be used for meat products.

agricultural property relief An allowance within the UK's INHERITANCE TAX on the transfer of agricultural property under certain conditions.

AIBD Abbreviation for the ASSOCIATION OF INTERNATIONAL BOND DEALERS.

AICPA Abbreviation for the AMERICAN INSTITUTE OF CERTIFIED PUBLIC ACCOUNTANTS.

AIM Abbreviation for the ALTERNATIVE INVESTMENT MARKET (of the UK).

AIMR Abbreviation for the ASSOCIATION FOR INVESTMENT MANAGEMENT AND RESEARCH.

AISG Abbreviation for the ACCOUNTANTS' INTERNATIONAL STUDY GROUP.

Aktiengesellchaft An Austrian, German or Swiss equivalent of a UK PUBLIC LIMITED COMPANY. It literally means a 'shares' company. There are about 2,000 such companies in Germany, most of which are not listed on a stock exchange.

AktG Abbreviation for the *Aktiengesetz*, a German law regulating AG companies.

all-inclusive income concept The inclusion of all items of profit and loss in the PROFIT AND LOSS ACCOUNT. For example, EXTRAORDINARY ITEMS would be included. In principle, no items should go directly to RESERVES. At present, UK, USA and INTERNATIONAL ACCOUNTING STANDARD accounting are loosely based on this concept, but nevertheless the profit and loss account still does not show COMPREHENSIVE INCOME.

allocation In the context of COST ACCOUNTING, the process of charging the whole of a cost to a COST CENTRE rather than leaving some or all as an OVERHEAD to be absorbed or apportioned. In the context of FINANCIAL ACCOUNTING, 'allocation' means the process of spreading costs over different accounting periods.

allotment The process of allocating the available shares to those who have applied to buy them.

allotted shares Newly issued shares allocated to particular applicants.

allowable capital loss In the context of the UK's CAPITAL GAINS TAX system, an amount that can be set against CAPITAL GAINS in order to reduce the amount of tax paid.

allowance for doubtful accounts US term for provision for BAD DEBTS.

allowances In the UK, a term used for amounts deducted from invoices to take account of such items as damaged goods.
In the US, an expression for PROVISIONS against the value of an ASSET, i.e. amounts charged against profit in anticipation of reductions in value. For an example, *see* BAD DEBTS.

all-purpose financial statements Similar term to GENERAL PURPOSE FINANCIAL STATEMENTS.

alternative accounting rules The legal requirements in the UK Companies Act 1985 on the subject of departures from HISTORICAL COST for the valuation of ASSETS. For example, TANGIBLE FIXED ASSETS may be valued at a market value (not necessarily a current one) or at CURRENT COST.

alternative budgets BUDGETS drawn up on a variety of different assumptions about future decisions and events.

Alternative Investment Market A secondary stock exchange in London designed for smaller companies with good growth prospects.

American Accounting Association A body whose primary membership is accounting academics in the USA. It organizes large conferences each summer, in a North American city, at which research is discussed and university recruitment carried out. It also publishes several academic journals including *The Accounting Review* and *Accounting Horizons*.

American depositary receipt (ADR) A document issued by a US bank acknowledging the deposit of a specified number of shares in a foreign company. An ADR can be traded on US stock markets without the company itself being listed on a US market. This enables the company to avoid the extensive requirements of the SECURITIES AND EXCHANGE COMMISSION.

American Institute of Certified Public Accountants (AICPA) The main US professional body of accountants. It was founded in 1887 (as a predecessor body) and has over 330,000 members. It is responsible for ethical guidance for the profession, for setting auditing standards that lead to GENERALLY ACCEPTED AUDITING STANDARDS and for an examination system. Until 1973, it was also responsible for ACCOUNTING STANDARDS, but that role has now been taken over by the FINANCIAL ACCOUNTING STANDARDS BOARD. However, the AICPA still provides comment on the agenda and exposure drafts of standard setters, and it issues its own Statements of Position.

Just as companies in the USA must be registered by state rather than federally, so CERTIFIED PUBLIC ACCOUNTANTS (CPAs) must belong to a state body of CPAs. The total number of such CPAs somewhat exceeds those who have joined the AICPA. The rules for entry to the state CPA societies varies from state to state.

american option An OPTION that can be exercised at any time before its expiry.

amortization A word used, particularly in North America, to refer to certain types of DEPRECIATION, particularly that relating to INTANGIBLE ASSETS. The term can also refer to any gradual expiration over time.

amortized cost A term that could mean either the amount of cost of an ASSET that has been amortized, or the amount of the cost after deducting what has already been amortized.

amortizing loan A loan which is repaid in several instalments rather than with one payment.

analysis of variance As a statistical term (often abbreviated (*see* ANOVA)), this means the segregation of the total variation in a dependent variable into the proportions accounted for by the explanatory variables and a residual. In a MANAGEMENT ACCOUNTING context, the term means the segregation of the VARIANCE in the total profit of an organization into sub-variances.

analytical auditing A technique of AUDITING that lays greater stress on those areas revealed to be weak by evaluations of INTERNAL CONTROL and by comparing a company's financial and non-financial data with internal and external reference points.

analytical review One method of audit testing, used as a complement to computations, verbal enquiries, inspection of records, etc. It involves the review of FINANCIAL STATEMENTS, accounting records and other documents for unusual items or for the reasonableness of totals. The AUDITOR should ensure that the financial statements show a picture consistent with his or her knowledge of the underlying circumstances of the business.

Anglo-Saxon accounting Financial reporting practices in the English-speaking
world. Although these vary from country to country within that world (just as
the use of the language does), there is a common origin and a common philosophy
behind them all. As with the predominant language, the financial reporting
practices of the USA, Canada, Australia, New Zealand and Ireland are British in
origin. In the case of the USA, the practices of London, Manchester, Glasgow and
Edinburgh were exported in the late nineteenth and early twentieth centuries in
the most obvious of ways, i.e. by British accountants emigrating. For example,
Arthur Young and James Marwick (names incorporated in BIG FIVE firms) moved
from Glasgow to the USA.

Perhaps the most obvious common characteristic is the emphasis on FAIR
PRESENTATION OF FINANCIAL STATEMENTS for the purpose of decision making
by investors. In the USA and Canada, this is expressed as a requirement for
FINANCIAL STATEMENTS to be fairly presented. In the other countries above, the
requirement is to show a 'TRUE AND FAIR VIEW'. This includes use of several
ACCOUNTING PRINCIPLES mentioned in that entry, and also substantial use of
the concept of MATERIALITY, whereby unimportant amounts are not shown or
not necessarily treated exactly correctly. Another relevant expression here is
'SUBSTANCE OVER FORM', whereby figures are shown in accordance with economic reality rather than legal form.

The Netherlands also tends to have accounting of a similar type as, of course,
do many members of the British Commonwealth. The obvious contrast is the
legal/tax basis of accounting in Germany.

The differences between these two main types of accounting probably arise
from the English common law system (as opposed to codified continental law),
the importance of private shareholders as providers of finance (as opposed to
bankers and governments), and the resulting lack of importance of tax rules for
financial reporting in the Anglo-Saxon world. Some evidence for the differences
may be seen under STOCK EXCHANGES and ACCOUNTANCY PROFESSION.

annual accounts UK term for those FINANCIAL STATEMENTS of an enterprise
that are prepared annually. For companies, such accounts must be filed with
the REGISTRAR OF COMPANIES. Compulsory elements of a company's annual
accounts are generally a BALANCE SHEET, PROFIT AND LOSS ACCOUNT, STATE-
MENT OF TOTAL RECOGNIZED GAINS AND LOSSES, CASH FLOW STATEMENTS
and notes. The DIRECTORS' REPORT and the AUDITORS' REPORT must also be
filed.

annual exemption Within the UK's INHERITANCE TAX system, the amount
that can be transferred each year without being taken into account when calculating liability to the tax.

annual general meeting (AGM) A meeting of the SHAREHOLDERS of a
company held once a year. (To be more exact under UK law, there must be a gap
of no more than 18 months between AGMs.) At the meeting, shareholders may

question directors on the contents of the ANNUAL REPORT and FINANCIAL STATE-MENTS, vote on the directors' recommendation for dividends, vote on replacements for retiring members of the board and conduct other business within the rules laid down by their company's MEMORANDUM OF ASSOCIATION and ARTICLES OF ASSOCIATION.

Under certain conditions, EXTRAORDINARY GENERAL MEETINGS are also held at the request of the directors or shareholders. Normally, they are due to some crisis.

The equivalent US expression is 'annual meeting of stockholders'.

annual percentage rate (APR) The equivalent in annual terms of a rate of interest specified for shorter periods. This rate must be disclosed by lenders or credit grantors under UK consumer law.

annual report A document sent to shareholders after a company's year end. It must contain a report by directors, the FINANCIAL STATEMENTS, and the report of the AUDITORS. Most large companies also include a less formal report in the form of a CHAIRMAN'S REPORT.

annual return In the UK, a legal document required to be filed by a company with the REGISTRAR OF COMPANIES after a company's ANNUAL GENERAL MEETING. The return includes details of the company, its shares and its directors. The FINANCIAL STATEMENTS must also be attached.

annuitant A person entitled to receive an ANNUITY.

annuity A series of equal payments at equal intervals for an agreed period. The agreed period might be a number of years or a person's lifetime, or it could be in perpetuity. An annuity can be purchased by paying a lump sum to, for example, a life assurance company.

annuity certain An ANNUITY which runs for a fixed period in terms of months or years rather than being perpetual or depending on the lifetime of a person.

annuity method A method of DEPRECIATION of ASSETS designed to take account of the time value of money. The intention is to produce a constant total annual charge for depreciation plus capital cost. As interest cost on the outstanding investment falls over the life of the asset, so depreciation cost is arranged to rise. In practice, this method is rarely used.

ANOVA Abbreviation for ANALYSIS OF VARIANCE.

anti-trust laws US laws designed to prohibit the restraint of trade. The laws are opposed to monopolies, cartels and price-fixing. In 2000, the Microsoft company was a famous target of such laws.

APB Abbreviations for the ACCOUNTING PRINCIPLES BOARD (of the US) or the AUDITING PRACTICES BOARD (of the UK).

APC Abbreviation for the AUDITING PRACTICES COMMITTEE (of the UK).

applicable accounting standards A UK legal term referring to ACCOUNTING STANDARDS issued by bodies prescribed by the COMPANIES ACT. From 1990, the relevant body has been the ACCOUNTING STANDARDS BOARD, but that body also approved the standards of its predecessor, the ACCOUNTING STANDARDS COMMITTEE. Large UK companies are required to state whether their FINANCIAL STATEMENTS are in compliance with applicable accounting standards, and to give details of, and reasons for, any departure from them.

application and allotment account An account within the DOUBLE-ENTRY BOOKKEEPING system designed to record the cash received from those applying to be SHAREHOLDERS. The account is cleared when the new sharesare allotted to successful applicants or the cash is returned to unsuccessful applicants.

application for listing A formal request by a company for its securities to be listed on a stock exchange. Such a company must comply with a number of procedures, including following the LISTING REQUIREMENTS of the appropriate exchange.

application for quotation The technical term for an APPLICATION FOR LISTING in the case of the London Stock Exchange.

applied research Original investigation designed to discover new scientific or technical knowledge related to a specific practical objective. This can be contrasted to pure research which has no specific practical objective, and to development which is designed to produce new or improved products, processes, etc. The accounting treatment for expenditure on applied research under UK, US and INTERNATIONAL ACCOUNTING STANDARD rules is to charge it immediately in the INCOME STATEMENT.

apportionment In the context of EXECUTORSHIP, the splitting of receipts and payments between types of beneficiaries under a will. In the context of COST ACCOUNTING, the charging of costs to COST CENTRES where the costs are not directly incurred by those centres.

appraisal The valuation of an ASSET or LIABILITY by a qualified expert.

appreciation An increase in value (usually some form of MARKET VALUE) of an ASSET. Under a strict HISTORICAL COST ACCOUNTING system, such appreciation is not recognized in the accounting records of the business until the asset is sold and the gain is realized. This is the case for most assets in the USA, Japan and

Germany, and the practice is partly followed because of CONSERVATISM and partly because of the need for OBJECTIVITY; before the asset is sold one cannot be sure exactly what its market value is. Also, in a GOING CONCERN, the market value of FIXED ASSETS is not necessarily of interest to the users of FINANCIAL STATEMENTS. However, most systems of INFLATION ACCOUNTING make adjustments to asset values to record appreciation.

In the UK and several other countries, the rules about recognizing appreciation are more permissive (*see* REVALUATION).

appropriation   The allocation of the NET PROFITS of an enterprise for an accounting period. For example, some part of the profits of a company may be allocated to the shareholders in the form of DIVIDENDS. In public sector accounting, an appropriation is an amount authorized to be spent for a particular purpose.

appropriation account   An expression sometimes used to describe that part of the PROFIT AND LOSS ACCOUNT where the NET PROFIT for the year is appropriated to the owners or ploughed back into the business. Appropriations are, then, ways of using up profit once it has been calculated. Dividends are appropriations, as are transfers to various RESERVES. Thus, these amounts are *not* expenses of the running of the business. It is not clear whether to regard taxation as an expense or as an appropriation, but it is generally treated as an expense.

In the published FINANCIAL STATEMENTS of UK companies, appropriations are made as a continuation of the profit and loss account. In the financial statements of PARTNERSHIPS the appropriation account will normally be a more obvious separate account, including, of course, the splitting up of the profit to the various partners.

In the USA, the expression 'statement of retained earnings' is more usual.

APR   Abbreviation for ANNUAL PERCENTAGE RATE.

ARB   Abbreviation for an ACCOUNTING RESEARCH BULLETINS.

arbitrage   Linked purchases and sales of items in more than one market where prices are different. The items may be currencies, commodities or securities. The 'prices' may include interest rates or currency rates. The price differential would have to be large enough in order to cover the costs of the transactions.

arbitrage pricing theory   A theory that uses several factors (not only a security's risk with respect to the market) to explain the movements in security prices. This can be contrasted to the CAPITAL ASSET PRICING MODEL.

arbitration   The settling of a dispute by using an arbitrator rather than through a court of law.

arm's length transaction A purchase, sale or other transaction where the parties involved are not related commercially or in other ways such that the price or other conditions could have been influenced away from a fair market price. Where transactions are not conducted on this basis, enterprises are required to make RELATED PARTY TRANSACTION disclosures.

arrears Liabilities not paid by their due date.

ARS Abbreviation for ACCOUNTING RESEARCH STUDIES.

Article of Incorporation A document setting out the name and nature of a US corporation. It is analogous to the MEMORANDUM OF ASSOCIATION in the UK.

Articles of Association A document drawn up at the foundation of a UK company, setting out the rights and duties of the shareholders and directors, and the relationship between one class of shareholders and another. (*See*, also, MEMORANDUM OF ASSOCIATION.) In the USA, similar rules will be found in the BYLAWS.

articulated accounts FINANCIAL STATEMENTS that form a coherent arithmetic whole. In the UK, for example, the PROFIT AND LOSS ACCOUNT, STATEMENT OF TOTAL RECOGNIZED GAINS AND LOSSES and BALANCE SHEET are articulated. Together, they summarize all the recorded amounts in the DOUBLE-ENTRY BOOK-KEEPING system.

artificial person An entity recognized in law as equivalent to a physical person. For example, for many purposes, a company is an artificial person in that it can own property, be sued and pay taxes in its own name.

ASB Abbreviation for the ACCOUNTING STANDARDS BOARD, the current UK standard setting body.

ASC Abbreviation for the ACCOUNTING STANDARDS COMMITTEE, a former UK standard setting body.

ASEAN Federation of Accountants A grouping of ACCOUNTANCY BODIES in the ASEAN region of east Asia.

A shares Generally, non-voting ORDINARY SHARES in a company. These are now unpopular.

ASIC Abbreviation for the AUSTRALIAN SECURITIES AND INVESTMENTS COMMISSION.

ASOBAT The abbreviation for *A Statement of Basic Accounting Theory*, which was an early (1966) attempt at a CONCEPTUAL FRAMEWORK for financial reporting. It stressed the needs of users of FINANCIAL STATEMENTS. It was published by the AMERICAN ACCOUNTING ASSOCIATION.

ASRs Abbreviation for ACCOUNTING SERIES RELEASES of the SECURITIES AND EXCHANGE COMMISSION.

ASRB Abbreviation for the Accounting Standards Review Board, a former standard setting body in Australia.

ASSC Abbreviation for the ACCOUNTING STANDARDS STEERING COMMITTEE, a former UK standard setting body.

asset Generally, in the English-speaking world, something controlled that has future economic benefits. However, it turns out that to define exactly what an accountant means by an 'asset' is exceptionally difficult. Various attempts have been made, particularly in the USA. A definition is contained in part of the CONCEPTUAL FRAMEWORK project in the USA (in *Statement of Financial Accounting Concepts*, 3). According to that document, the existence of an asset relies upon 'probable future economic benefits obtained or controlled by a particular entity as a result of past transactions or events'. The INTERNATIONAL ACCOUNTING STANDARDS COMMITTEE (IASC) and UK standard setters use a similar definition.

When all the assets in the BALANCE SHEET are added together, the result will be the 'TOTAL ASSETS'. When the amounts due to outsiders (the LIABILITIES) are deducted, what remains is the NET ASSETS or NET WORTH of the business. Of course, because of the unrecorded assets and the sometimes curious valuation conventions of accountants, the 'net worth' is probably much less than the business is worth! (*See* below and, also, ASSET VALUATION.)

There are several problems with the definition of assets. For example, are machines which are on long LEASES to be considered as assets of the lessee? Legally they still belong to the LESSOR, but in many cases the economic substance of the initial leasing transaction is very similar to a purchase plus a loan. The practice in the USA and the UK has moved towards treating many leased assets as those of the LESSEE.

A second example is a new highway. It may be of great benefit to a company, and some of the company's taxes may have helped to pay for it. Also the company has rights to its use. However, the highway is not controlled by the company, and is fairly clearly not the company's asset. Equally straightforwardly, substantial expense may be involved in the drilling of an oil well, only to discover that it is a 'dry hole'. Since it will bring no future benefits, it is not counted as an asset.

In the case of some companies, such as Coca-Cola, the most important 'assets' do not appear at all on the balance sheet. The value of such companies rests on their future earning power which rests upon customer loyalty, brand names, trained staff, skilled management and so on. These items are generally not recognized as assets by accountants because their cost cannot be identified and their valuation would not have OBJECTIVITY. It is not at all clear exactly what they are worth or exactly what has been spent to create them. Yet, they will bring future benefit, and amounts are constantly expended to create or preserve them. However, when a business is sold, an amount in excess of the accounting value of the assets may be paid. In the FINANCIAL STATEMENTS of the purchaser, this excess is recorded as an asset called GOODWILL.

Thus, the accounting definition of an asset (and whether to recognize assets) is heavily hemmed-in by a number of conventions, all of which have good reasons behind them. However, the net result is not necessarily easily comprehensible or satisfactory.

asset-backed fund A FUND containing mainly assets other than MONETARY ASSETS.

asset classification The categorization of assets on a BALANCE SHEET. For example, in UK law, assets must first be classified as FIXED ASSETS or CURRENT ASSETS. Within those two classes, assets are further split into groups. To some extent, MEASUREMENT of the value of the assets follows from this. For example, current assets are generally valued at the lower of cost and NET REALIZABLE VALUE.

asset cover A ratio that shows the number of times that an enterprise's debt is covered by its NET ASSETS. A high cover is one indication of SOLVENCY.

asset deficiency An excess of LIABILITIES over ASSETS. In other words, an enterprise's NET ASSETS are negative, which suggests that it may not be financially viable.

asset register A record of an enterprise's FIXED ASSETS, showing such items as the cost, depreciation and date of purchase.

asset revaluation reserve A part of EQUITY which records the amount by which ASSETS have been revalued in excess of their cost.

asset stripping Asset stripping or financial surgery was particularly popular in the UK in the late 1960s and early 1970s. It is normally associated with the purchase of a business by financial entrepreneurs who have calculated that the asking price for the business as a going concern is lower than the total amount that could be raised by selling the assets separately.

asset valuation The MEASUREMENT of assets for the purpose of recording them in a BALANCE SHEET. The traditional method of valuation is HISTORICAL COST ACCOUNTING, whereby ASSETS are valued at purchase price or production cost, less DEPRECIATION, i.e. at net HISTORICAL COST. There are good reasons for this, such as CONSERVATISM and a desire for OBJECTIVITY. However, particularly when prices have risen, the historical cost of an asset may be misleading, given that many non-accountants assume that assets are recorded at a market price. In some countries, including the UK but not the USA, land and buildings are sometimes revalued to reflect the increase in what they could be sold for. The problem is that there are few rules: some companies revalue annually, some every five years, some never.

FIXED ASSETS other than land and buildings tend to be more uniformly shown at net historical cost, though it should be remembered that depreciation is not an exact measurement.

CURRENT ASSETS are valued at the lower of cost and NET REALIZABLE VALUE, though in North America REPLACEMENT COST is sometimes used where it is even lower. DEBTORS/ACCOUNTS RECEIVABLE are valued at what the enterprise prudently expects to receive, and CASH is valued at its FACE VALUE.

asset value (per share) The total value of the ASSETS of a company in its BALANCE SHEET divided by the number of issued ORDINARY SHARES. It should be remembered that some of a company's assets are not recognized and many others are measured at something other than MARKET VALUE.

assignment The legal transfer of the rights and duties under a contract, including a FINANCIAL INSTRUMENT or a LEASE.

associate A term used to include an ASSOCIATED COMPANY but which could also include analogous enterprises that are not companies.

associated company A UK term for a company in which another has a PARTICIPATING INTEREST and over which the other has significant influence. The 'equity method' (described below) is used to account for such companies in CONSOLIDATED FINANCIAL STATEMENTS. An enterprise will be presumed to be an associate if it is owned to the extent of from 20 to 50 per cent of the voting equity. Above 50 per cent ownership, it is almost certainly a subsidiary; under 20 per cent ownership, it normally becomes a trade investment. Companies held as joint ventures with other owners are treated as associated companies in the UK or USA.

The equity method (*see* EQUITY ACCOUNTING) as used in consolidated financial statements, involves recording the associate in the BALANCE SHEET as a single line, called 'investment in ASSOCIATED UNDERTAKINGS'. This is valued at the cost of the investment in the associate at the time of purchase *plus* the appropriate proportion of the UNDISTRIBUTED PROFITS made by the associate since that date (in the UK, the cost will be split into the appropriate proportion of the FAIR VALUE of the assets and the implied GOODWILL).

Dividends passing from the associated company to its owner cause cash to increase and 'investment in associated undertakings' to decrease by the same amount. Profits earned by the associate cause the owner's consolidated profits to be increased by the appropriate share, and 'investment in associated undertakings' to rise by the same amount.

associated undertakings A term used to include an ASSOCIATED COMPANY but which also includes analogous enterprises that are not companies.

Association for Investment Management and Research A body, based in the US, which acts as a professional society for investment analysts.

Association of Accounting Technicians A UK-based body whose members are less well qualified than those belonging to ACCOUNTANCY BODIES. Such bodies also exist in other countries and are sometimes called second-tier accountancy bodies.

Association of Authorized Public Accountants A UK-based body, some of whose members can become REGISTERED AUDITORS under the COMPANIES ACT. It is not a member of the CONSULTATIVE COMMITTEE OF ACCOUNTANCY BODIES.

Association of Chartered Certified Accountants One of the six chartered bodies of accountants in the UK and Ireland. The association's earliest predecessor body was founded in 1891. Many of the association's members live outside the UK.

Association of International Accountants One of the bodies of accountants, based in the UK, some of whose members can become REGISTERED AUDITORS under the COMPANIES ACT. It is not a member of the CONSULTATIVE COMMITTEE OF ACCOUNTANCY BODIES.

Association of International Bond Dealers A body whose name was self-explanatory, and has been renamed the INTERNATIONAL SECURITIES MARKET ASSOCIATION.

assurance A term whose technical meaning relates to a type of insurance against inevitable events (e.g. life assurance), but which can be used more generally to mean various forms of checking, including AUDIT.

assured As a technical term, a person or sum involved in a life assurance policy.

ATII Abbreviation for an Associate of the CHARTERED INSTITUTE OF TAXATION (of the UK).

attainable standard A cost (or other measure) that is possible under the most efficient operating conditions, but which includes normal amounts of wastage.

attest To witness (generally in written form) a signature or other event.

attest function The process of providing a written AUDIT OPINION on the compliance of FINANCIAL STATEMENTS with various requirements, such as that to give a TRUE AND FAIR VIEW.

at-the-money option A contract giving the holder the right to buy securities or other assets at a price which is now the current price.

attributable profit The profit earned so far on a construction contract, calculated on the basis of the proportion of work done.

attribute-based costing A framework to increase the efficiency of an organization by integrating ACTIVITY-BASED COSTING with market research and other techniques.

attributes sampling In an AUDIT context, an examination of a proportion of a population of items (e.g. invoices) to determine whether a particular QUALITATIVE CHARACTERISTIC (e.g. a proper signature) is generally present.

audit *See* AUDITING.

Audit Commission A government agency in England and Wales responsible for the appointment of AUDITORS and the oversight of audits of local authorities.

audit committee A committee to which those undertaking a company's EXTERNAL AUDIT report. This committee's members may be, in the majority, non-executive directors of the company. It is recommended practice for listed companies to establish an audit committee.

audit completion checklist A list of items to be checked at the end of an AUDIT, including such items as whether the FINANCIAL STATEMENTS being audited include all DISCLOSURES required by law and by ACCOUNTING STANDARDS.

audit evidence Information gathered by auditors in order to arrive at their AUDIT OPINION on FINANCIAL STATEMENTS. Such evidence includes that directly obtained by the AUDITOR (e.g. attendance at a physical count of INVENTORIES), that supplied by management (e.g. the BOOKS OF ACCOUNT), and that supplied by third parties, e.g. confirmation by DEBTORS of amounts owed to the company.

audit exemption Exemption by law from the requirement to appoint an AUDITOR to give an AUDIT OPINION on FINANCIAL STATEMENTS. In the UK, PRIVATE LIMITED COMPANIES below a certain size are so exempt. The size level has been raised several times. In 2000, it was raised to £1 m turnover.

audit expectations gap *See* EXPECTATIONS GAP.

audit fee The remuneration receivable by an AUDITOR specifically for work on the audit. In the UK, the fees for the audit of a company must be agreed by the ANNUAL GENERAL MEETING. The fee must be disclosed, in the notes included in the FINANCIAL STATEMENTS, separately from any amounts payable to the auditors for non-audit work.

auditing Generally, the monitoring by independent experts of the reports by managers on their STEWARDSHIP of resources. The basic aim of a modern AUDIT in the UK is to give an opinion to the shareholders on whether the FINANCIAL STATEMENTS drawn up by the directors of a company give a TRUE AND FAIR VIEW. In order to do this, an AUDITOR needs to check the physical existence and valuation of important assets, and to examine the systems of INTERNAL CONTROL to ensure that transactions are likely to have been recorded correctly. If internal control is poor, the auditor will ask for it to be improved and will increase the amount of checking done on sample transactions. If the control systems look good, relatively small samples of various types of transactions may be checked.

The auditor would generally be expected to circularize a sample of some of the debtors to confirm that they exist. The auditor would normally attend the count of the INVENTORIES (in the UK, the annual stock take), and would try to spot and to question unusual items in the BOOKS OF ACCOUNT or financial statements. The rules for auditing vary from firm to firm, but are to some extent found in AUDITING STANDARDS.

The directors and auditors will be hoping that the AUDIT REPORT can be 'unqualified', as a result of the relevant laws and standards being followed, and the overall impression of a fair view being given. In order to achieve this, the auditors will try to persuade the directors to make any necessary changes to the PUBLISHED ACCOUNTS.

Auditing is a very ancient activity. By derivation, it means 'hearing' (*audit* is derived from the Latin for 'he hears'). Auditing was thus originally the process whereby the owner heard the account given by his steward of the use of the owner's resources for a period (*see* STEWARDSHIP). By the nineteenth century, the many owners of a large company would appoint one of their number to be a specific auditor of the financial statement prepared by the directors whom they had appointed to manage the company. This was partly because the process of auditing had become more complicated as business itself became more complicated.

In the UK, audit became compulsory for limited liability banks as a result of the Companies Act 1879 which followed the spectacular failure of the City of Glasgow Bank in 1878. The Companies Act 1900 made audit compulsory for all companies. Since the 1980s, certain smaller companies are exempted. In the USA, audit is compulsory for companies registered with the SECURITIES AND EXCHANGE COMMISSION.

The qualifications that company auditors must have are also set down: membership of a CERTIFIED PUBLIC ACCOUNTANT (CPA) body in the USA, or in the UK membership of one of four of the bodies of the CONSULTATIVE COMMITTEE OF

ACCOUNTANCY BODIES (or some other individuals recognized by the Department of Trade and Industry). This provides a large amount of government-required work for accountants of recognized institutes. It is the single most important type of work for the members of these bodies, although many members work in other fields. Auditing is now very complex, so high standards of training are necessary. Entry standards and examinations are now of high quality.

In Anglo-Saxon countries, auditing is carried out by individuals or by firms which vary greatly in size. Some firms have thousands of partners and many more staff. However, the audit is always the ultimate responsibility of a member of one of the appropriate professional bodies. *See*, also, INTERNAL AUDIT.

auditing guidelines Statements in the UK which supplement AUDITING STANDARDS.

Auditing Practices Board The committee of the CONSULTATIVE COMMITTEE OF ACCOUNTANCY BODIES that is responsible for preparing AUDITING STANDARDS and Guidelines in the UK and Ireland.

Auditing Practices Committee A former committee of the CONSULTATIVE COMMITTEE OF ACCOUNTANCY BODIES that was responsible for preparing AUDITING STANDARDS in the UK until 1991. It was replaced by the AUDITING PRACTICES BOARD.

auditing standards Rules for the practice of AUDITORS which detail the work to be covered by an audit and the standard practice for the AUDIT REPORT. The UK rules are drawn up by the AUDITING PRACTICES BOARD.

Auditing Standards Board A US body responsible for preparation and publication of AUDITING STANDARDS.

audit manual A written set of internal procedures and policies governing the conduct of an AUDIT. Each firm of AUDITORS maintains such a manual, and some of them publish their manuals.

audit opinion A statement by AUDITORS concerning their view about compliance by an enterprise with a particular set of regulations or standards. In the context of a UK company, the auditors give an opinion on whether the company's FINANCIAL STATEMENTS comply with the Companies Act 1985 and give a TRUE AND FAIR VIEW.

If there are problems, the auditors may provide a QUALIFIED AUDIT REPORT.

auditor A person or firm appointed to carry out the AUDIT of an enterprise. For a UK company, the shareholders appoint the auditor on the recommendation of the directors. The law requires companies above a certain size to appoint a REGISTERED AUDITOR.

auditors' remuneration *See* AUDIT FEE.

auditors' report *See* AUDIT REPORT.

audit planning memorandum A document prepared by AUDITORS which outlines the overall plan for an AUDIT, including the degree to which SUBSTAN-TIVE TESTS are to be carried out on particular areas of a company's accounting system and FINANCIAL STATEMENTS.

audit programme A document detailing the work to be done on an AUDIT to carry out the strategy of an AUDIT PLANNING MEMORANDUM.

audit qualification *See* QUALIFIED AUDIT REPORT.

audit report A written document included with a company's FINANCIAL STATE-MENTS in which the auditors explain their work done and give an AUDIT OPINION on compliance by the company with various requirements. The report is addressed to the members (i.e. generally the shareholders) of the company.

audit risk The degree of probability that the auditor will fail to discover a material error or misstatement and thereby incorrectly give an unqualified AUDIT OPINION.

audit rotation The principle whereby an AUDITOR (or firm of auditors) of a particular company should be appointed for a fixed term. The aim is to increase the independence of auditors from the enterprise's managers. However, there would be costs in terms of learning and disruption. Audit rotation is not common in the UK but is so in some continental European countries.

audit trail The path of a transaction or event through all the stages of an ACCOUNTING SYSTEM, from being recorded to appearance in FINANCIAL STATE-MENTS. AUDITORS will wish such a trail to be clearly visible in a series of documents with cross-references.

Aufsichtsrat German for SUPERVISORY BOARD.

Australian Accounting Research Foundation (AARF) A joint institution of the two main Australian accountancy bodies that co-ordinates the profession's contribution to setting ACCOUNTING STANDARDS. At one time the AARF was the major component of the Australian standard-setting system.

Australian Securities and Investments Commission A government agency responsible for the oversight of such matters as the financial reporting and audit-ing of listed corporations in Australia. It is an approximate equivalent of the SECURITIES AND EXCHANGE COMMISSION in the USA.

authorized auditor A person who is not a REGISTERED AUDITOR but is nevertheless allowed by law to be appointed as an auditor of an unlisted company.

authorized investments Investments on a list of those legally suitable for trustees of trust funds to purchase.

authorized minimum share capital The minimum share capital allowed by law. In the case of a UK PUBLIC LIMITED COMPANY, this is presently £50,000. In the UK, there is no minimum share capital for PRIVATE LIMITED COMPANIES, but there are such requirements in many continental European countries.

authorized share capital The maximum amount of a particular type of SHARE in a particular COMPANY that may be issued. The amount is laid down in the company's MEMORANDUM OF ASSOCIATION.

available-for-sale financial assets Those FINANCIAL ASSETS that are not: (a) loans and receivables originated by the enterprise, (b) HELD-TO-MATURITY investments or (c) held for trading. Under the rules of INTERNATIONAL ACCOUNTING STANDARD 39, such assets are held at FAIR VALUE in a BALANCE SHEET.

AVCO In the context of STOCK (inventory) valuation, a method of determining the HISTORICAL COST of a particular type of inventory. As its name suggests, the cost of any unit of inventory or material used is deemed to be the average of the unit costs at which the inventory was bought. Generally, the average would be weighted by the different volumes of purchases. The average can be worked out at set intervals or each time there is a further purchase. AVCO is a minority practice in the UK and the USA.

In the context of COST ACCOUNTING, the term 'AVERAGE COST' means the total cost of production divided by the number of units produced.

average cost See AVCO.

avoidable costs Costs that would not be incurred if particular options were not taken by an enterprise. In the short term at least, FIXED COSTS are not avoidable but VARIABLE COSTS may be if particular products are not made.

avoidance of tax The re-arrangement of a taxpayer's affairs, within the letter of the law, in order to reduce tax liabilities. Compare to EVASION OF TAX.

BAA Abbreviation for the BRITISH ACCOUNTING ASSOCIATION.

back duty An amount of tax relating to a past period that was unassessed because fraud or error led to lack of full DISCLOSURE by the taxpayer.

backflush costing A method of costing of products which attaches costs to output rather than to the flow of products through production. This method is associated with the JUST-IN-TIME production system.

backlog depreciation In the context of a company that bases DEPRECIATION on current values, the amount of extra depreciation that would be necessary in a particular year in order to make up for the fact that previous years' depreciation provisions had been based on values that are now out-of-date.

BADC Abbreviation for the BUSINESS ACCOUNTING DELIBERATION COUNCIL of Japan.

bad debt allowance/provision/reserve A separate record in the accounting system of the amount by which the DEBTORS are overstated due to the possibility of debts that will not be paid. On a BALANCE SHEET, the allowance has generally already been deducted from the gross amount of debtors.

The clearest of the three terms in the heading is 'allowance'. The term 'PROVISION' is often used in the UK, but is misleading because it is also used to refer to a type of LIABILITY. The term 'RESERVE' is sometimes used in the USA in this context, but that is also confusing because it is also used outside the USA to mean an element of EQUITY.

bad debts Amounts of DEBTORS (UK)/accounts receivable (USA) that have become uncollectable. However, there are various levels of doubt that an enterprise may have. Normally, one would hope and expect that a great majority of debts would eventually be received. However, PRUDENCE requires that all reasonably likely losses be anticipated when valuing the debtors. Thus: (a) debts which are almost certainly uncollectable are deducted from the total; (b) debts which are reasonably likely to be uncollectable have a specific allowance made against them and (c) in addition, a general allowance is made against the total remaining figure of debts, based on previous experience with unexpected bad debts. Often, the word 'PROVISION' is used rather than 'allowance', although this is confusing because that former term is also used to refer to a type of LIABILITY.

In each of the three above cases, there will be an expense charged against income, and a reduction in the figure of Debtors/Accounts Receivable shown on the BALANCE SHEET.

bad debts recovered The collection of money from DEBTORS despite the fact that their debts had been written off as BAD DEBTS.

badwill A term sometimes used informally, or by those whose first language is not English, to refer to NEGATIVE GOODWILL.

bailment The delivery of goods from one person to another on condition that they will be returned.

balance In a DOUBLE-ENTRY BOOKKEEPING context, the difference between the two sides of an ACCOUNT. For example, an excess of DEBITS over CREDITS leads to a DEBIT BALANCE. At the end of an ACCOUNTING PERIOD, the balances on all the accounts are shown on a BALANCE SHEET.

balanced scorecard An approach to the provision of information to external users or to management whereby all the relevant areas of performance are addressed. This broadens the reporting to include non-financial elements and to cover such issues as customer satisfaction and employee relations.

balance off The process of totalling the two sides of an ACCOUNT in order to determine the balance. For example, if there is an excess of DEBITS over CREDITS, a balancing item is entered as a credit so that the account is balanced. The double entry for that credit is an equal sized debit shown underneath the balanced off account. It is a debit balance 'brought down'.

balance sheet A snap-shot of the accounting records of ASSETS, LIABILITIES and EQUITY of a business at a particular moment, most obviously the accounting year end. The balance sheet is the longest established of the main FINANCIAL STATEMENTS produced by a business. As its name suggests, it is a sheet of the balances from the DOUBLE-ENTRY BOOKKEEPING system at a particular time. It is important to note that it is probably not a snap-shot of what the business is *worth*. This is because not all the business's items of value are recognized by accountants as ASSETS, and because the ASSET VALUATION methods used are mostly based on past costs rather than on present market values.

Initially, the balance sheet was not designed as a statement of worth at all; it was merely a mechanical by-product of the periodical closing of books in the double-entry bookkeeping system. (In some sense, the balance sheet is the graveyard of the double-entry bookkeeping system; it balances because the double-entry bookkeeping system creates equal totals of debits and credits.) The worth of a business was more sensibly calculated by taking a quite separate 'inventory' of all the assets and liabilities at a date.

In the modern CONCEPTUAL FRAMEWORK, it is important to check that the balances meet the appropriate definitions. For example, any debit balance shown in the balance sheet should meet the definition of an asset.

Annual balance sheets are compulsory requirements of COMPANY LAW (UK) and the SECURITIES AND EXCHANGE COMMISSION (USA). *See*, also, BALANCE SHEET FORMATS.

balance sheet audit An AUDIT of the RECOGNITION, MEASUREMENT and PRESENTATION aspects of the items shown in a BALANCE SHEET. The objective is to confirm that the requirements of laws and standards have been complied with.

balance sheet equation *See* ACCOUNTING EQUATION.

balance sheet formats Prescribed or optional layouts for the presentation of items in a BALANCE SHEET. Before the Companies Act 1981 in the UK (and still in some other English-speaking countries) formats and terminology varied substantially. In the USA, many balance sheets use an 'account format' with assets on the left and capital and liabilities on the right. The CURRENT ASSETS are shown above the other assets (*see* Figure 1). Even the title of the balance sheet may be expressed instead as 'STATEMENT OF FINANCIAL POSITION' or some variation.

Figure 1 An account form balance sheet (USA)

JCN Inc
Balance Sheet, December 31, 200x ($000)

Current Assets			Current Liabilities		
Cash		300	Loans Payable		800
Accounts Receivable		1850	Accounts Payable		1200
Inventories		1500	Accrued Expenses		400
Total		3650	Dividends		600
			Total		3000
Investments		800	Deferred Taxes		500
Property			Long-term Debt		3000
Land	2000		Shareholders' Equity		
Buildings	2000		Common Stock	1500	
Machinery	3000		Paid-in Capital	500	
Total		7000	Retained Earnings	2,950	
			Total		4950
Total Assets		11,450	Total Liabilities and Equity		11,450

In the UK, account form balance sheets were the norm until the second half of the twentieth century, and are still found for partnerships and sole traders. However, unlike US and continental European balance sheets, the assets were on the *right* and the capital and liabilities on the *left*.

However, long before the Companies Act 1981, large companies in the UK had taken to using a statement (or vertical) format. This is because it enables the presentation of NET CURRENT ASSETS (or working capital), and because it

Figure 2 A statement form balance sheet (UK)

D & D Piranha plc
Balance Sheet 31.12.200x (£000)

Fixed Assets			
Tangible Assets			
Land and Buildings			4000
Plant and Machinery			2000
Fixtures and Fittings			1000
			7000
Investments			800
			7800
Current Assets			
Stocks	1500		
Debtors	1850		
Cash at Bank and in Hand	300		
		3650	
Creditors: falling due within one year			
Bank Loans and Overdrafts	800		
Trade Creditors	1200		
Corporation Tax	800		
Proposed Dividends	600		
Accruals	100		
		3500	
Net Current Assets			150
Total Assets less Current Liabilities			7950
Creditors: falling due after one year			
Debenture Loans			3000
Net Assets			4950
Capital and Reserves			
Called-up Share Capital		1500	
Share Premium		500	
Profit and Loss Account		2950	
Shareholders' Funds			4950

avoids the confusion that undistributed profit might appear to be a liability. UK company law (now the Companies Act 1985) sets out two balance sheet formats and allows companies to choose (consistently) between them. One of these formats is shown as Figure 2, which uses the same numbers as Figure 1. The other format has very similar headings but is in account form, with the assets on the left, starting with fixed assets. The headings (as in Figure 2) must be shown in the order laid down. There is a further level of sub-headings which must either be shown on the balance sheet or, where clearer, in the notes to the balance sheet. The NOTES TO THE ACCOUNTS will also include other compulsory disclosures connected with balance sheet items, like cumulative amounts of DEPRECIATION.

balance sheet total When used in the UK COMPANIES ACT as part of identifying one of the size thresholds for types of company, this term refers to the total of the ASSETS in a BALANCE SHEET.

balancing allowance In the UK CAPITAL ALLOWANCES system, a SET-OFF against taxable income when the sale proceeds of an asset are less than the written down value for tax purposes.

balancing charge In the UK CAPITAL ALLOWANCES system, an addition to taxable income when the sale proceeds of an asset exceed the written down value for tax purposes.

balancing figure A number which, if added into a series of other numbers, would cause the total to equal another total. For example, if the total of the DEBITS in an ACCOUNT exceeds the total of the CREDITS, the balancing figure would be the extra credit needed to make the total credits equal the total debits.

BALO Abbreviation for the *Bulletin des annonces légales obligatoires*, a French government gazette which includes the FINANCIAL STATEMENTS of public companies.

bank Technically, an enterprise licensed by law as a taker of deposits and regulated by Banking Acts.

bank certificate In the context of an AUDIT, a document signed by an official of a bank which confirms the balances due or from an enterprise.

bank confirmation In the context of an AUDIT, the written agreement of a bank that an enterprise's bank balances are as listed by the AUDITOR.

bank (or banker's) draft A cheque drawn by a bank on itself. Assuming that the bank is of good standing, such a cheque would normally be accepted as as good as cash, without waiting for clearance.

banker's cheque *See* BANK (OR BANKER'S) DRAFT.

banker's order An instruction to a bank from a customer to pay particular amounts at particular times to a particular party.

banker's reference A written report by a bank on the CREDITWORTHINESS of one of its customers.

bank giro A system for transferring amounts between bank accounts without the use of cheques.

Bank of England Although originally a private sector bank, now the central bank of the UK. Its independence from the government was increased in 1997 when it was given sole authority for setting base interest rates.

bank reconciliation statement A detailed numerical reconciliation explaining any differences between an enterprise's records of its bank balances at a particular date and the statements provided by the bank. Enterprises generally carry out such reconciliations frequently (sometimes daily) in order to identify any errors in their own or their banks' records.

bankrupt As a noun, a person against whom a BANKRUPTCY order has been made by a court, generally because of inability to meet financial OBLIGATIONS. The order removes property from the bankrupt so that it can be sold to pay CREDITORS.

bankruptcy The legal status of a person declared BANKRUPT by a court. A CREDITOR may 'sue for bankruptcy' in order that a court may declare the person legally bankrupt which will affect his ability to undertake commercial transactions. *See*, also, INSOLVENCY.

bank statement The periodic summary of transactions between a bank and its customer. For private individuals, such statements are commonly prepared on a monthly basis, but for businesses they are often more frequent.

bargain purchase The acquisition of an enterprise (or of its NET ASSETS) at less than the FAIR VALUE of those assets. Such a purchase may be possible if the seller is badly informed about the value of its assets or if the seller is unable or unwilling to sell the assets separately. A bargain purchase gives rise to the recognition of NEGATIVE GOODWILL.

bargain purchase option In the context of LEASES, an option in a lease contract for the LESSEE to buy the leased assets at a price below the MARKET VALUE.

barometer stock A share whose price (or movement in price) on a stock exchange is regarded as a good indicator of the state of the market as a whole.

barter The trading of goods or services without the use of money as the medium of exchange. Such trading may be common where money is unreliable (perhaps because of high inflation), where the financial system is primitive, or where traders prefer to avoid records of transactions (possibly for tax reasons).

base rate In the UK, the rate of interest used by banks as a benchmark for the calculation of various rates for lending and borrowing. The rate is under the control of the BANK OF ENGLAND.

base stock A volume of INVENTORY assumed to be necessary for the operations of a business. In the context of INVENTORY VALUATION, the 'base stock method' treats the base stock as a FIXED ASSET at a cost valuation. The effect is somewhat similar to using 'last in, first out' (LIFO), and is not generally acceptable in the UK.

base year In the context of a series of indices over time, the year for which the index is set at 100.

basic earnings per share The amount of NET PROFIT for a period that is attributable to the holders of ORDINARY SHARES divided by the weighted average number of the ORDINARY SHARES outstanding during the period.

basic rate of income tax In the UK income tax system, the MARGINAL RATE OF TAX paid by a large majority of taxpayers. A small band of taxable income is taxed at a starting rate, and a small proportion of taxpayers suffers a higher rate on taxable income above the top limit of the basic rate band.

basic wage rate The level of wages relating to work for a specified number of hours in a week. Added to this would be overtime payments and other incentive pay.

basis of apportionment The method of calculation used for the spreading of OVERHEAD COSTS among COST CENTRES when they cannot be allocated to one particular centre.

basis of assessment The way in which periods for a particular type of income are related to TAX YEARS in the UK. For example, interest income is assessed for tax on the basis of the amount for the tax year, whereas the taxable income of companies is assessed on the basis of their accounting years. The appropriate basis of assessment is laid down in the TAX SCHEDULES for each type of income.

basis period In the context of the UK tax system, the period (generally a year) for which its taxable income forms the BASIS OF ASSESSMENT for a particular tax year.

basis point In the context of rates measured in percentage terms, one-hundredth of 1 per cent.

batch costing In the context of COST ACCOUNTING, a system used when products can easily be identified into groups that are processed together.

b/d (or b/f) Abbreviation for 'brought down' (or 'brought forward'), as used when explaining in a DOUBLE-ENTRY BOOKKEEPING account that an amount comes from the balance of a previous period on the same account.

bean counters A pejorative term for accountants, particularly those employed within companies.

bear An investor on a STOCK EXCHANGE who anticipates falls in prices. A 'bear market' is a pessimistic state of affairs at a stock exchange. The opposite is a BULL, who charges ahead, anticipating price rises (*see*, also, STAG). Successful bears are those who agree to 'sell' shares that they do not yet own, in order to cover the sale by buying later when the price has fallen.

bearer biological assets Those living animals and plants that meet the other aspects of the definition of ASSET and are used to bear agricultural produce rather than to become the produce themselves. For example, if a herd of sheep is used mainly for the production of wool, the sheep are bearer biological assets and the wool is agricultural produce.

bearer security SHARES or BONDS that pass from one owner to the next by delivery rather than by registration.

bed and breakfast A transaction involving the sale and almost immediate repurchase of a security in order to gain a tax advantage. For example, this might be useful in order to realize annual gains small enough to be exempt under a CAPITAL GAINS TAX.

behavioural accounting An approach to the study of accounting that stresses the reactions of preparers and users of accounting to the accounting process itself.

below-the-line The 'line' in question is that showing the 'NET PROFIT after tax' in a PROFIT AND LOSS ACCOUNT (UK) or the 'NET INCOME' in an INCOME STATEMENT (US). *See* ABOVE THE LINE.

benchmark accounting policy In the context of an INTERNATIONAL ACCOUNTING STANDARD (IAS), a policy labelled as a benchmark rather than an 'allowed alternative'. Generally, when there is a choice within an IAS, the two policies are labelled in this way. In most cases, there is no suggestion that the benchmark is preferred. The exception is the use of PROPORTIONAL CONSOLIDATION for joint venture entities in IAS 31. Also, there is no requirement for numerical reconciliation from use of an allowed alternative to the benchmark, except in the usage of the 'last in, first out' (LIFO) INVENTORY VALUATION method under IAS 2.

benchmarking The setting of targets based on best practices (perhaps by observing other enterprises), whereby areas of under-performance can be identified.

beneficial owner The person who benefits from a security in cases where the legal owner is a NOMINEE.

benefit–cost ratio *See* COST–BENEFIT ANALYSIS.

benefits in kind Employment remuneration other than in the form of cash. Typical examples of such benefits are the use of a company car for private, rather than business, purposes, or the use of accommodation at reduced or zero rental. In the UK income tax system, mechanisms are in place to tax many of these benefits.

bequest A gift resulting from a provision in a will.

beta coefficient The 'beta coefficient' of a SHARE is an indication of one aspect of the risk attached to it. The beta shows the sensitivity of the price of a share to changes in the price of shares generally. *See* CAPITAL ASSET PRICING MODEL.

BFH Abbreviation for the *Bundesfinanzhoj*; the supreme tax court in Germany, whose decisions have a major effect on financial reporting because of the closeness in that country of tax and financial reporting rules and practice.

bid price The price on a stock market at which a SHARE would be bought by a dealer from a shareholder. The dealer would sell at a higher price (the offer price or the ask price). The difference is a 'turn' or the bid–offer spread.

Big Bang Colloquial expression for a series of major changes in 1986 to the practices on the London Stock Exchange. For example, the DUAL CAPACITY SYSTEM was adopted.

big bath Colloquial expression for writing off ASSETS and taking as many expenses as possible in a particular year. The objective is to put all the bad news in one year, so that subsequent years will look better. A newly installed management might wish to take a big bath in its first year.

Big Board Colloquial expression for the New York Stock Exchange, as opposed to other US exchanges.

Big Five An expression used to describe the world's largest accounting firms, which have offices virtually throughout the world. The Big Five (in alphabetical order) are:

(a) Andersen
(b) Deloitte Touche Tohmatsu
(c) Ernst & Young
(d) KPMG (Klynveld Peat Marwick Goerdeler)
(e) PricewaterhouseCoopers

Exactly in which order of size the firms ought to be depends on whether you count the numbers of offices, numbers of partners, numbers of staff, total fee incomes, etc. It also depends on which year, what the exchange rates are, and whether it is for the world, the UK, the USA or some other context.

These firms are very well established throughout the Anglo-Saxon world, and increasingly in Europe. In some countries, there is resistance to their success, and firms have to operate under local names or have local partners, or they have to work through similar, legally separate, national firms.

Most of the firms began in the UK and in the USA, and later merged. The exception is Andersen which has spread from the USA. In many cases the founders of the US parts of these multinational firms were expatriate Britons. The role of such firms outside the UK and the USA was originally to AUDIT subsidiaries of UK or US multinationals. However, in many countries their work has now expanded to include much domestic auditing and consultancy.

Big GAAP Colloquial expression for the financial reporting regulations applied to large (or perhaps to listed) companies. 'GAAP' stands for GENERALLY ACCEPTED ACCOUNTING PRINCIPLES.

bilan social The French term for a partly numerical report relating to data about the employees of an enterprise.

bill of exchange An order in writing drawn by one party (e.g. a supplier) and signed by another (e.g. a customer) requiring the latter to pay an amount. The bill is an acknowledgement of DEBT by the DEBTOR, e.g. as a result of a non-cash transaction. A company may have 'BILLS PAYABLE' or 'BILLS RECEIVABLE'. Bills can be passed from one person to another, i.e. they are negotiable. Banks may be willing to 'discount' a bill, i.e. to give cash in exchange for the bill at a discount on its face value. The US expression is 'notes'.

bill of lading A document acknowledging the loading of goods on to a ship and recording the conditions under which they will be transported.

bill of sale A document transferring the ownership of goods from vendor to purchaser.

bills payable UK term for NOTES PAYABLE.

bills receivable UK term for NOTES RECEIVABLE.

bin card A card, relating to the storage area for a particular INVENTORY, on which quantities of receipts and issues are recorded. The bin card therefore shows the amount of stock that should be in the bin at any time.

biological assets Living animals and plants that meet the other aspects of the definition of ASSET. After harvest, the assets become agricultural produce. Under INTERNATIONAL ACCOUNTING STANDARDS, biological assets are required to be measured on the BALANCE SHEET at a market value.

BiRiLiG Abbreviation for the *Bilanzrichtliniengesetz*, the German accounting directives law of 1985.

black economy That part of a national economy that is not recorded for tax or other official purposes.

black market An illegal market for a particular good or service.

block grant An amount of money allocated to a public sector organization that the organization can decide by itself how to spend.

blocked funds Money which cannot be transferred from one place to another, generally because of exchange controls imposed by the government in the country of the prospective sender of the funds.

blue chip Colloquial term for a well-established and well-regarded company (or a SHARE in such a company) listed on a stock exchange.

blue-sky laws State laws in the USA that govern trading in securities, e.g. designed to protect the public from traders who would try to sell them the blue sky.

Board of Customs and Excise The department of the UK Treasury responsible for the administration of certain taxes, generally INDIRECT TAXES, such as customs duties and value added tax.

Board of Inland Revenue The department of the UK Treasury responsible for the administration of certain taxes, generally DIRECT TAXES, such as income tax and corporation tax.

body corporate An association treated in law as though it were a person, i.e. achieving incorporation. Companies are bodies corporate as are some other institutions.

bona fide Latin term for 'good faith', as used in the context of honest sales that do not involve collusion or fraud.

bona vacantia Latin term for 'goods without an owner', such as those goods of a deceased person with no traceable living relatives and no will. In the UK, such property passes to the Crown, i.e. to the State.

bond covenant Part of a bond contract between the lenders and borrowers of money. The lender will promise in the covenant not to do certain things, such as borrowing beyond particular limits.

bonds A word used to cover many sorts of (usually) long-term loans to a company or other body, where there is a contract between the borrower and the lender. For details, *see* DEBENTURES. The expressions 'LOAN STOCK' or, in the USA, 'OBLIGATIONS' or 'DEBT' are also used. Bonds usually have a fixed life, a fixed interest return and a fixed REDEMPTION value.

bonus dividend A one-off DIVIDEND paid in excess of the amounts normally expected.

bonus issue An issue of BONUS SHARES.

bonus shares Shares issued to existing shareholders of a company, in proportion to their shareholdings. Such shares are free, as their name suggests – no cash changes hands. The purpose is usually to lower the share price, perhaps for the psychological reason that it seems high in relation to other shares or has gone into two digits, i.e. above £10 or $10. If a one-for-one issue is made, the result would be a doubling of shares. Since nothing else about the company has changed, the share price ought to halve, but sometimes it falls less, perhaps because of favourable attention drawn to the company.

Accounting for the issue is straightforward; reserves of various kinds can be relabelled 'SHARE CAPITAL' to the total value of the PAR VALUE of the shares.

Bonus issues are sometimes called 'SCRIP ISSUES' or 'CAPITALIZATION ISSUES' (because reserves are being capitalized).

book of original (or prime) entry A chronological record of the common transactions in a business, such as sales or cash movements. Each type of transaction has a separate book devoted to it from which entries are generated for the DOUBLE-ENTRY BOOKKEEPING system.

bookkeeper The person in an enterprise who is responsible for the BOOKS OF ACCOUNT.

bookkeeping Day-to-day recording of transactions of a business or other body (*see* DOUBLE-ENTRY BOOKKEEPING for a detailed description). Bookkeeping describes the more mechanical, everyday, aspects of accounting.

bookkeeping barter The exchange of goods without the use of money as the means of exchange but using monetary measures for the UNIT OF ACCOUNT and thus for the recording of the transactions.

books of account The detailed records of all the transactions of a business, kept on a daily basis. They include the ACCOUNTS. Some types of transactions are so numerous that the DOUBLE-ENTRY BOOKKEEPING system would be swamped if they were recorded individually, e.g. credit sales, credit purchases and cash transactions. For these, special subsidiary 'books of original/or prime entry' are used to record all the details and then to pass summary totals through to the main system. Thus, there may be a 'SALES DAY BOOK', a 'PURCHASES DAY BOOK' and a 'CASH BOOK'.

The accounting records are generally divided up into 'ledgers' of similar types. For example, there may be a SALES LEDGER and a PURCHASES LEDGER to which totals from the day book are 'posted'. Traditionally, there would have been PERSONAL LEDGERS (for amounts owed to or by persons), real ledgers (for land, buildings, etc.), and NOMINAL LEDGERS (for those things that were neither personal nor physical, like interest charges, DEPRECIATION, and so on). However, the expression 'nominal ledger' has come to be used by some to describe all the main accounts. These days, accounting records in many businesses are kept on computer files, so that physical 'books' and 'ledgers' are beginning to go the way of quill pens.

book value The amount of which an ASSET or LIABILITY is shown in a BALANCE SHEET. In practice, for most assets, this generally means 'NET BOOK VALUE', which takes account of DEPRECIATION. Other synonyms are 'CARRYING VALUE' and 'WRITTEN DOWN VALUE'.

borrowing costs INTEREST and other costs incurred by an enterprise in connection with loans and other borrowing of funds. In US accounting, such costs are added to the total cost of a FIXED ASSET under construction, i.e. the borrowing costs are capitalized. In UK or INTERNATIONAL ACCOUNTING STANDARD rules, this is an option.

bottom line The conclusion of the accounting process in terms of calculating performance for the period, i.e. the NET PROFIT after tax. Colloquially, therefore, the term means 'the conclusion of an argument'.

bought day book One expression for the JOURNAL in which records of purchases are recorded. Synonymous terms are purchases day book and purchases journal.

bought ledger The ACCOUNTS relating to the CREDITORS of the enterprise. The bought ledger collects together these accounts. It can also be called the 'creditors' ledger'.

branch accounts The accounting records or the FINANCIAL STATEMENTS relating to separate parts of an enterprise; generally geographically separate parts. Originally, overseas operations were often accounted for as branches but now they are generally set up as legally separate SUBSIDIARY companies.

brand A name or symbol used as a means of distinguishing a product from other products and to suggest quality. When legally protected, brands are 'TRADE MARKS'. For financial reporting purposes, brands can be capitalized as INTANGIBLE ASSETS if purchased separately or as part of a larger acquisition.

In the UK, it was common for large amounts to be allocated to brands until the end of the 1990s because there were no rules requiring AMORTIZATION. However, now the rules are the same as for GOODWILL.

It was even common for internally generated brands (*see* INTANGIBLE ASSETS) to be capitalized based on estimates by brand valuing consultants, but this is not now acceptable.

breakeven analysis The comparison of projected sales against projected costs at various levels of activity in order to estimate how much volume is necessary before a PROFIT can be made. The key point is that some costs are FIXED COSTS and some are VARIABLE COSTS.

The technique can also be called COST–VOLUME–PROFIT ANALYSIS.

breakeven chart A graph on which estimated REVENUES, FIXED COSTS and VARIABLE COSTS are plotted at increasing levels of activity.

breakeven point The level of activity at which an enterprise makes neither a profit nor a loss, as shown on a BREAKEVEN CHART. This is the point at which total revenue equals total cost.

break-up value The expected market selling price of an ASSET or of a whole business if a sale were necessary because the business could not continue to trade. This value might be lower than NET SELLING PRICE or NET REALIZABLE VALUE because those values assume the normal course of business and an orderly market.

British Accounting Association The UK's main body that brings together academic accountants for the fostering of research and other purposes. It organizes conferences and issues the journal, *The British Accounting Review*.

broker An agent who brings together two parties to make a contract. For example, the contract might be for insurance or for the trading of shares.

brought down (or brought forward) An expression used in an ACCOUNT when an amount has been calculated to balance the account. The amount brought down to start a new period is the DOUBLE-ENTRY BOOKKEEPING for the amount needed to balance the account.

budget A financial plan, usually expressed in money terms and divided into periods. For example, a business may have a cash budget for the coming year, detailing the planned inflows and outflows of cash on a monthly basis. This will involve the calculation of the planned surplus cash at the end of each month. There will also be sales, production, purchases, expense and other budgets. The purpose of a budgeting system is to help to plan, monitor and control the business throughout the year.

In the context of the UK government, the Budget is the annual statement of planned expenses and revenues for the year.

budgetary control A process by which financial control is exercised over an enterprise by establishing a detailed monetarily quantified plan for parts of the enterprise and then reviewing and adjusting activities in the light of subsequent performance compared to the plan.

budget centre A part of an enterprise for which BUDGET records are separately kept.

budget committee A group within an enterprise that has overall responsibility for the BUDGETS and for the monitoring process connected to them.

budget cost (or budget allowance) The amount of expenditure that, according to the BUDGET, is allowed to be spent in a period by a BUDGET CENTRE. Generally, the managers of budget centres are consulted when the budgeted amounts are established, and they are then assessed on actual performance compared to budgeted amounts.

budget director The person in an enterprise who is operationally responsible for the running of the whole system of BUDGETS.

budgeted capacity The available level of output in an enterprise expressed, for example, in MACHINE HOURS, for a particular period according to the BUDGET.

budgeted revenue The income scheduled to be received by a BUDGET CENTRE for a particular period.

budget manual A written set of instructions, internal to an enterprise, which controls all the aspects of BUDGETS and BUDGETARY CONTROL.

budget period A period for which a BUDGET is drawn up, typically a year but broken down into months or quarters. Generally, there are close links between this aspect of MANAGEMENT ACCOUNTING and the FINANCIAL ACCOUNTING, so the budget year is usually the accounting year.

buffer stock A level below which an organization would not wish its STOCKS to fall, so that it is protected from surprising increases in use or decreases in supply of them.

bull An investor on a STOCK EXCHANGE who anticipates a rise in prices. Thus, a 'bull market' is an optimistic state of affairs at a stock exchange. Successful bulls are those who 'buy' shares, intending to sell them soon afterwards when prices have risen. The buying and selling may not be *settled* on the same day. Thus, 'buying' can be achieved without the apparently necessary resources. The opposite of a bull is a BEAR. *See*, also, STAG.

bullet loan A borrowing which must be repaid in a single amount at a particular date.

burden A US term for OVERHEAD costs.

Business Accounting Deliberation Council A Japanese committee, under the control of the Ministry of Finance, that makes regulations concerning the CONSOLIDATED FINANCIAL STATEMENTS of listed companies.

business combinations A US (and now INTERNATIONAL ACCOUNTING STANDARDS COMMITTEE) expression for ACQUISITIONS or MERGERS involving two or more companies. The accounting treatments can be varied and complex.

business entity concept *See* ENTITY CONVENTION.

business name In the UK, a technical legal term for the name under which an enterprise trades.

business plan A detailed plan, including monetary projections, setting out the objectives and prospects of a business for a number of years into the future. This term is particularly associated with new or proposed enterprises when they are seeking support from banks or other providers of finance.

business property relief   In the context of the UK's INHERITANCE TAX, a reduction in the amounts brought in to tax when the ASSETS of a donor are business assets.

business rates   A UK tax paid by businesses and calculated on the basis of a valuation of the property occupied. The rate of tax is set centrally, but collected locally.

business segment   A distinguishable component of a business that provides a product or service that is subject to risks and returns that are different from those of other business segments. There are SEGMENT REPORTING rules for listed companies which require disclosure of such items as SALES, NET PROFIT and ASSETS on a segmental basis. These items can be segmented on a geographical market basis and on a product (line-of-business) basis.

buy-out   Purchase of a company by a group of people containing some of the former managers of it; *see* MANAGEMENT BUY-OUT.

BV   Abbreviation for *besloten vennootschap met beperkte aansprakelijheid*, a Dutch or Belgian private limited company.

bylaws   The rules relating to the operation of an organization. For UK companies, these are called the ARTICLES OF ASSOCIATION.

by-product   Items produced incidentally to the main products of an enterprise's commercial activities. In a sense, such products are scrap or waste, but can sometimes be sold for significant amounts. Consequently, for the purposes of COST ACCOUNTING, one approach is to deduct the NET REALIZABLE VALUE of the by-product from the costs of the main product.

C

CA Abbreviation for CHARTERED ACCOUNTANT.

Cadbury Report The report of a UK committee which produced proposals for good CORPORATE GOVERNANCE in 1993.

callable bonds Bonds where the issuer has the right at specified times to redeem the bond.

called-up share capital The total amount so far due from all shareholders to an issuing company, whether the amounts have been paid or not. Newly issued shares are sometimes paid for in several instalments or calls.

call option A contract which gives the holder the right to buy specified FINANCIAL ASSETS or commodities at a particular price and time.

Canadian Institute of Chartered Accountants (CICA) The senior professional body of accountants in Canada, whose predecessor body was founded in 1880. A committee of the CICA is responsible for setting ACCOUNTING STANDARDS in Canada.

cap A top limit on certain charges (e.g. interest rates) included in a contract.

CAPA Abbreviation for the Confederation of Asian and Pacific Accountants, a body that can be traced back to 1957 but was formally organized in 1976. It is an umbrella body for a large number of ACCOUNTANCY BODIES in the Asia–Pacific region.

capacity The level of activity that an enterprise (or part of it) can sustain, measured perhaps in terms of output of units or MACHINE HOURS.

capacity usage variance A measure of the gain or loss in a period, compared to a BUDGET, caused because the hours worked are longer or shorter than planned.

Caparo case The decision in a 1990 case under English law that auditors owe a duty of care to existing shareholders only (not to prospective shareholders) and to the shareholders as a body (not individually). This seems to be a rather old-fashioned decision which runs counter to the CONCEPTUAL FRAMEWORK which stresses the use of FINANCIAL STATEMENTS by investors and others for decision making.

The full name of the case was Caparo Industries plc *v* Dickman and others.

capital A word used somewhat loosely in the business world in general, and even by accountants, to mean the company's finance. This might include all SHARE CAPITAL, past profits, long-term loans and CURRENT LIABILITIES. Such an aggregation might be called 'TOTAL CAPITAL'. It would, of course, equal 'TOTAL ASSETS'.

However, 'capital' might also be used to mean the long-term finance, i.e. the above total less current liabilities. Yet another meaning might be all the elements of capital belonging to shareholders (SHAREHOLDERS' EQUITY), or even just the amount of money contributed in the past by the shareholders. Unfortunately, the reader will have to determine the exact meaning by the context.

The expression 'CAPITAL EMPLOYED' is also seen on balance sheets and in profitability RATIOS. It tends to mean the total long-term capital, although such an aggregate might be called 'net capital employed' because it does not include current liabilities.

Worse still, economists tend to use the word 'capital' to refer to items on the other side of the balance sheet, particularly FIXED ASSETS and INVENTORIES.

capital account The account within a DOUBLE-ENTRY BOOKKEEPING system that records the interest of the owners, particularly in the case of SOLE TRADERS or PARTNERSHIPS.

capital allowances A system of DEPRECIATION used in the determination of taxable income that is unique to the UK and Ireland. The rates are specified in annual Finance Acts; they tend to be more generous than the depreciation that accountants would charge for financial accounting purposes. There are two main reasons for the existence of capital allowances. First, the subjective nature of depreciation is thereby removed from the tax system. Accountants can charge the most appropriate depreciation in their accounts, without being worried that it will affect taxation. In a sense, the reverse problem occurs in most continental countries, in that tax-based depreciation rates determine accounting depreciation. Secondly, generous capital allowances can be used as an investment incentive. This ACCELERATED DEPRECIATION for tax purposes lowers the tax bill quickly and thus is a cash incentive.

From 1986 in the UK there have been 25 per cent annual WRITING DOWN ALLOWANCES for plant, cars, patents and 'know how'. Small companies receive larger allowances. The allowances use the DECLINING (OR REDUCING) BALANCE METHOD. For industrial buildings, there is a 4 per cent allowance on a straight-line basis. However, there are no allowances for commercial buildings, such as shops or offices, and none for land, which generally does not wear out.

When assets are sold, capital allowances are, in effect, reclaimed by the Inland

Revenue to the extent that the sale price exceeds the tax written down value, which will usually be zero for plant and machinery.

capital asset An alternative name, used more by economists than by accountants, for FIXED ASSET.

capital asset pricing model (CAPM) A theory, which may be expressed by equations, about the determination of the price of marketable securities, such as shares in LISTED COMPANIES. The model is built up on a number of assumptions, some of which are not very realistic. It is designed to show, for a particular security, the relationship between its expected return and its risk. The total risk attached to a security can be broken down into that which is systematic (related to the rest of the securities market) and that which is unsystematic (related only to the particular security). SYSTEMATIC RISK cannot be avoided by diversification, but unsystematic risk can be.

In algebraic terms, the following equation is descriptive of the CAPM:

$$E(R_j) = R_f + B_j (ER_M - R_f)$$

where $E(R_j)$ is the expected return on security j; R_f is the risk-free rate of return, B_j represents systematic risk (the beta coefficient), and ER_M is the expected return on the market portfolio.

capital budget A detailed monetary plan for a particular period for the acquisition of FIXED ASSETS.

capital budgeting The process whereby an enterprise selects and monitors its investments in FIXED ASSETS. Capital budgeting therefore includes the identification of investment projects, the appraisal and ranking of the projects by their likely outcomes, the process of approval for projects to be included in the CAPITAL BUDGET and then the checking of performance compared to budget. The INVESTMENT APPRAISAL part is extensively discussed in the academic literature.

capital commitments Future commitments that will entail CAPITAL EXPENDITURE. For example, a company may have contracted to purchase, at a future date, a new office building. At the BALANCE SHEET date, it may have no ASSET and no LIABILITY or cash expended as a result of the commitment. However, the commitment may be of interest to users of financial statements, particularly those concerned with the LIQUIDITY of the company. Thus, capital commitments are recorded in the NOTES TO THE ACCOUNTS.

capital consumption In the context of NATIONAL INCOME ACCOUNTING, a measure of DEPRECIATION of FIXED ASSETS based on REPLACEMENT COSTS.

capital costs Expenses related to the purchase of FIXED ASSETS rather than current expenses for the operations of an enterprise.

capital employed The aggregate finance used by a business. Sometimes the expression is used to refer to the total of all liabilities and capital, sometimes it excludes current liabilities (*see* CAPITAL).

capital expenditure Expenses of an enterprise on FIXED ASSETS that are capitalized rather than those current expenses that are charged immediately in the calculation of PROFIT. To the extent that the assets bought by capital expenditure wear out in a period, the DEPRECIATION is charged against profit.

capital expenditure budget Synonym for CAPITAL BUDGET.

capital gain The increase in MARKET VALUE of an ASSET. Sometimes the term is used to refer to those gains that are realized on the sale of an asset. For the purposes of CAPITAL GAINS TAX, only REALIZED GAINS are taxed.

capital gains tax A personal tax on the increase in value of certain ASSETS when realized. In the UK such a tax has operated on most assets since 1965. It was indexed for inflation from 1982 to 1998, but now the rate of tax declines as an asset is held for longer periods. For companies, capital gains are included in income charged to CORPORATION TAX.

capital gearing *See* GEARING.

capital instruments Contracts whereby an enterprise raises finance. For example, a company might issue shares or DEBENTURES in exchange for the receipt of money. Shares are EQUITY INSTRUMENTS and debentures are examples of FINANCIAL LIABILITIES, a category of FINANCIAL INSTRUMENTS.

capital intensive Reliant on a large amount of FIXED ASSETS, as opposed to when an enterprise relies on a large amount of staff and so is 'labour intensive'.

capital investment Synonym for CAPITAL EXPENDITURE.

capital investment appraisal *See* INVESTMENT APPRAISAL.

capital investment budget *See* CAPITAL BUDGET.

capitalization (or market capitalization) The aggregate market price on a stock exchange of all the listed shares of a company, or perhaps all its ORDINARY SHARES. It is, in a sense, what the company is worth, which may considerably exceed the balance sheet NET ASSETS. This is because balance sheets do not include all valuable assets (e.g. customer loyalty or trained staff; *see* ASSET), and because accounting ASSET VALUATION is often not based on market prices.

The term could also be used as the noun related to the verb 'to CAPITALIZE'.

capitalization issue *See* BONUS SHARES.

capitalization of borrowing costs The inclusion in the cost of an ASSET being constructed by an enterprise of the interest expense on the money borrowed by the enterprise.

capitalize To include as an element in the BALANCE SHEET. For example, if an enterprise spends money on the purchase of an item that meets the criteria for RECOGNITION as an ASSET, then those expenses are capitalized.

capital lease US term for a FINANCE LEASE; one that is capitalized by a lessee as an ASSET and a LIABILITY.

capital loss The shortfall of the net proceeds from the sale of an ASSET below its original cost. This implies that the term is used once the loss has been realized because of a sale and, in the context of CAPITAL GAINS TAX, that is certainly the case.

capital maintenance concept A concept used to determine the definition of PROFIT. It is variation in this that underlies the differences in systems of INFLATION ACCOUNTING.

Under HISTORICAL COST ACCOUNTING, the profit of a period is recognized as any excess of the money capital at the end of the period over the money capital at the beginning of the period (after correcting for additions or reductions of capital, such as share issues or dividends). However, it might well be argued that there is no *real* profit unless the shareholders' capital is maintained in *real* terms, i.e. after adjustment to take into account the fall in value of money due to inflation. An accounting system based on this concept of capital maintenance is called CURRENT PURCHASING POWER (CPP) ACCOUNTING in the UK, or CONSTANT DOLLAR ACCOUNTING or GENERAL PRICE LEVEL ADJUSTED in the USA. Such systems use retail price indices to adjust accounting figures from historical cost. This is a relatively simple set of adjustments, which does take *inflation* into account. It was the method favoured by the accountancy professional bodies in the English-speaking world in the late 1960s and early 1970s. In several highly inflationary economies, such as some in South America, CPP systems have been adopted.

An alternative view of the maintenance of capital is to concentrate not on the shareholders' money capital (historical cost) or on the shareholders' real capital CPP, but on the physical capital of the business. This would be an ENTITY VIEW rather than a PROPRIETARY VIEW. This point of view is taken on the grounds that the business is a GOING CONCERN and does not intend to return capital to the shareholders. Thus, for the decisions of managers and investors, the present worth, past progress and future prospects of a business can best be indicated by measuring current values and then calculating the resultant profit implications. A version of such a system, called CURRENT COST ACCOUNTING (CCA) was introduced as a requirement for SUPPLEMENTARY FINANCIAL STATEMENTS of large and listed companies in the UK in 1980 (until 1985), although its exact capital maintenance concept is not crystal clear. Other English-speaking countries have adopted similar requirements. In The Netherlands, some companies published REPLACEMENT COST based financial statements for decades.

Thus, how exactly one measures profit depends upon which concept of capital one has adopted.

capital market The various stock exchanges and other markets for long-term finance. The finance is sought by companies, governments and other institutions, and is provided particularly by PENSION FUNDS, life assurance companies and private investors.

capital redemption reserve An amount of RETAINED PROFITS set aside as legally undistributable when shares are bought back by a company.

capital reduction *See* REDUCTION OF CAPITAL.

capital reserve A former term for those accounts representing amounts which are not legally distributable or are not intended to be distributed by a company. Examples of such reserves are the SHARE PREMIUM ACCOUNT, which represents amounts paid in when shareholders bought their shares from the company; the CAPITAL REDEMPTION RESERVE, which represents amounts that have been substituted for share capital when shares were redeemed from their owners by the company; the LEGAL RESERVE, as required in many countries other than the UK or the USA; and the REVALUATION reserve, which represents increases in the value of ASSETS which have been recorded in the accounts but have not yet been realized by the sale of the assets.

These 'reserves', like all others in accounting, are not, of course, amounts of cash. The latter is an asset; the reserves are on the other side of a BALANCE SHEET showing who has funded the assets. The reserves are part of SHAREHOLDERS' EQUITY.

The equivalent US expression is 'RESTRICTED SURPLUS'.

capital stock US expression for SHARE CAPITAL.

capital structure The relationship between the various sources of finance of an enterprise. These sources may be EQUITY or DEBT in nature, and they may be long-term or short-term. In general, it is sensible to increase GEARING by relying on debt up to the point that it becomes too risky in terms of unavoidable interest payments.

capital surplus One of the US expressions for SHARE PREMIUM, although the term 'additional paid-in capital' is more common.

capital transactions Transactions affecting non-current items (such as FIXED ASSETS or LONG-TERM DEBT) rather than 'REVENUE' items.

capital transfer tax A UK personal tax on transfers of wealth which operated from 1975 to 1986 and was replaced by INHERITANCE TAX.

capital turnover The RATIO of sales of an enterprise for a period to the capital employed during the period. The capital employed might be measured as NET ASSETS or as TOTAL ASSETS less CURRENT LIABILITIES. The ratio gives an indication, when compared to other periods or to similar enterprises, of the efficiency of use of resources.

CAPM Abbreviation for the CAPITAL ASSET PRICING MODEL.

captive finance company A finance company (perhaps a bank or a leasing company) which is a SUBSIDIARY of a non-finance company.

captive insurance company An insurance company which is controlled by a non-insurance company (or jointly controlled by more than one). One of the objectives of such a captive company would generally be to act as insurer for the risks of the commercial or industrial parent company.

carriage inwards Expenses of delivery incurred by an enterprise related to goods purchased by it.

carriage outwards Expenses of delivery incurred by an enterprise related to goods sold by it.

carried down (or carried forward) An expression used in an ACCOUNT when an amount has been calculated to balance the account. The balancing item is labelled 'carried down', and an equal amount is created as a double entry (*see* DOUBLE-ENTRY BOOKKEEPING) which is brought down as the opening entry in the same account for the next period.

carrying amount *See* CARRYING VALUE.

carrying cost The cumulative expenses of holding INVENTORIES, including such costs as insurance and warehousing.

carrying value The amount at which an item is shown in a BALANCE SHEET. For an ASSET, depending on the country and the company, this might be a written-down value of depreciated HISTORICAL COST or a more recent revaluation. For depreciated assets, another equivalent term is 'NET BOOK VALUE'.

cash Amounts of money on hand and in the bank. In the UK, a CASH FLOW

STATEMENT uses the term 'cash' to refer to cash in hand and deposits with up to 24 hours notice.

cash accounting This term might be used to refer to CASH FLOW STATEMENTS or to the CASH BASIS OF ACCOUNTING. As a technical term, it is used in the UK's VALUE ADDED TAX system to refer to a basis allowed for smaller businesses whereby amounts actually received are taken into account, thus allowing immediate relief for BAD DEBTS.

cash at bank Amounts belonging to an enterprise that are held in demand deposits at a bank. In a UK CASH FLOW STATEMENT, a 24-hour notice cut-off is used.

cash basis of accounting A way of accounting that stresses the receipts and payments of cash rather than the REVENUES and EXPENSES calculated according to the ACCRUAL BASIS OF ACCOUNTING. Normally, cash and bank transactions are treated in the same way for this purpose. Since payments are recorded when they are made, this implies not only that 'expenses' are not recorded but also that 'ASSETS' are not recorded.

cash book A chronological listing of all receipts and payments of cash. This includes (and might be restricted to) those receipts and payments made via bank accounts. The cash book might include several columns for particular common receipts and payments.

    The cash book is part of the DOUBLE-ENTRY BOOKKEEPING system in that its balance at the end of a period is included in the TRIAL BALANCE and then in the BALANCE SHEET.

cash budget A detailed numerical plan for the future cash receipts and payments of an enterprise, often prepared on a monthly basis. The cash budget should have predicted any operating shortages or surpluses of cash, and included plans to cope with them.

cash cow A product or part of an enterprise which generates a reliable and substantial flow of sales (and therefore inflow of cash). There is generally an implication that the cash cow is unexciting.

cash cycle The regular process within an enterprise whereby cash is used to pay the suppliers of raw materials or other INVENTORIES which then turn into sales and eventual receipts of cash.

cash discount A reduction in the amount to be received or paid for goods or services if cash is used, or perhaps if invoices are paid rapidly.

cash dividend The normal way whereby a company pays a return to its shareholders out of the profit for a period. In the UK, such dividends are paid by a company without deduction of income tax, and the term 'cash dividend' can be used to clarify this. Also, the term can be used to distinguish such a dividend from one paid by transferring extra shares to the shareholders.

cash equivalents Short-term investments that are readily convertible to known amounts of cash and which are subject to an insignificant risk of changes in value. Generally, some limit on the length of the investment is presumed, such as three months.

cash float Physical cash (notes and coins) held by a trader for the purposes of being able to give change to customers or to pay small bills.

cash flow Sometimes used to refer very loosely to the amount of cash coming into or out of a business in a particular period. However, it can be used as a more precise accounting term, particularly in North America, to refer to NET PROFIT with DEPRECIATION charges added back. The latter will have been deducted in the calculation of the former, but is not, of course, a cash payment of the period in question. *See*, also, CASH FLOW STATEMENT.

cash flow accounting *See* CASH FLOW STATEMENT.

cash flow forecast *See* CASH BUDGET, although the term could be used to refer to a forecast *before* plans for dealing with anticipated surpluses or deficits of cash from operations are included.

cash flow projection *See* CASH BUDGET.

cash flow risk The risk that future cash flows associated with a MONETARY ASSET or LIABILITY will fluctuate.

cash flow statement One of the main annual FINANCIAL STATEMENTS in many countries, including the UK and the USA. This statement uses a CASH BASIS OF ACCOUNTING rather than an accrual basis. The INTERNATIONAL ACCOUNTING STANDARD and US version of the statement concentrates on the cash flows relating to operations, financing, investment; and it reconciles to a wide total including CASH and CASH EQUIVALENTS. In the UK, there are eight headings including the use of cash for tax payments and the use of cash in the management of liquid resources. There is a reconciliation to a narrow concept of 'cash'.

cash generating unit The smallest set of assets for which it is possible to measure cash inflows and outflows separately. In a manufacturing industry, this might be a whole factory rather than an individual machine. An IMPAIRMENT is measured on the basis of cash generating units.

cash payments journal A JOURNAL recording chronologically all the payments out of an enterprise's bank account. There may be several columns for different types of payments, particularly one for payments to suppliers, i.e. to TRADE CREDITORS.

cash ratio In the context of a bank, the relationship between the available physical cash and the sum of the deposits of customers, i.e. their bank accounts. A country's CENTRAL BANK will demand that banks keep at least a minimum level.

cash receipts journal A JOURNAL recording chronologically all the receipts into an enterprise's bank account. There may be several columns for different types of receipts, particularly one for receipts from account customers, i.e. from TRADE DEBTORS.

cash sale A sale for cash rather than one to be recorded in a customer's account for later payment.

CCA Abbreviation for CURRENT COST ACCOUNTING.

CCAB An abbreviation for the CONSULTATIVE COMMITTEE OF ACCOUNTANCY BODIES (of the UK and Ireland).

ccc The Welsh equivalent to the abbreviation 'plc' for PUBLIC LIMITED COMPANY.

c/d (or c/f) Abbreviation for carried down (or carried forward), as used in an ACCOUNT when an amount is entered to balance off the account. An equivalent double entry (*see* DOUBLE-ENTRY BOOKKEEPING) is brought down to begin the next period in the same account.

central bank The government's bank that also implements a country's monetary policy and may supervise the banking sector. Examples include the Bank of England (for the whole of the UK, not just for England), the Federal Reserve Bank in the USA and the Bundesbank in Germany.

certificate of deposit The written acknowledgement by a bank that it holds a sum of money and will repay it at a particular date and will also pay a particular rate of interest. Such certificates can be traded from one person to another, i.e. they are 'NEGOTIABLE INSTRUMENTS'.

certificate of incorporation A written acknowledgement by the REGISTRAR OF COMPANIES (or a similar official in a country other than the UK) that a company has complied with the necessary formalities and has begun legal existence.

certificate to commence business In the UK, a written acknowledgement by the REGISTRAR OF COMPANIES that a PUBLIC LIMITED COMPANY has complied with the rules concerning AUTHORIZED MINIMUM SHARE CAPITAL.

certified accountant A member of the ASSOCIATION OF CHARTERED CERTI-FIED ACCOUNTANTS.

certified public accountant In the USA, a member of one of the state authorities of public accountants. Many such members volunteer to join the AMERICAN INSTITUTE OF CERTIFIED PUBLIC ACCOUNTANTS. The state authorities grant licences to practise public accounting.

cessation In the context of taxation, the discontinuation of a business.

CGT Abbreviation for CAPITAL GAINS TAX.

chairman In the context of a UK company, the chairman of the board of directors. Good CORPORATE GOVERNANCE suggests that the chairman should not be the same person as the managing director (or chief executive officer). Consequently, the chairman is often a part-time non-executive director. The chairman also presides at the company's ANNUAL GENERAL MEETING.
   The equivalent US term is 'president'.

chairman's report (chairman's statement) A statement in the ANNUAL REPORT of most large UK companies in which the chairman of the board of directors reviews the progress of the past year and the prospects for the future. It will often contain acknowledgement of support from staff, suppliers, customers or shareholders; it may make some political points about taxation, investment or inflation. The report is not a mandatory requirement; thus, it neither obeys particular rules nor follows a standard format.

Chapter 11 In American law, the rules under which a business that is in financial difficulties applies to a court for protection from its CREDITORS. This procedure may enable the business to survive and eventually to repay the creditors wholly or partly.

charge In the context of an ASSET, a legal right over the proceeds of sale. A CREDITOR might be given a charge over some or all assets of a company as an inducement to lend money. However, the term can also mean an EXPENSE.

chargeable assets In the context of the UK's CAPITAL GAINS TAX, assets whose disposal would be relevant for the calculation of the tax. Exempted assets include a taxpayer's principal residence, motor cars and betting winnings.

chargeable gain In the context of the UK's CAPITAL GAINS TAX, certain gains on the disposal of CHARGEABLE ASSETS. Gains are reduced in various ways, e.g.

by deducting costs of purchase and sale. The same term applies to the gains of companies that are added into CORPORATION TAX calculations.

chargeable transfer In the context of the UK's INHERITANCE TAX, certain gifts that are taxable on the donor. Some other transfers are exempt, e.g. because they are made more than seven years before death.

charge account The facility whereby a customer can buy from a retailer on CREDIT rather than for CASH. The rules of the account may require payment each month if interest expense is to be avoided. The term can also be used for the listing of the amounts due to the retailer and those paid by the customer.

charge and discharge accounting A system of BOOKKEEPING whereby an individual charges himself or herself with amounts to be received, and credits (discharges) himself or herself with amounts paid. Such a system was used particularly before DOUBLE-ENTRY BOOKKEEPING when accounting for manors or monasteries in medieval times.

charitable contribution A donation by a company to a charitable organization. In the UK, certain donations have to be disclosed in the DIRECTORS' REPORT. Some donations are not deductible expenses for the purposes of calculating TAXABLE INCOME.

charity accounts The FINANCIAL STATEMENTS prepared and published by charities, as filed with the Charity Commissioners. There are requirements on this subject in the Charities Act 1993 and in a STATEMENT OF RECOMMENDED PRACTICE. The financial statements include a STATEMENT OF FINANCIAL ACTIVITIES rather than a PROFIT AND LOSS ACCOUNT.

chartered accountant In the UK and Ireland, a person who is a member of one of three institutes of accountants that has a royal charter.

Chartered Association of Certified Accountants Former name of the ASSOCIATION OF CHARTERED CERTIFIED ACCOUNTANTS.

chartered company In the UK, a company incorporated by royal charter rather than by another means such as the now normal route under the COMPANIES ACT.

Chartered Institute of Management Accountants A UK-based professional accountancy body whose earliest predecessor body was founded in 1919. Its members mainly work in commerce and industry, and membership does not enable work as a COMPANY AUDITOR. A large and increasing proportion of the Institute's members live outside the UK. The designatory letters for members are ACMA for associates and FCMA for fellows.

Chartered Institute of Public Finance and Accountancy A UK professional accountancy body founded (under another name) in 1885. Many of its members work in local and central government. The designatory letters for members are CPFA.

Chartered Institute of Taxation A UK professional association whose members generally work in the field of taxation. The designatory letters for associates are ATII, and for fellows, FTII.

chartist A financial analyst who believes that company share prices move over time in a way that can be recorded on graphs and charts in order to predict future price changes.

chart of accounts A German invention that provides a detailed, standardized arrangement of account codes for ASSETS, LIABILITIES, CAPITAL, REVENUES and EXPENSES. The system may be decimalized, and varies industry by industry. Its original purpose was to allow companies to record and prepare accounting information in a uniform, and therefore comparable, way. This would enable inter-firm comparisons, and would enhance the efficiency of industry.

Charts were used as a uniform system in France during the Second World War, and proved sufficiently successful that they were permanently adopted there as part of the *plan comptable général* (general accounting plan). Thus, throughout France, an auditor or tax inspector or industrialist can easily feel at home in a company's accounting system because uniform coding and definitions are in use.

In Germany, there are voluntary charts of accounts, which are still useful for original inter-firm comparative purposes.

In the UK or the USA the term is sometimes used to describe the listing of the LEDGER ACCOUNTS in a company's BOOKKEEPING system.

check US term for CHEQUE, but *see*, also, INTERNAL CHECK.

cheque A written instruction to a banker to pay on demand a specified amount of money from the writer's bank account to a party named in the instruction.

chinese wall A notional barrier between two departments in the same business designed to stop the flow of client or other information between the departments. This might be necessary to avoid various conflicts of interest or INSIDER DEALING.

CICA Abbreviation for the CANADIAN INSTITUTE OF CHARTERED ACCOUNTANTS.

CIMA Abbreviation for the CHARTERED INSTITUTE OF MANAGEMENT ACCOUNTANTS (of the UK).

CIPFA Abbreviation for the CHARTERED INSTITUTE OF PUBLIC FINANCE AND ACCOUNTANCY (of the UK).

circularization of debtors The sending of letters by an AUDITOR to the DEBTORS of a client in order to seek confirmation of the existence and size of the client's assets.

circulating capital Those assets of an enterprise that change regularly from one form (e.g. INVENTORY) to another (e.g. CASH) as a result of the normal trading operations of the enterprise. There is no precise definition of this term, which could therefore mean the same as CURRENT ASSETS or as NET CURRENT ASSETS or WORKING CAPITAL.

City Code on Takeovers and Mergers A written set of practices expected to be observed by all parties before and during BUSINESS COMBINATIONS in the UK. The Code does not have the force of law but is an example of an attempt at self-regulation. The Code is designed to protect shareholders from unfair treatment by directors.

class action A civil law action by one or more persons on behalf of a whole class of similar persons.

classical system of corporation tax A system of CORPORATION TAX whereby companies and their owners are taxed as fully separate taxable entities. As a result a company's taxed income is paid out to shareholders who are then taxed on it again. Such a system operates in the USA and The Netherlands, as it did in the UK until 1973 when it was replaced by an IMPUTATION SYSTEM.

classification In the context of FINANCIAL STATEMENTS, the arrangement of items into classes of similar items. For example, the assets in a UK BALANCE SHEET are classified into FIXED ASSETS and CURRENT ASSETS.

class of assets Grouping of assets of a similar nature and use in an enterprise's operations. The relevance of this is that the revaluation of TANGIBLE ASSETS and INTANGIBLE ASSETS is not allowed in the UK or under INTERNATIONAL ACCOUNTING STANDARDS COMMITTEE rules by individual asset but only for a class of assets.

clean opinion/report In the context of an independent AUDIT, a report by the auditors that is not qualified in any way.

clean surplus concept The idea that an enterprise's performance statement (e.g. an INCOME STATEMENT) should show all gains and losses rather than any of them being taken directly to EQUITY.

clientele effect The preference by particular groups of investors for companies with particular types of DIVIDEND POLICY. For example, some investors may prefer to hold shares in companies that pay low dividends because they hope instead for large increases in share price due to the accumulation of wealth in the companies.

close company Companies which are controlled by their directors or by five or fewer participators or their associates (i.e. five or fewer shareholders or their families or partners). Such companies are likely, of course, to be small. They may have a similarity to PARTNERSHIPS in their management but are incorporated for legal and tax purposes.

A LISTED COMPANY is required to note whether or not it is a close company in its ANNUAL REPORT.

The term 'close company' is defined in tax legislation and, under certain circumstances, involves a higher level of taxation.

close-ended funds Investment companies whose capital is fixed rather than such entities as UNIT TRUSTS where there is no particular limit on contributions by investors.

closely held corporation A company whose shares are owned by a small number of investors.

closing balance The excess of the DEBITS over the CREDITS, or vice versa, in an ACCOUNT at the end of a period.

closing entries Entries made in a DOUBLE-ENTRY BOOKKEEPING system at the end of an accounting period in order to balance and close the REVENUE and EXPENSE accounts. The other halves of the balancing entries appear in the PROFIT AND LOSS ACCOUNT.

closing rate The spot exchange rate of two currencies at the BALANCE SHEET date.

closing rate method UK term for the normal method of FOREIGN CURRENCY TRANSLATION, whereby the FINANCIAL STATEMENTS of FOREIGN SUBSIDIARIES are translated into the parent's currency at current exchange rates. In particular, the exchange rate at the BALANCE SHEET date is used to translate balance sheet items (except for items in EQUITY). The same rate can be used for PROFIT AND LOSS ACCOUNT items, although the actual rates or the average rate for the year could be used instead. Gains and losses resulting from the use of this method are taken to RESERVES.

closing stock The stock/INVENTORIES remaining in an enterprise at the date of the BALANCE SHEET. The amount is shown in the balance sheet and also taken into account in the calculation of GROSS PROFIT.

cluster sampling In the context of an AUDIT, the division of a population of items (e.g. invoices) into groups which are then sampled. The selected group is then checked in detail by looking at all its members.

CNC Abbreviation for the CONSEIL NATIONAL DE LA COMPTABILITÉ (of France).

CNCC Abbreviation for the COMPAGNIE NATIONALE DES COMMISSAIRES AUX COMPTES (of France).

COB Abbreviation for the COMMISSION DES OPÉRATIONS DE BOURSE (of France).

CoCoA *See* CONTINUOUSLY CONTEMPORARY ACCOUNTING.

COGS Abbreviation for COST OF GOODS SOLD.

collar A contractual feature within a FINANCIAL INSTRUMENT whereby the maximum and minimum rates of interest are fixed.

collateral Assets used to secure a loan. If the borrower defaults, the collateral can be seized by the lender.

collectors of taxes UK officials responsible for the collection but not for the assessment of amounts of various DIRECT TAXES. The assessment is made by the INSPECTOR OF TAXES.

columnar accounts LEDGER accounts with several columns for different categories of items.

combined financial statements FINANCIAL STATEMENTS of two or more enterprises that are added together. The implication is that these are not CONSOLIDATED FINANCIAL STATEMENTS, perhaps because they do not relate to a group of controlled enterprises or because some of the procedures of consolidation have not been carried out. For example, there may have been no elimination of intercompany transactions.

comfort letter A written confirmation from AUDITORS or other reporting accountants on some issue. For example, in the context of issuing a PROSPECTUS, stockbrokers may seek confirmation from accountants that a company has sufficient CAPITAL.

Comité de la Réglementation Comptable French committee with the power to amend accounting regulations.

commercial code Part of the legal system in most of continental Europe and in countries influenced by codified law, e.g. Japan. Commercial codes usually contain detailed accounting rules applying to enterprises. They are amended by COMPANIES ACTS or equivalent.

commercial paper A written acknowledgement by a company that it will pay back money that was borrowed for the short term and in an unsecured manner.

commercial substance The economic reality behind a possibly complex set of legal arrangements. For example, if a company sells a machine and immediately leases back the same machine for most of its expected life, the substance of the arrangement may be that the machine has not been sold. *See*, also, SUBSTANCE OVER FORM.

commission A payment made, usually on a percentage of value basis, to a provider of intermediary services, such as an agent, stockbroker or auctioneer.

Commission des Opérations de Bourse (COB) The approximate French equivalent of the SECURITIES AND EXCHANGE COMMISSION of the USA. It was founded in 1968 by the French government and charged with supervising and improving the financial capital market. As with all continental European bourses, there are relatively few shares listed on the Paris Bourse (*see* STOCK EXCHANGES). The government and banks are important providers of finance in France.

Perhaps the most obvious impact that the COB had on the financial reporting of French listed companies resulted from its campaign in favour of CONSOLIDATED FINANCIAL STATEMENTS. Consolidation was virtually unknown in France in 1968, but a majority of French listed companies prepared consolidated statements by the time it became compulsory for them in 1986.

Commissione Nazionale per le Società e la Borsa The approximate Italian equivalent of the SECURITIES AND EXCHANGE COMMISSION in the USA. It regulates the financial reporting and auditing of companies whose securities are publicly traded in Italy. It was founded in 1974, and has pushed accounting for LISTED COMPANIES towards ANGLO-SAXON ACCOUNTING.

Commissioners of the Inland Revenue UK officials who are appointed by the Inland Revenue to hear appeals by taxpayers against tax assessments. *See*, also, GENERAL COMMISSIONERS and SPECIAL COMMISSIONERS.

commitment fee The price charged by a bank for making available loan finance that has not yet been called upon.

commitments basis In the context of PUBLIC SECTOR ACCOUNTING, a method which records expenditure when an organization is committed to it rather than when it is spent.

commitments for capital expenditure Proposed purchases of FIXED ASSETS to which a company is committed. In the UK, the COMPANIES ACT requires directors to disclose in the ANNUAL REPORT the amount of commitments and any amounts in excess of this that the directors have been authorized to commit.

committed costs Long-run expenditures that the management of an enterprise cannot reasonably avoid, such as payments on an uncancellable lease.

Committee on Accounting Procedure A former committee of the AMERICAN INSTITUTE OF CERTIFIED PUBLIC ACCOUNTANTS that issued, between 1939 and 1959, documents called ACCOUNTING RESEARCH BULLETINS. Several of these are still in force in the USA, and therefore form part of GENERALLY ACCEPTED ACCOUNTING PRINCIPLES.

commodities Primary materials (e.g. coffee beans, copper or sugar) that are traded on an exchange.

commodity contract A legal arrangement for the delivery by one party and the receipt by another party of COMMODITIES.

common costs The costs that are borne by all the output of a process, or those costs shared by a number of departments.

common seal The official signature of a company in the form of an impression that can be formed on paper (or on wax). Certain documents have to be sealed in this way.

common-size financial statements FINANCIAL STATEMENTS in which all the items are expressed as percentages of some total. For the BALANCE SHEET, the denominator is usually TOTAL ASSETS; for the income statement, it is SALES.

common stock US term for the ORDINARY SHARES in a corporation. Normally a majority of the ownership capital will comprise issues of common stock, though PREFERENCE SHARES/PREFERRED STOCK are also issued. Stock usually has a PAR VALUE, which is little more than a label for the type of stock. The amount that would have to be paid for one share will be determined, in the case of a listed share, by the daily price on the STOCK EXCHANGE. The total of common stock is part of the SHAREHOLDERS' FUNDS of a company. The return to common stock is a DIVIDEND. In the long run, the size of dividends depends on the profitability of the company.

commorientes Latin term for two or more persons who die at the same time. In the context of inheritance law, it is assumed that the oldest person died first, and so on.

Compagnie National des Commissaires aux Comptes A French body, responsible to the Minister of Justice, that regulates EXTERNAL AUDIT.

Companies Act The Acts of Parliament that regulate companies. In the UK, there is now one main Act, the Companies Act 1985. In some countries, such as Germany, COMPANY LAW has been the main source of general and detailed requirements in accounting. In other countries, such as the USA, there is virtually nothing on accounting in state or federal law; instead, accounting rules are set by the SECURITIES AND EXCHANGE COMMISSION, by an independent committee, the profession, or some combination. In the UK, before the EU's FOURTH DIRECTIVE led to the provisions of the Companies Act 1981, there were only general requirements in the law concerning accounting. For example, proper BOOKS OF ACCOUNT had to be kept, annual FINANCIAL STATEMENTS audited, published and give a 'TRUE AND FAIR VIEW', and a number of detailed DISCLOSURES made.

In the UK, company law really began with the 1844 Act which enabled companies to be easily formed, and the 1855 Act which allowed LIMITED LIABILITY. Compulsory independent audit for banks followed in 1879, and for all LIMITED COMPANIES in 1900. Not until the 1929 Act did PROFIT AND LOSS ACCOUNTS become compulsory. GROUP ACCOUNTS were required by the 1947 Act (consolidated into the 1948 Act).

Company law in the UK was consolidated again in the Companies Act 1985. Before that, the principal Act of 1948 had been supplemented by Acts of 1967, 1976, 1980 and 1981. The 1981 Act added requirements for the formats of the BALANCE SHEET and the profit and loss account, extended disclosure requirements, provided certain exemptions from publication for smaller PRIVATE COMPANIES and introduced detailed compulsory ACCOUNTING PRINCIPLES. Many of these provisions came, via the Fourth Directive, from German law (particularly the public companies law of 1965). The Companies Act 1989 amended the 1985 Act by implementing into UK law the requirements of the SEVENTH and EIGHTH DIRECTIVES (on group accounting and on AUDITORS).

On several matters other than accounting, UK law has traditionally been fairly detailed. For example, there are many provisions on AUDIT, directors' duties, rights of SHAREHOLDERS and CREDITORS, conduct of ANNUAL GENERAL MEETINGS, and so on. The law also contains many provisions on BUSINESS NAMES and INSIDER DEALING.

Companies House The registry, in Cardiff, which maintains records on all English and Welsh companies and to which those companies must send their ANNUAL REPORTS. This information is available to the public.

company A legal entity separate from its owners, the SHAREHOLDERS. Thus, companies can own ASSETS, can sue and be sued at law, can have 'PERPETUAL SUCCESSION', i.e. there need be no limit to their lives, irrespective of the lives of, or changes to, the owners. Also, most companies have LIMITED LIABILITY; to be more exact, the owners of the company have limited liability for the DEBTS of the company. In effect, the owners' liability is usually limited to the money contributed (or to be contributed) for their shareholdings. Because owners may be granted limited liability (in the case of the UK, from the Companies Act, 1855 onwards), many investors are prepared to risk their money and become co-owners. This enables very large amounts of capital to be raised, and therefore makes very large companies possible. If there were no limited liability (as with most PARTNERSHIPS) it would be much more difficult to persuade investors to become co-owners, without their insisting on becoming co-managers so that they could safeguard their own investments and potential liabilities. Most investors have no desire to become co-managers of businesses, and most businesses have no desire for vast numbers of co-managers. Thus, limited liability is essential for large businesses.

In the UK, before the 1844 Act, it had been necessary to have an Act of Parliament or a Royal Charter in order to set up a company. Now companies are commonplace in the UK and throughout the world. They are set up with a series of legal transactions and registration with government (or state government) offices. In the UK, the MEMORANDUM OF ASSOCIATION and ARTICLES OF ASSOCIATION outline the rules of the company; in the USA the analogous documents are the CERTIFICATE OF INCORPORATION and the BYLAWS.

Throughout much of the Western developed world (though not in the USA) the law distinguishes between PRIVATE COMPANIES and PUBLIC COMPANIES. Table 1 gives abbreviated designations in certain countries which will be seen as part of the names of companies.

Table 1 Abbreviated company names

	Private	Public
France	Sàrl	SA
Germany	GmbH	AG
Italy	Srl	SpA
Japan	YK	KK
The Netherlands	BV	NV
UK	Ltd	plc

It is necessary for a company to be public in order for there to be a market in its SECURITIES (shares or loans). The extreme example of a public market is a STOCK EXCHANGE listing. Thus, public companies tend to be larger than private companies. The law imposes greater restrictions on public companies. In the UK, for example, public companies must have a minimum issued capital of £50,000. The definition of DISTRIBUTABLE PROFITS is stricter for them. They are not allowed the exemptions from publication granted to certain private companies.

There are about 12,000 public companies in the UK, about a quarter of them listed. There are about 950,000 private companies. In some countries, such as Germany and The Netherlands, public companies are required to have a two-tier board structure comprising a SUPERVISORY BOARD (containing some employee representation) and a MANAGEMENT BOARD.

In the USA, there is no such legal distinction between public and private. However, the analogous companies to public ones are those that are registered with the SECURITIES AND EXCHANGE COMMISSION (SEC). Companies must register with the SEC in order for there to be a market in their securities. The SEC lays down AUDIT and DISCLOSURE requirements. Further, it provides the backing for ACCOUNTING STANDARDS. Thus, the rules for registered companies are greatly more extensive than those for unregistered companies. *See*, also, CLOSE COMPANIES and CORPORATION TAX.

company auditor A person (or firm) appointed as AUDITOR under the provisions of the COMPANIES ACT. Such a person must be a REGISTERED AUDITOR.

company formation The legal procedures to be adopted when creating a COMPANY. In the UK, this involves sending various documents to the REGISTRAR OF COMPANIES.

company law *See* COMPANIES ACT.

company limited by guarantee A type of COMPANY for which the members have liability limited to the amounts specified in the MEMORANDUM OF ASSOCIATION. These amounts could be called upon in the event that the company were wound up. Such companies are fairly rare in the UK, but some charities adopt this legal form.

company limited by shares A type of COMPANY for which the members have liability limited to the amounts unpaid on their shares. This is by far the most common type of company in the UK.

company officers The directors of a COMPANY, but also including the COMPANY SECRETARY if that person is not a director.

company seal *See* COMMON SEAL.

company secretary An officer of a COMPANY, generally appointed by the directors, who is responsible for the minutes of board meetings and for sending ANNUAL RETURNS to the REGISTRAR OF COMPANIES. The company secretary may also be put in charge of a large number of other administrative and legal issues.

comparability A characteristic of FINANCIAL STATEMENTS (or of items in the statements) of more than one enterprise that would enable them to be assessed side by side in a way that is not misleading.

comparative figures *See* CORRESPONDING AMOUNTS.

compensated absences Absences by an employee from work, in those cases where the employer nevertheless pays the employee's remuneration.

compensating error A mistake in a DOUBLE-ENTRY BOOKKEEPING system which is cancelled out in a TRIAL BALANCE by another error of equal size.

compilation A US term for the preparation (as opposed to the audit) of the FINANCIAL STATEMENTS of an enterprise by independent accountants.

completed contract method A technique of accounting for the costs and revenues connected to a CONTRACT whereby no profit is recognized until the contract has been completed and the resulting product has been delivered. Such a method is required under UK, US and INTERNATIONAL ACCOUNTING STANDARDS COMMITTEE rules where the outcome of a contract cannot be reliably assessed. In some other countries, it is the normal method for all contracts. *See*, also, PERCENTAGE-OF-COMPLETION METHOD.

compliance costs The costs to those subject to laws of complying with the laws. For example, the compliance costs of CAPITAL GAINS TAX are said to be very high because of the complications of the rules.

compliance tests In the context of an AUDIT, investigations of the effectiveness of the INTERNAL CONTROLS of a company. If the controls are found to be effective, then a small amount of testing of the transactions will be necessary.

composition A legal agreement between a company and its CREDITORS when the company is unable to pay the creditors in full.

compound discount The difference between the nominal amount of a future sum and its discounted PRESENT VALUE.

compound instrument A FINANCIAL INSTRUMENT that, from the issuer's perspective, contains both a LIABILITY and an EQUITY element. Under the rules of INTERNATIONAL ACCOUNTING STANDARD (IAS) 32, such an instrument must be shown in a BALANCE SHEET as partly a liability and partly equity. However, this is not the case under UK or US rules, which follow the legal form of the instrument. For example, a CONVERTIBLE DEBENTURE is shown as partly DEBT and partly equity under IAS rules but as debt under UK and US rules.

compound interest Interest calculated on the aggregate of the original loan and the interest on it unpaid by the borrower; cf. SIMPLE INTEREST.

compound journal entry A JOURNAL entry involving something more than equally matched single DEBIT and CREDIT amounts.

comprehensive auditing *See* VALUE FOR MONEY AUDIT.

comprehensive income The income of an entity for a period including all recognized gains and losses, not just those included in a conventional INCOME STATEMENT. In the USA, companies are required to disclose comprehensive income, but several formats for this are allowed. In the UK, it can be seen in the STATEMENT OF TOTAL RECOGNIZED GAINS AND LOSSES.

comprehensive tax allocation Accounting for DEFERRED TAX on all temporary differences (or timing differences).

comptroller A US title for the person in charge of a company's accounting functions.

Comptroller and Auditor General A UK official reporting directly to Parliament on the subject of the AUDIT of government departments.

conceptual framework A theoretical structure to underlie the making and use of technical rules in accounting.
Perhaps the best way to explain the idea of a conceptual framework is to refer to the efforts of the FINANCIAL ACCOUNTING STANDARDS BOARD in the USA, which began a conceptual framework project after the TRUEBLOOD REPORT of 1973 had criticized the *ad hoc* nature of accounting standards. The project has led to several 'STATEMENTS OF FINANCIAL ACCOUNTING CONCEPTS'. The first statement concerned the OBJECTIVES OF FINANCIAL STATEMENTS. It was concluded that the most important aim was to provide investors with useful information for making financial decisions. Then, the ELEMENTS OF FINANCIAL STATEMENTS were identified and defined. For example, ASSETS, LIABILITIES and INCOME were discussed. These are, of course, very difficult to define with precision.
Another statement concerned the qualitative characteristics of accounting information. In order to achieve the desired objectives, it was concluded that RELEVANCE and RELIABILITY were the two most important features. 'Relevance' would be determined with respect to the decisions to be made by users; 'reliability' would increase with objectivity.
The INTERNATIONAL ACCOUNTING STANDARDS COMMITTEE and UK standard setters have adopted similar frameworks.

Confederation of Asian and Pacific Accountants A regional association of ACCOUNTANCY BODIES covering a large number of countries in Asia and others bordering the Pacific Ocean.

conglomerate A group of companies engaged in diverse commercial activities.

connected persons In the context of the disclosure requirements of the COM-

PANIES ACT, certain persons related to a company's directors. Such persons include a spouse, a child, a business partner and a trustee of a TRUST that benefits a director or a connected person.

Conseil National de la Comptabilité A French government committee responsible, since 1947, for the accounting plan, the PLAN COMPTABLE GÉNÉRAL.

consent letter A letter from an expert (such as an accountant, a valuer or an ACTUARY) which confirms permission to include the expert's report in a PROSPECTUS.

conservatism *See* PRUDENCE.

consideration Something valuable that is offered by a purchaser in a contract. At its simplest, the consideration would be a sum of money (or a promise of money), or it could be another ASSET or relief from a LIABILITY or some other promise. A consideration is necessary for a contract to be valid.

consignment Generally, a number of goods sent together as a package. However, the specific term 'sent on consignment' refers to goods sent to an agent for the purposes of sale. The goods remain the property of the sender (the consignor) until sale.

consignment accounts LEDGER accounts which record transactions relating to goods sent to another party (an agent) for the purpose of sale. The goods remain part of the sender's INVENTORY.

consistency The concept that an enterprise should use the same rules of RECOG-NITION, MEASUREMENT and PRESENTATION from year to year in its FINANCIAL STATEMENTS. This is now well established in most countries. A company may be allowed to change its policies in special circumstances, such as an alteration in ACCOUNTING STANDARDS, but the change should always be disclosed in the ANNUAL REPORT. The purpose of consistency is to enable a better comparison of a year's profits and values with those of previous years. The concept that different *companies* should use the same rules to assist inter-company comparisons might be called UNIFORMITY.

Consistency is required in the UK by FINANCIAL REPORTING STANDARD 18 and by COMPANY LAW.

CONSOB Abbreviation for the COMMISSIONE NAZIONALE PER LE SOCIETÀ E LA BORSA (Stock Exchange Commission, Italy).

consolidated accounts A term often used in the UK for CONSOLIDATED FINANCIAL STATEMENTS.

consolidated balance sheet A BALANCE SHEET prepared by a group of enterprises under common control on the basis that the group is a single entity. *See* CONSOLIDATED FINANCIAL STATEMENTS.

consolidated cash flow statement A CASH FLOW STATEMENT prepared by a group of enterprises under common control on the basis that the group is a single entity. *See* CONSOLIDATED FINANCIAL STATEMENTS.

consolidated financial statements A means of presenting the financial position, results and cash flows of a parent and its subsidiary companies as if they were a single entity. Consolidation ignores the separation of parents and subsidiaries due to legal and geographical factors; it accounts for the group of companies as a single entity. Approximately, the FINANCIAL STATEMENTS of all the companies in the group are added together, with adjustments to extract INTRA-GROUP TRANSACTIONS and indebtedness, to achieve FOREIGN CURRENCY TRANSLATION, and to ensure uniform ACCOUNTING POLICIES throughout.

consolidated fund In the context of accounting by the UK government, an account recording tax revenues and other receipts that are not specifically recorded in another account.

consolidated income statement An INCOME STATEMENT prepared by a group of enterprises under common control on the basis that the group is a single entity. *See* CONSOLIDATED FINANCIAL STATEMENTS.

consolidated profit and loss account *See* CONSOLIDATED INCOME STATEMENT.

consolidation The process of preparing CONSOLIDATED FINANCIAL STATEMENTS by combining together the statements of group enterprises as though they were a single entity.

consolidation adjustments The eliminations and other adjustments to the statements of group enterprises as part of the process of preparing CONSOLIDATED FINANCIAL STATEMENTS. For example, INTRA-GROUP TRANSACTIONS and indebtedness are eliminated, and adjustments are made to ensure UNIFORM ACCOUNTING POLICIES.

consolidation difference One way of describing the difference, which arises as part of the process of CONSOLIDATION, between the price paid to buy a SUBSIDIARY and the values of the individual ASSETS and LIABILITIES thereby obtained. Normally, the difference is positive, i.e. the price paid exceeds the value of the NET ASSETS. This difference could also be called GOODWILL arising on consolidation.

consortium Two or more independent enterprises that choose to operate together for particular purposes.

consortium relief In the context of UK CORPORATION TAX, a way of giving tax reductions for members of a CONSORTIUM (limited to twenty members) by enabling the sharing of losses.

constant dollar accounting US term for CURRENT PURCHASING POWER ACCOUNTING.

constraint In the context of production, a restriction or limitation caused by a shortage of a particular input. For example, forecasts may suggest that a type of skilled labour or raw material may be in insufficient supply to fit in with production plans, so attempts must be made to increase supply or to make other adjustments.

construction contract A contract specifically negotiated for the construction of an ASSET or group of related assets. The accounting for this would follow either the PERCENTAGE-OF-COMPLETION METHOD or the COMPLETED CONTRACT METHOD.

constructive obligation An obligation that arises because an enterprise has created a valid expectation on the part of other parties that it will discharge certain responsibilities by an established pattern of past practice or published policies.

Consultative Committee of Accountancy Bodies A co-ordinating body set up by the six professional accountancy bodies in the UK and Ireland after proposals for their merger failed in 1970. These bodies, in order of size, are shown in Table 2.

Table 2 Professional accountancy bodies in the UK and Ireland

	Designatory letters
The INSTITUTE OF CHARTERED ACCOUNTANTS IN ENGLAND AND WALES (ICAEW)	ACA, FCA
The ASSOCIATION OF CHARTERED CERTIFIED ACCOUNTANTS (ACCA)	ACCA, FCCA
The CHARTERED INSTITUTE OF MANAGEMENT ACCOUNTANTS (CIMA)	ACMA, FCMA
The INSTITUTE OF CHARTERED ACCOUNTANTS OF SCOTLAND (ICAS)	CA
The CHARTERED INSTITUTE OF PUBLIC FINANCE AND ACCOUNTANCY (CIPFA)	CPFA
The INSTITUTE OF CHARTERED ACCOUNTANTS IN IRELAND (ICAI)	ACA, FCA

consumable materials Materials that are used up in the production process but which are not directly associated with particular output, so they do not form part of DIRECT COSTS. For example, small items (such as screws) or materials (such as lubricating oil) would be treated in this way.

Consumer Price Index The US term for the RETAIL PRICE INDEX as prepared by a government department and published monthly.

Contact Committee An EU committee set up by the FOURTH DIRECTIVE on company law designed to discuss possible amendments to the accounting requirements of the Directives.

contingencies *See* CONTINGENT ASSET and CONTINGENT LIABILITY.

contingency theory of management accounting The theory that the appropriate MANAGEMENT ACCOUNTING system for an organization depends upon the particular circumstances of the organization, such as its structure and competitive environment.

contingent asset A possible ASSET that arises from past events and whose existence will be confirmed only by the occurrence or non-occurrence of one or more uncertain future events. Such items are not recognized as assets but are disclosed in NOTES TO THE ACCOUNTS if they are MATERIAL and PROBABLE.

contingent consideration A payment, by the purchaser as part of a CONTRACT, that is dependent on certain future events such as the performance of a purchased enterprise.

contingent gain A possible gain that depends upon the occurrence of some future event. Such gains are not recognized in the INCOME STATEMENT but might be disclosed in the NOTES TO THE ACCOUNTS in the form of information on a related CONTINGENT ASSET.

contingent liability An obligation that is not recognized or a possible OBLIGATION whose existence will be confirmed only by the occurrence or non-occurrence of one or more uncertain future events. The reasons that an obligation would not be recognized are: (a) that it is not probable that an outflow of resources will be required to settle the obligation, or (b) that the amount of the obligation cannot be measured reliably. Contingent liabilities should be disclosed in the NOTES TO THE ACCOUNTS.

contingent loss A possible loss that depends upon the occurrence of some future event. Such losses are not recognized in the INCOME STATEMENT but are disclosed in the NOTES TO THE ACCOUNTS in the form of information about a CONTINGENT LIABILITY.

contingent rent That portion of a lease payment that is variable depending on a factor other than just the passage of time, e.g. percentage of sales or amount of usage.

continuity assumption *See* GOING CONCERN.

continuous budget A BUDGET which is up-dated every month or quarter as another such period passes, and a further future period is added to the end.

continuous inventory A system of physically counting all INVENTORIES/stock on a regular and rotating basis throughout the year and reconciling it to the accounting records such as BIN CARDS. Discrepancies will reveal errors in the records or losses of stock. The records are adjusted to conform to the physical reality. This may avoid the need for an annual simultaneous count of all the stock at the year end.

continuously contemporary accounting (CoCoA) A system of financial reporting whereby ASSETS and LIABILITIES are measured at their CURRENT CASH EQUIVALENTS. Since all items are measured in the same way, the totals on a BALANCE SHEET have a clear meaning. Gains and losses are measured in terms of changes in their values rather than at the point of sale or by using the ACCRUAL BASIS OF ACCOUNTING.

This system was invented and elaborated in the 1960s by the late Professor R J Chambers of the University of Sydney.

continuous stocktaking *See* CONTINUOUS INVENTORY.

contra *See* CONTRA ENTRY.

contra accounts Entries in the LEDGER accounts of two different enterprises that can be offset. For example, if two companies owe money to each other, complete or partial offsetting can be arranged without full payments.

contract An agreement between two or more parties. In English law (and similarly throughout much of the English-speaking world), a legally binding contract requires one party to make an offer, another to accept the offer, and valuable CONSIDERATION to pass. Contracts are often in writing but do not need to be in order to be legally binding, except for contracts related to certain items such as the sale of land.

contract accounting *See* LONG-TERM CONTRACT.

contract cost The total expected cost of a CONSTRUCTION CONTRACT to the enterprise that is to fulfil the contract for a customer.

contract costing The collection of costs on a contract-by-contract basis for the purpose of COST ACCOUNTING. It will also involve the assessment of the total costs of contract work in progress at the end of a period.

contracting costs The costs which arise because there is a separation between the owner and the manager (or the principal and the agent). For example, in the case of a LISTED COMPANY, the shareholders appoint directors, but then have to pay for mechanisms to check up on, and to control, the directors, such as the costs of AUDIT.

contract note A written confirmation of the purchase or sale of a security such as a SHARE.

contract of employment *See* EMPLOYMENT CONTRACT.

contra entry An entry in a LEDGER account representing the reversal of an earlier entry in the same account. The objective is to cancel the earlier entry without crossing it out.

contribution In the context of BREAKEVEN ANALYSIS, the excess of REVENUES over VARIABLE (or MARGINAL) COSTS. This amount will contribute towards covering FIXED COSTS and then providing PROFIT.

contribution income statement A variation of a normal published INCOME STATEMENT, whereby sales and variable costs are recorded in columns by product in order to show contributions, and then the total FIXED COSTS are deducted from the total contribution. Such a format might be used as part of MANAGEMENT ACCOUNTING.

contribution margin ratio The contribution margin of a particular product (i.e. SALES minus VARIABLE COSTS) divided by the sales of that product. An enterprise can rank its different products by their relative profitability by using their contribution margin ratios.

contributory pension A PENSION for which the employee makes some or all of the contributions to the fund that will eventually pay the pension.

control The power to obtain the future economic benefits that flow from an ASSET or an enterprise. In the case of the latter, this means the power to govern the financial and operating policies of the enterprise so as to obtain the benefits from its activities. The definition of an asset includes reference to control, and so does the definition of a SUBSIDIARY.

control account A LEDGER account in which the balance is kept equal to the balances on a number of more detailed accounts. For example, there may be a large number of separate accounts for DEBTORS, and it may be more convenient to have a single account in the DOUBLE-ENTRY BOOKKEEPING system as a summary of all these. It would be called the SALES LEDGER CONTROL ACCOUNT (or total debtors control account). The individual accounts of the debtors would then not be part of the double-entry system.

control contract A CONTRACT which gives one enterprise the legal right to control the financial and operating policies of another enterprise. In the UK, such a contract would generally disenfranchise the shareholders, so it would not be legal. However, in other countries (e.g. Germany) such contracts can operate and would mean that the controlled enterprise was a subsidiary of the controlling enterprise.

controllable costs COSTS that could be controlled by managers at a particular level of an enterprise within a particular time span. The higher up the enterprise and the longer the span, the more costs are controllable.

controllable variance A VARIANCE between actual and budgeted amounts that is regarded as being within the control of the manager who is responsible for the BUDGET CENTRE.

controlled non-subsidiary An enterprise which does not meet the definition of SUBSIDIARY but is nevertheless controlled by another. Under INTERNATIONAL ACCOUNTING STANDARDS COMMITTEE rules, there should be no such enterprises, because the definition of 'subsidiary' rests solely on control. However, in some national laws, including that of the UK, such a company could be contrived. However, it would nevertheless be required to be treated as a subsidiary for the purpose of CONSOLIDATION (*see* QUASI-SUBSIDIARY).

controller *See* COMPTROLLER.

controlling interest An investment in an enterprise that in practice enables control over the financial and operating policies of that enterprise. At its simplest, ownership of more than half of the voting shares of a company would amount to a controlling interest.

As a technical legal term in the case of a company director's holding, a 20 per cent interest is labelled a 'controlling interest'.

control period The length of the periods within the financial year for which separate totals are included in a BUDGET. Often this period will be one month.

control risk That part of the AUDIT RISK related to a client's INTERNAL CONTROL system.

convenience translation A set of FINANCIAL STATEMENTS (and perhaps other elements of an ANNUAL REPORT of a company) which have been adjusted not only for language but in other ways. For example, some large Japanese companies publish convenience translations in American English, with dollar as well as yen amounts, and with certain re-arrangements of the financial statements and notes.

convention In an accounting context, a practice customarily adopted. For example, it is the convention in the UK for the PROFIT AND LOSS ACCOUNT to precede the BALANCE SHEET.

conversion In the context of foreign currency, the changing of one currency into another (not just an accounting activity, *see* FOREIGN CURRENCY TRANSLATION). In the context of law, a civil wrong equivalent to the crime of theft.

conversion cost The costs of turning raw materials into finished products. This would include all manufacturing expenses, whether DIRECT or INDIRECT COSTS, and both VARIABLE and FIXED COSTS.

conversion ratio The exchange ratio to be used at the conversion of CONVERTIBLE LOAN STOCK into shares, i.e. it expresses the number of shares that an owner of a quantum of DEBT would obtain.

conversion right The legal right contained in a CONTRACT whereby the holders of CONVERTIBLE LOAN STOCK are allowed to opt to convert their DEBT into SHARES.

convertible Changeable from one legal form into another. For example, certain DEBTS are legally arranged as CONVERTIBLE LOAN STOCK, which can be changed into SHARES.

convertible currency A currency that can be freely exchanged for other currencies at publicly available RATES OF EXCHANGE.

convertible debenture *See* CONVERTIBLE LOAN STOCK.

convertible loan stock Long-term DEBTS/DEBENTURES/BONDS that are convertible, at some future date at the option of the lender, into EQUITY, i.e. ORDINARY SHARES of the borrowing company. This means that investors can have the safety of debt finance (in that there is fixed annual interest and preferential repayment of capital if a company is wound up), with the profit-sharing aspects of equity if the company does well. For the company, the advantages are that it will be easier to attract finance at a reasonable annual cost of capital, and that the returns to the providers of finance will initially be in the form of interest, which is tax-deductible.

convertible unsecured loan stock A type of CONVERTIBLE LOAN STOCK where the contract makes available no particular assets for the lender if the borrower defaults.

conveyancing The transfer of title to the ownership of land.

cooking the books Colloquial expression for manipulating the accounting records or the FINANCIAL STATEMENTS of an enterprise in order to mislead the readers of such documents.

core deposit intangible The asset owned by a bank in the shape of the ability to use money for profitable purposes that is technically payable to the bank's depositors but which most of them will not call on most of the time.

corporate assets In the context of the measurement of IMPAIRMENT, assets that cannot be directly allocated or reasonably apportioned to any particular CASH GENERATING UNIT.

corporate failure prediction The assessment of the likelihood of the LIQUI-DATION of a company. Various models have been designed for this purpose which use RATIOS calculated from the company's FINANCIAL STATEMENTS as input.

corporate governance The processes by which companies are governed and held accountable to their owners. Good corporate governance might involve the separation of the job of chairman from that of managing director, the use of an AUDIT COMMITTEE and the appointment of a number of NON-EXECUTIVE DIRECTORS. The London Stock Exchange requires listed companies to state whether they comply with various codes of practice (*see* CADBURY REPORT and GREENBURY REPORT).

corporate modelling The simulation of a business in the form of a computer-based model in order to predict the outcomes of various possible decisions.

Corporate Report A discussion paper published in 1975 by the UK's standard-setting body (then called the ACCOUNTING STANDARDS STEERING COMMITTEE) concerning the objectives, uses and users of FINANCIAL STATEMENTS. Some of its contents can be found in CONCEPTUAL FRAMEWORKS. The Report also recommended the publication of a number of extra financial statements by companies (*see*, for example, VALUE ADDED STATEMENTS) but there was no direct action on these recommendations.

corporate social reporting Publication of reports by companies on social rather than financial matters. This might include EMPLOYEE REPORTING (simplified reporting to employees) and EMPLOYMENT REPORTS (reporting about the status, etc. of employees). It might also include ENVIRONMENTAL ACCOUNTING.

corporation A succession of persons treated as an artificial person for legal purposes. For example, a succession of kings or bishops can be distinguished from any particular physical person who occupies the post at one moment. Similarly, an association of persons (most obviously a LIMITED COMPANY) can be a corporation.

corporation sole A CORPORATION involving only one physical person.

corporation tax In the UK, the tax on the income of companies. The tax was introduced in 1965 as a separate tax. Before that, companies paid income tax on their business profits (as sole traders and partners still do) plus a special profits tax. In the USA, companies still pay 'income tax'.

correcting entry An entry made in a DOUBLE-ENTRY BOOKKEEPING system designed to correct for an error. Depending on the nature of the error, the correcting entry might or might not be a double entry.

corresponding amounts Amounts reported in FINANCIAL STATEMENTS but relating to previous periods. For example, UK and INTERNATIONAL ACCOUNTING STANDARDS COMMITTEE rules require all figures in a PROFIT AND LOSS ACCOUNT to be shown with corresponding amounts for the previous year. In the USA, two years of corresponding figures must be shown for this statement.

The British term is normally 'CORRESPONDING AMOUNTS'.

corridor A range around an enterprise's best estimate of POST-EMPLOYMENT BENEFIT obligations. In INTERNATIONAL ACCOUNTING STANDARD and US accounting rules, the corridor is equivalent to 10 per cent of the greater of the PRESENT VALUE of the obligation and the FAIR VALUE of the fund. If ACTUARIAL GAINS AND LOSSES go outside this corridor, they must start to be recognized as income or expense.

COSA Abbreviation for COST OF SALES ADJUSTMENT.

cost The amount of CASH or CASH EQUIVALENTS paid or the FAIR VALUE of the other consideration given to acquire an ASSET. Also included would be subsequent costs to bring the asset into its present condition and location.

Valuation practices in many countries are based on HISTORICAL COST, i.e. the purchase price or production cost of assets. INVENTORIES (stocks) are valued at the 'LOWER OF COST OR MARKET'. OIL AND GAS ACCOUNTING is often based on a 'FULL COST' METHOD. Cost can also be used to mean CURRENT REPLACEMENT COST.

The profit of a business is calculated by setting the costs (or EXPENSES) of the period against its REVENUES.

There are also many ways of analysing costs for COST ACCOUNTING or MANAGEMENT ACCOUNTING purposes.

cost absorption In the context of COST ACCOUNTING, the adding to the production cost of particular output the relevant OVERHEAD COST.

cost accounting The breaking down of various COSTS and REVENUES by product, location or manager. The purpose is to assist managers in working out which is the most profitable product, or which is the cheapest location, or how much should be charged for particular products. Costs are allocated directly to production where possible. If not, they are apportioned to various COST CENTRES for OVERHEAD. Then, these can be absorbed into production on a pre-arranged basis.

Cost Accounting Standards Board US government body that sets regulations for the operation of federal government contracts.

cost accumulation The recording of the COSTS of production for a particular product as it progresses towards completion. This enables the total costs to be calculated and examined in detail.

cost allocation The assignment of COST directly to a product or a COST CENTRE.

cost apportionment The assignment of COST to two or more COST CENTRES on a pre-arranged basis because the cost cannot be directly allocated. For example, property taxes for a large factory may be split up among various cost centres on the basis of floor area used.

cost ascertainment The process of calculating the cost relating to a particular unit, COST CENTRES, etc.

cost attribution The various processes (such as COST APPORTIONMENT and COST ABSORPTION) whereby costs are eventually related to particular units of output.

cost behaviour The effects on total costs of changes in the level of activity within a business. Certain costs are FIXED COSTS, others are VARIABLE COSTS and some are in-between. The behaviour of total costs can be studied in BREAKEVEN ANALYSIS.

cost–benefit analysis A detailed numerical comparison of the expected costs and benefits of particular proposed projects in order to decide which ones to proceed with, and possibly to rank projects in order of usefulness. In a business context, this is part of CAPITAL BUDGETING.

cost centre The sections of an organization for which costs are collected. Each cost centre should be the clear responsibility of one manager. Cost centres come in two main types: (a) production, and (b) service. In costing systems that try to associate all costs with particular units of output, the costs of the cost centres have to be absorbed into units of production.

cost classification The splitting up of costs into categories, such as DIRECT COSTS versus INDIRECT COSTS, or VARIABLE COSTS versus FIXED COSTS.

cost code A reference number for any ACCOUNT which relates to costs.

cost control The process of managing costs, particularly in order to keep them in line with (or below) BUDGET.

cost driver A factor within an organization that causes COSTS. For example, the cost driver for machine set-up costs is the number of different jobs that the machine has to do. Cost drivers need to be identified as part of ACTIVITY-BASED COSTING.

cost estimation In the context of COST ACCOUNTING, the processes whereby the predicted costs of particular products or services are calculated.

cost flow assumptions In the context of INVENTORY (stock) valuation, the assumptions made about the method of flow of particular inventories through the production process in an organization. Such an assumption is necessary when individual units of an inventory cannot be (or cannot conveniently be) separately identified. One possible assumption is 'first-in, first-out' (FIFO). This assumes, for accounting purposes, that the oldest inventory purchased that is still on hand will be the first one used in production. Other possible assumptions are WEIGHTED AVERAGE COST METHOD and 'last-in, first-out' (LIFO).

In the UK, LIFO is not normally allowed by STATEMENT OF STANDARD ACCOUNTING PRACTICE 9 on the ground that the remaining inventory in the BALANCE SHEET will be valued at unreasonably out of date costs. However, LIFO is allowed by US and INTERNATIONAL ACCOUNTING STANDARDS COMMITTEE standards.

cost function The relationship between costs and other variables, such as the level of production. The function can be expressed in terms of a formula or equation. Such a relationship is examined in BREAKEVEN ANALYSIS.

costing methods The techniques used in COST ACCOUNTING.

cost ledger The set of those ACCOUNTS within a DOUBLE-ENTRY BOOKKEEPING system that relate to COSTS.

cost ledger control account The CONTROL ACCOUNT in the main DOUBLE-ENTRY BOOKKEEPING records of an organization that keeps the detailed cost accounts in a subsidiary ledger which is not itself part of the main records.

cost method Accounting for investments by recording them at cost (less any IMPAIRMENT). The INCOME STATEMENT reflects income from the investment only to the extent that the investor receives dividends.

This is the normal UK method of accounting for investments in the FINANCIAL STATEMENTS of investors, as opposed to CONSOLIDATED FINANCIAL STATEMENTS. Even in the latter statements, it is used for investments that are not controlled or significantly influenced. Under INTERNATIONAL ACCOUNTING STANDARD or US rules, and by UK financial institutions, certain investments are shown at FAIR VALUE instead.

cost of acquisition The FAIR VALUE of the consideration given to buy something. In the case of an immediate payment of money, this is the FACE VALUE of the money. However, where the CONSIDERATION includes non-monetary items or future money, a valuation is necessary in current terms.

cost of capital The rate of return that an enterprise would be expected to pay for extra capital raised to finance its activities. Therefore, the cost of capital is also the minimum required RATE OF RETURN on proposed new investment. Usually, the WEIGHTED AVERAGE COST OF CAPITAL of existing long-term sources of capital is used.

cost of conversion Costs of work in progress or finished goods STOCKS (INVENTORIES). These include costs directly related to the units of production, such as direct labour, and a systematic allocation of fixed and variable production overheads that are incurred in converting materials into finished goods.

cost of goods manufactured The costs during a period related to the production of goods, whether sold or not. This cost includes PRODUCTION OVERHEADS.

cost of goods sold *See* COST OF SALES.

cost of purchase *See* COST OF ACQUISITION.

cost of sales The cost of goods sold during a period. This is calculated, for a simple retail business, as the costs of the goods available for sale (i.e. the OPENING STOCK plus the purchases of goods) less the goods remaining at the end of the period, i.e. the CLOSING STOCK. For a manufacturing business, the cost of sales also includes all DIRECT COSTS and INDIRECT COSTS of production.

cost of sales adjustment (COSA) An adjustment in the CURRENT COST ACCOUNTING system to take account of the fact that the costs of INVENTORIES (stocks) are changing. For example, suppose that a business has the same physical quantity of OPENING STOCK and CLOSING STOCK but that prices of the stock are rising. The *value* of the closing stock will be higher, so profit will be higher.

However, the profit is tied up in the stock. The COSA adjusts profit downwards for this. The profit then reflects the success of the business after taking account of replacing the stock used up at current prices.

cost-plus contract A CONSTRUCTION CONTRACT in which the contractor is paid for defined costs, plus a percentage of the costs or a fixed fee.

cost-plus method A method of pricing a product which adds a mark-up to the cost of producing or buying the product.

cost pool In the context of ACTIVITY-BASED COSTING, an aggregation of costs which will be charged to products on the basis of a common COST DRIVER.

cost savings In the context of rising prices, the reduction in costs caused by buying goods and services early. To put it another way, these are the HOLDING GAINS related to ASSETS that will be used in production.

cost sheet A form, used in COST ACCOUNTING, on which all the costs of a particular product or service are shown.

costs of disposal Incremental costs directly attributable to the disposal of an ASSET, e.g. agent's or lawyer's fees.

cost standard A pre-determined expected level of cost.

cost unit The smallest unit of production for which an organization calculates the cost. Depending on the complexity and value of the output, the cost unit might be a single physical item (e.g. a table) or parts of an item (e.g. a wing of an aeroplane) or multiple items, e.g. 100 nails.

cost–volume–profit analysis The analysis of the behaviour of profits as costs change in response to changes in levels of activity. *See* BREAKEVEN ANALYSIS.

council tax A UK tax paid on domestic property by its owners (or occupiers) to local government. The tax varies in bands by value of property and also varies by local authority.

country risk The economic, social or political risks attached to locating ASSETS, production or SALES in a particular country. An extreme example of country risk would be the EXPROPRIATION of assets without compensation by a foreign government.

coupon A piece of paper attached to a BEARER SECURITY which the holder can use to claim interest or DIVIDEND payments. The term can also be used as an abbreviation for COUPON RATE.

coupon rate The contracted rate of interest on a DEBT expressed as a percentage of the FACE VALUE (or PAR VALUE).

coupon stripping The de-coupling of the COUPONS from their BEARER SECURITIES so that the two elements can be sold separately.

covenant A legally binding promise to perform (or not to perform) an action. For example, as part of a DEBENTURE deed, the borrowing company might agree with the lenders that it would never borrow so much money that particular GEARING RATIOS would be exceeded.

covering The reduction or elimination of a risk of loss that had been caused by having promised to deliver or pay something in the future.

CPA Abbreviation for a CERTIFIED PUBLIC ACCOUNTANT.

CPP Abbreviation for CURRENT PURCHASING POWER ACCOUNTING.

Cr Abbreviation for CREDIT (in DOUBLE-ENTRY BOOKKEEPING).

CRC Abbreviation for the COMITÉ DE LA RÉGLEMENTATION COMPTABLE (of France).

CRC Abbreviation for CURRENT REPLACEMENT COST.

creative accounting The inventive use (or stretching of) accounting rules by enterprises in order to present misleadingly good FINANCIAL STATEMENTS. There is a well-known story about a large company that was interviewing several applicants for a senior accounting job. The applicants were given masses of accounting data and asked to calculate the profit. The applicant who got the job was the one who asked: 'What profit had you in mind?' There are so many subjective elements in the measurement of value or profit, that a wide range of answers is often legal and in conformity with GENERALLY ACCEPTED ACCOUNTING PRINCIPLES. Thus, there is the opportunity to be 'creative'. A rather more old-fashioned and more limited expression is 'window-dressing'.

It was concern along these lines that helped to lead to the establishment of the bodies that set ACCOUNTING STANDARDS.

credit In the context of DOUBLE-ENTRY BOOKKEEPING, one of the two types of entry, denoting in this case increases in LIABILITIES, EQUITY or REVENUES or decreases in ASSETS or EXPENSES. The origin is that *credit* is the Latin for 'he/she believes' or 'he/she trusts'. When the only accounting records of a business were those of people who owed the business money, or were owed money by it, the simple entries would have been *debit* for 'he/she owes' and *credit* for 'he/she trusts' or is owed. Thus, a creditor is someone who is owed money.

As record-keeping developed into double-entry, a debit and a credit were invented for all transactions. Thus, for example, a purchase of raw materials from a supplier who is not yet to be paid is recorded as: *debit* purchases; *credit* the supplier (the creditor). Similarly, a sale to a customer who is not yet to pay cash is recorded as: *debit* the customer (the debtor); *credit* sales. In the full system, any increase in revenues, liabilities or capital is a credit entry, as is any decrease in assets or expenses. If the system is working properly, the total of all the debits will equal the total of all the credits. The credit side of an ACCOUNT is conventionally the right-hand side.

The other meaning of credit is closely connected. To 'extend credit' or to 'make sales on credit' is to trust another person. The lender becomes the creditor, i.e. the one who trusts.

credit account The facility whereby a customer can buy from a retailer on trust rather than for CASH. The US term is CHARGE ACCOUNT, under which entry there is some more detail.

credit balance The arithmetical difference between the sums of all the CREDIT entries and all the DEBIT entries in an ACCOUNT, in those cases where there is an excess of credit.

credit control The system used by a business to manage the receipt of money from those of its customers who do not pay immediately in cash. For example, it would be normal to prepare analyses of the ages of outstanding debts and to follow up unpaid debts in particular ways.

credit note A written acknowledgement by a business to a customer of a reduction in the DEBT of the customer. This would be the result, for example, of the return of goods by the customer.

creditor As explained under CREDIT, a creditor is a 'truster', someone to whom a business owes money. The US expression for the amounts owed is ACCOUNTS PAYABLE. Creditors are created by purchases 'on credit' or other amounts owing, e.g. to the tax authorities. Short-term creditors are included under 'CURRENT LIABILITIES' on a BALANCE SHEET; they are expected to be paid within the year. If credit purchases are the cause, the title used might be 'TRADE CREDITORS'.

Long-term creditors are those who are not expected to be paid within the year. These might be trade creditors but would more likely be holders of bonds or DEBENTURES. The latter would normally be entitled to receive interest, whereas trade creditors are not. However, trade creditors often offer discounts for prompt payment, which is an implied way of charging interest.

creditor–days ratio The relationship between the size of the balance of money due to suppliers and the purchases on credit. This is a measure of the average number of days that a business waits before paying its suppliers.

creditors ledger The set of accounts within a DOUBLE-ENTRY BOOKKEEPING system in which are recorded the amounts due to suppliers. This can also be called the 'purchase ledger' or the 'bought ledger'.

creditors ledger control account An ACCOUNT which summarizes the entries in the CREDITORS LEDGER. In a DOUBLE-ENTRY BOOKKEEPING system, the creditors ledger control account can take the place of the many accounts for individual creditors, leaving the latter as memorandum accounts rather than as part of the double-entry system.

creditors' voluntary liquidation The legal closing down of a company caused by insolvency. The shareholders start the process off, but the law gives a number of rights to the creditors.

credit rating The assessment of the ability (and willingness) of a business or an individual to pay DEBTS at the due date.

credit rating agency A business that assesses the CREDITWORTHINESS of other businesses, institutions or individuals. The rating may be carried out privately, but some agencies publish their ratings of governments or large companies.

credit risk The risk that the other party to a FINANCIAL INSTRUMENT will not discharge an OBLIGATION and will thereby cause a financial loss.

credit sale A sale to a customer who does not immediately pay cash.

creditworthiness The degree to which it is wise to provide goods on CREDIT or to lend money to an organization or an individual. The measurement of this would be based on an assessment of the organization's ability and willingness to pay DEBTS when due.

critical event In the context of CRITICAL-PATH ANALYSIS, an event that lies on a critical path.

critical-path analysis A quantitative method for the control of a project which involves estimating the time taken to complete the longest set of activities which form an essential part of the project. Then efforts can be made to shorten, or at least to avoid delays on, this critical path.

cross-holding A mutual holding of shares by two or more companies in each other. However, under UK law, a SUBSIDIARY cannot hold shares in its parent.

cross rate The exchange rate between two currencies, as measured by reference to a third.

cross-sectional analysis Comparisons between enterprises rather than comparisons across time.

CTT Abbreviation for CAPITAL TRANSFER TAX.

cum dividend In the context of the sale of a SHARE, the share is cum dividend (or cum div.) if the purchaser would receive the next payment of dividend. This is normal. The opposite is *ex dividend*, which may apply for a short period around the dividend date. In that case, the seller intends to keep the next dividends, presumably to be received soon.

cum rights In the context of the sale of a share, the share is cum rights if the purchaser (rather than the seller) is entitled to participate in any future RIGHTS ISSUE of shares.

cumulative preference shares The normal type of PREFERENCE SHARES, on which any arrears of dividends have to be settled before the ORDINARY SHAREHOLDERS can be paid a dividend.

cumulative preferred stock US term for CUMULATIVE PREFERENCE SHARES.

currency exposure The degree to which an enterprise is subject to a risk of loss if exchange rates change.

currency risk In the context of a FINANCIAL INSTRUMENT, the risk that the value of the instrument will change due to fluctuations in foreign exchange rates.

currency translation *See* FOREIGN CURRENCY TRANSLATION.

current account In the context of a DOUBLE-ENTRY BOOKKEEPING system, an account that records amounts (resulting from day-to-day transactions) due to and from different companies in a group or to and from a PARTNERSHIP and its PARTNERS.

current asset Under UK law, an ASSET which is not intended for continuing use in the business. Such assets include STOCKS, DEBTORS and CASH. Also, a BALANCE SHEET may include current asset investments, i.e. those designed to be held for a short period. Just as investments can be fixed or current, so automobiles can be fixed (if part of a fleet of company cars) or current (if part of the trading stock of a car dealer). A company is required to show current assets separately from FIXED ASSETS, at least in its NOTES TO THE ACCOUNTS.

Under INTERNATIONAL ACCOUNTING STANDARDS COMMITTEE requirements, this distinction is not necessary, and anyway could be based on a 12-month cut-off.

current asset investment Under UK law, an investment which is not intended for continuing use in the business.

current cash equivalent The amount of cash for which an ASSET could be sold or a LIABILITY settled. If an asset could not be sold or, like GOODWILL, could not be sold separately, it would have a CURRENT CASH EQUIVALENT of zero.

current cost The amount that would have to be paid if the same or an equivalent ASSET were to be acquired currently. This is another term for CURRENT REPLACE-MENT COST.

current cost accounting (CCA) One of many possible systems designed to adjust accounting for changing prices. It is often included under the generic heading INFLATION ACCOUNTING, although it does not involve adjustments for inflation, but for specific price changes relating to the business's ASSETS. In the UK, STATEMENT OF STANDARD ACCOUNTING PRACTICE (SSAP) 16 was operational in the first half of the 1980s, requiring supplementary CCA information from large companies.

BALANCE SHEETS under CCA contain assets which are normally valued at net CURRENT REPLACEMENT COST. This is what it would cost to buy an identical replacement (or, if necessary, a similar replacement after adjustment for the differences). The replacement cost is reduced to the extent that the asset has been depreciated – hence, 'net' current replacement cost. In practice, index numbers might be used as estimates for actual replacement costs.

A CCA PROFIT AND LOSS ACCOUNT contains several adjustments compared to an HISTORICAL COST one. There is a DEPRECIATION adjustment to reflect the fact that depreciation based on a current cost would be higher (when prices of the assets are rising), and a COST OF SALES ADJUSTMENT to recognize the effect of changing prices on INVENTORIES (STOCKS). However, the most controversial adjustments in CCA systems are for monetary items. In SSAP 16, there was a MONETARY WORKING CAPITAL ADJUSTMENT to take account of the effect of price changes on DEBTORS and CREDITORS, and a GEARING ADJUSTMENT which was an adjustment for the fact that the business gains at the expense of lenders when the value of money falls due to rising prices.

current cost depreciation The measure of the DEPRECIATION of an ASSET by allocating the CURRENT COST of the asset (less expected disposal value) over its expected useful life.

current cost operating profit The profit before interest and taxation as calculated in the context of CURRENT COST ACCOUNTING. This is the conventional operating profit adjusted for such items as the current cost of depreciating FIXED ASSETS.

current investment Under INTERNATIONAL ACCOUNTING STANDARDS COM-

MITTEE definitions, an investment that is readily realizable and is intended to be held for not more than one year from the BALANCE SHEET date.

Under UK accounting, such assets are generally held at the lower of cost and NET REALIZABLE VALUE, although UK banks and companies following INTERNATIONAL ACCOUNTING STANDARD or US rules value some of these investments at FAIR VALUE. *See* AVAILABLE-FOR-SALE FINANCIAL ASSETS and TRADING.

current liabilities Those amounts on a BALANCE SHEET that are expected to be paid by the business within one year. They will include TRADE CREDITORS (UK)/ACCOUNTS PAYABLE (US), certain tax LIABILITIES, and PROPOSED DIVIDENDS. Bank overdrafts are included on the grounds that they fluctuate in size and are technically recallable at short notice.

current/non-current method A method of translating the FINANCIAL STATEMENTS of a foreign subsidiary into a parent's currency for the purposes of preparing CONSOLIDATED FINANCIAL STATEMENTS, whereby current items are translated at the closing rate of exchange and non-current items are translated at historical rates of exchange.

current purchasing power accounting A UK term for a method of adjusting FINANCIAL STATEMENTS prepared under HISTORICAL COST ACCOUNTING to take account of inflation. Basically, items in financial statements are up-dated by applying changes in RETAIL PRICE INDEX.

current rate method US term for the method of FOREIGN CURRENCY TRANSLATION whereby a foreign subsidiary's BALANCE SHEET items are translated at the closing rate of exchange, and income statement items are translated at actual rates or average rates for the year.

current ratio The relationship between the CURRENT ASSETS and the CURRENT LIABILITIES of a business. It is a measure of LIQUIDITY that can be used when comparing one company with another or one year with another. A higher ratio means greater liquidity and a greater probability that CREDITORS can be paid. However, it may mean that the resources of the business are inefficiently tied up in unproductive assets such as CASH or DEBTORS. This ratio can also be called the 'working capital ratio'.

For an even more short-run test of liquidity, one could calculate the QUICK RATIO or acid test. This omits the less current assets, such as STOCKS (INVENTORIES).

current replacement cost The amount that would have to be paid to replace an ASSET at any moment, including costs of purchase. Often a problem will arise in that an exact replacement is no longer available. The replacement cost of a 'MODERN EQUIVALENT ASSET' will then have to be used, adjusting for differences in the services provided. In practice, replacement cost is often estimated by applying price indices for the particular asset to its ORIGINAL COST.

current service cost The increase in the discounted value of a defined benefit OBLIGATION resulting from employee service in the current period.

The context is accounting for pensions and other POST-RETIREMENT BENEFITS. The current service cost is treated as an expense of the current period. It may be contrasted with PAST SERVICE COST.

current tax The amount of income tax in respect of the taxable profit (or loss) for a period. The amount of current tax that is unpaid relating to the current and prior periods is recognized as a LIABILITY. The tax expense recorded for a period includes both the current tax and the DEFERRED TAX.

current value accounting A particular version of price-change adjusted accounting. Its main adjustments (from HISTORICAL COST ACCOUNTING) are for the price changes of the business's assets, not for general inflation. *See* INFLATION ACCOUNTING.

current year basis In the context of the taxation of income and profits in the UK, the charging of tax in a fiscal (i.e. tax) year on the basis of profits of the accounting year ending in the fiscal year. An alternative would be the PRECEDING-YEAR BASIS.

curtailment A rearrangement of a PENSION PLAN that reduces the OBLIGATION of the company. The curtailment occurs because an enterprise makes a material reduction in the number of employees covered by a plan, or amends the terms of a DEFINED BENEFIT PLAN such that a material element of future service by current employees qualifies for lower benefits.

Gains or losses on curtailments should be recognized in income when they occur.

Customs and Excise The UK government department responsible for the assessment and collection of certain INDIRECT TAXES, such as VALUE ADDED TAX and CUSTOMS DUTIES.

customs duties Taxes levied on the import of certain goods into a country.

customs invoice Documentation prepared by a seller which records prices and other details specifically for the purposes of import or export formalities.

cut-off date In the context of an enterprise's accounting, the day beyond which transactions are not considered when preparing the FINANCIAL STATEMENTS for a particular period.

CVP Abbreviation for COST–VOLUME–PROFIT ANALYSIS.

cwmni cyfyngedig cyhoeddus (ccc) The Welsh language equivalent of PUBLIC LIMITED COMPANY (plc).

cycle billing The sending of invoices to customers at different dates throughout a month rather than all on the same day.

damages An amount of money required by a court of law to be paid to a person who has suffered loss or damage by the person responsible for that loss or damage.

dangling debit An informal term for a treatment of GOODWILL whereby it is shown as a deduction from reserves rather than as an ASSET. This is not now acceptable in the UK or under INTERNATIONAL ACCOUNTING STANDARDS COMMITTEE requirements.

database management system A suite of computer programs designed to organize, up-date and provide access to a collection of data.

data capture The recording of information at the source of a transaction.

data protection The safeguarding of personal information stored on electronic systems from misuse.

date of acquisition The date on which control of the NET ASSETS and operations of an acquiree enterprise is transferred to an acquirer. This is the date from which subsidiaries are consolidated into GROUP FINANCIAL STATEMENTS.

dawn raid The surprise purchase of a large quantity of SHARES in a COMPANY as a prelude to attempting to take over the company.

day books Part of the DOUBLE-ENTRY BOOKKEEPING system, these are the BOOKS OF ACCOUNT which initially record the very frequent transactions of a business, such as sales and purchases, so that the main accounting records are not swamped with masses of detail. Thus, there may be the 'SALES DAY BOOK', the 'PURCHASES DAY BOOK' and so on. These 'BOOKS OF ORIGINAL ENTRY' are totalled periodically, perhaps daily, and the totals taken to the main ACCOUNTS.

days' sales in inventory The level of INVENTORY in an enterprise expressed in terms of the number of days that it would take to sell that amount.

days' sales in receivables The level of RECEIVABLES (debtors) expressed in terms of the number of days of selling that would generate that amount.

DCF Abbreviation for DISCOUNTED CASH FLOW.

dealing securities Marketable securities that are acquired and held with the intention of reselling them in the short term. This is essentially the same as a TRADING ASSET.

Dearing Report A UK report of 1988 entitled *The Making of Accounting Standards* written by a committee chaired by Sir Ron Dearing. The report led to the setting up of the ACCOUNTING STANDARDS BOARD.

death duty A general term for taxation that falls due on the death of a person, usually as a result of the transfer of wealth from the deceased (*See*, for example, INHERITANCE TAX).

debenture Certain types of loans, usually long-term, made to a company. Normally, debentures are 'secured' on the ASSETS of the company by mortgage deeds. Thus, a debenture holder would be able to persuade a court of law to force a company to sell those assets if the company was otherwise unable to meet the terms of the loan.

debenture redemption reserve An element of a company's EQUITY containing amounts of profits voluntarily set aside as not to be distributed. The amounts are arranged to rise so that they reach the size of the debenture by the time it is redeemed.

debenture trust deed A written legal agreement which records the rights of the lenders of money to a company.

debit In the context of DOUBLE-ENTRY BOOKKEEPING, one of the two types of entry, denoting in this case increases in ASSETS or EXPENSES, or decreases in LIABILITIES, EQUITY or REVENUES. The word 'debit' is naturally associated with the double-entry system, but pre-dates it. It derives from the Latin for 'he/she owes'. Thus, when a merchant's only records were of the amounts owed to him and by him, the *debit* was one of the two types of record. An entry in the accounting records of 'Smith *debit* 100' merely records that Smith owes 100, perhaps for a sale to Smith without immediate receipt of cash.

In the full double-entry system, all increases in ASSETS and EXPENSES and all decreases in EQUITY, LIABILITIES or REVENUES are debits. If the recording has been done correctly, the total of the debits will always equal the total of the credits.

The debits are to be found on the left-hand side of ACCOUNTS. This has always been the case, and may be due to the fact that the left (*sinister* in Latin) is regarded as 'bad' (Judas sat on the left side of Jesus at the Last Supper; the damned are on the left at the Last Judgement, etc.). The 'bad' people who have not paid the business yet are shown on the left. The 'good' people who extend credit to the business are shown instead on the right.

debit balance The arithmetical difference between the sums of all the DEBIT entries and all the CREDIT entries in an account, in those cases where there is an excess of debits.

debit note A written notification to a customer that a business has charged the customer's account with an amount.

debt An amount owed by one party to another. In the USA, the term 'debt' (as opposed to 'a debt') is often used to refer to a company's long-term borrowings.

debt capital The long-term borrowings of an enterprise; to be distinguished from equity capital, as provided by the shareholders.

debt collection agency A business which offers, for a fee, to assist in the collection of cash from its clients' customers.

debt–equity ratio The relationship between an enterprise's debt finance and its equity finance. Usually, only long-term finance is considered. This is one measure of GEARING.

debt instrument Another way of saying 'a debt', but this term implies a debt evidenced by a specific legal contract. A debt instrument is to be contrasted with an EQUITY INSTRUMENT, such as a SHARE.

debtor collection period The average time (usually measured in days) that it takes an enterprise to collect its debts from customers.

debtors By derivation, 'debitors', i.e. those with DEBIT balances in the BOOKS OF ACCOUNT of a business. In a BALANCE SHEET, debtors are usually mostly trade debtors, i.e. customers who have not yet paid cash. Such amounts are shown as CURRENT ASSETS because they are not intended for continuing use in the business.

In a balance sheet, debtors are valued at what is expected to be received, bearing in mind the principle of CONSERVATISM. Thus, BAD DEBTS are written off, and allowances are made against debts that may not be collectable. The allowances (often called provisions) may be either specific (against particular suspect debts) or general (based on the average experience of bad debts).

debtors' ledger The set of accounts within a DOUBLE-ENTRY BOOKKEEPING system in which are recorded the amounts owed by customers. This can also be called the SALES LEDGER.

debtors' ledger control account An account which summarizes the entries in the DEBTORS' LEDGER. In a DOUBLE-ENTRY BOOKKEEPING system, the debtors' ledger control account can take the place of the many accounts for individual debtors, leaving the latter as memorandum accounts rather than as part of the double-entry system.

debt restructuring The re-arrangement of an enterprise's borrowings in order to change interest payments or the repayment dates. If an enterprise is having difficulties in paying its debts, the lenders might agree to lessen or postpone the enterprise's burden in some way in order to improve the chances of the debt being settled eventually.

decentralization The delegation of responsibilities down to lower levels of an organization.

decision model A simulation of the elements involved in a business decision, used in order to help the choice among various possible courses of action.

decision table A written statement in tabular form of various possible actions and the probabilities of particular outcomes from them.

decision tree A diagram showing, as branches in a tree, various possible decisions and their probable outcomes at each subsequent stage.

declared dividend A forthcoming payment to the shareholders of a company out of its past profits, once the payment has been formally approved (in the UK, by the SHAREHOLDERS). The precise steps necessary for approval depend on the national law and on the company's own ARTICLES OF ASSOCIATION. However, generally in the UK, a final dividend is declared when the shareholders vote in favour of a recommendation by the directors at the company's ANNUAL GENERAL MEETING.

declining (or reducing) balance method An arithmetic technique for calculating the depreciation of an ASSET whereby a period's DEPRECIATION EXPENSE is calculated as a constant percentage of the net undepreciated amount (NET BOOK VALUE) at the end of the previous period. This method causes depreciation expenses to be larger in the earlier years of an asset's life.

decommissioning costs The COSTS involved in closing down an installation at the end of its useful economic life. For example, there may be very substantial decommissioning costs involved at the end of the life of a nuclear power station. An estimate of these (discounted for the time value of money) is added to the cost of the ASSET at the beginning of its life, and this is balanced by the recognition of a PROVISION for the costs.

deductible temporary difference In the context of DEFERRED TAX, a TEMPORARY DIFFERENCE leading to amounts that will be deductible in determining taxable profit (or loss) of future periods. Such a temporary difference would result, for example, when a liability for future pension payments is recognized before it is taken into account by the tax authorities. The deductibility for tax will arise when the accounting carrying amount of the LIABILITY is settled. The deductible temporary difference leads to the recognition of a DEFERRED TAX ASSET.

deed of arrangement A written contract between an insolvent person or company and the creditors, whereby the former agrees to settle debts (or proportions of them) and the latter agree to give up certain legal claims.

deed of covenant *See* COVENANT.

deed of partnership *See* PARTNERSHIP AGREEMENT DEED.

deed of variation A written agreement that allows, under certain conditions, for a deceased person's will to be changed.

deep discounted bonds Loans carrying low interest and therefore sold at well below the FACE VALUE of their REDEMPTION.

deep market A market for shares, commodities or other items where there is considerable volume, so that even a large transaction would not move the market price.

deep pocket An informal term for the capacity of a person or organization to pay large sums, particularly in the context of litigation. Large audit firms are said to have deep (insured) pockets, and therefore to be worth suing.

defalcation Misappropriation of property belonging to another person or organization.

default Failure to comply with the terms of a contract; most obviously, failure to pay a DEBT when it falls due.

defeasance Making a contract void. *See* IN-SUBSTANCE DEFEASANCE.

defective accounts A UK legal term for company FINANCIAL STATEMENTS that do not comply with legislation, and in particular do not give a TRUE AND FAIR VIEW. Failure to follow ACCOUNTING STANDARDS will therefore normally mean that the accounts are defective. The FINANCIAL REPORTING REVIEW PANEL can take companies to court if it believes that they have published defective accounts.

defensive interval ratio A measure (in days) of the ability of an enterprise to pay its debts as they fall due. It is calculated by comparing 'quick assets' (i.e. CURRENT ASSETS apart from INVENTORIES) with some measure of daily estimated operating EXPENSES to be paid in cash.

deferral method One of two main methods for calculating DEFERRED TAX ASSETS and DEFERRED TAX LIABILITIES. The deferral method uses tax rates that were ruling when the deferred tax balances originated. In contrast, the liability method uses current tax rates. The latter method is now required under UK, US and INTERNATIONAL ACCOUNTING STANDARDS COMMITTEE rules.

deferred annuity A contract involving the payment of a lump sum in order to get in exchange an annual series of cash receipts, starting at some future date.

deferred asset An asset involving cash expected to be received beyond one year from the balance sheet date.

deferred charges *See* DEFERRED COSTS.

deferred consideration agreement A contract to purchase something (generally a business) where the payment of some of the purchase price is delayed until a particular future date or event.

deferred costs Generally, costs of an enterprise that have not yet been charged as expenses in the profit and loss account and therefore are shown in the balance sheet as ASSETS, but do not meet the definition of (or RECOGNITION tests for) that term. Consequently, such practice is not allowed in the UK or under INTERNATIONAL ACCOUNTING STANDARDS COMMITTEE rules, but in some countries various items (such as advertising expenditure or set-up costs of a business) may be treated in this way.

deferred credit *See* DEFERRED INCOME.

deferred income An amount recognized in the FINANCIAL STATEMENTS but not yet treated as a realized gain in the PROFIT AND LOSS ACCOUNT. The deferred credit or income is stored as a CREDIT BALANCE on the BALANCE SHEET while waiting to be treated as income. Government grants related to the purchase of ASSETS can be treated in this way.

deferred income tax US term for DEFERRED TAX.

deferred shares Shares in a company which only have rights to dividends after other shareholders have been paid.

deferred tax In the UK, this is caused by a timing difference between when an

EXPENSE or REVENUE is recognized for financial reporting purposes and when it is recognized for TAXABLE INCOME. For example, suppose that DEPRECIATION for tax purposes (i.e. CAPITAL ALLOWANCES) is more rapid than for accounting purposes; in such a case, in early years of an ASSET's life, tax depreciation will be larger than accounting depreciation (and vice versa later). Thus, there are timing differences. In order to account fully for deferred tax, an additional deferred tax charge would be recorded to represent tax at current rates on the excess of the tax allowance over the accounting charge for depreciation. A deferred tax LIABILITY is also recorded in this amount. In the US and under INTERNATIONAL ACCOUNTING STANDARDS COMMITTEE rules, there is a requirement to account for TEMPORARY DIFFERENCES rather than for TIMING DIFFERENCES.

deferred tax assets Under INTERNATIONAL ACCOUNTING STANDARDS COMMITTEE or US rules, the income taxes recoverable in future periods in respect of DEDUCTIBLE TEMPORARY DIFFERENCES and the carry forward of unused tax losses.

deferred tax liabilities Under INTERNATIONAL ACCOUNTING STANDARDS COMMITTEE or US rules, the income taxes payable in future periods in respect of TAXABLE TEMPORARY DIFFERENCES.

deficit An excess of expenditure over revenue. This term is generally used by not-for-profit organizations.

defined benefit employee obligation The discounted present value of expected future payments required to settle an EMPLOYEE BENEFIT OBLIGATION resulting from employee service in the current and prior periods. This obligation would be reduced by a pension fund so that the net amount would be shown on the BALANCE SHEET as a LIABILITY.

defined benefit liability Approximately, under INTERNATIONAL ACCOUNTING STANDARDS COMMITTEE rules, the net total of the PRESENT VALUE of the defined benefit obligation minus the FAIR VALUE of any PLAN ASSETS out of which the OBLIGATIONS are to be settled. However, the amount would be increased by ACTUARIAL GAINS that had not yet been taken to INCOME, and similarly decreased by any unrecognized actuarial losses and PAST SERVICE COST. The context is accounting for DEFINED BENEFIT PLANS for post-retirement obligations.

defined benefit plans Post-employment benefit plans (including pensions) other than DEFINED CONTRIBUTION PLANS. Such plans, including plans for PENSION and POST-RETIREMENT MEDICAL BENEFITS, involve a contractual right for the employee to receive specified future benefits, such as fixed lump sums or payments linked to final salary. This involves considerable estimation of the employer's obligations, involving ACTUARIAL ASSUMPTIONS.

defined contribution plans POST-EMPLOYMENT BENEFIT PLANS under which an enterprise currently pays contributions into a separate fund and will have no OBLIGATION to pay further contributions, even if the fund does not hold sufficient assets to pay all promised employee benefits. These plans involve few accounting problems compared to DEFINED BENEFIT PLANS.

deflation A general decrease in prices.

del credere agent An agent who deals between a seller and a buyer, in those cases where the agent bears the risk that the customer will not pay for the goods.

del credere commission A payment by a seller to an agent to cover the risk that the buyer will not pay the agent.

delinquent account receivable US term for an amount unpaid by a customer at the due date.

delivery lead time The period between placing an order for INVENTORIES and their arrival.

Delphi technique A mechanism for arriving at the best prediction of some future event by asking a group of experts for separate opinions, revealing them to the group, then seeking consensus.

demand deposit An amount of money deposited with a bank which can be reclaimed without notice.

demerger The splitting up of a company or group into two or more legally separate units.

demonstrably committed The position of being able to show that there is no commercially realistic possibility of withdrawing from a plan of action. If an enterprise is demonstrably committed to a likely future payment as a result of a past event, then there is an 'OBLIGATION' and a LIABILITY is recognized.

department As a formal term, a separately identifiable part of an organization for which costs and responsibility can be identified.

departmental accounting The process of preparing financial information on costs and revenues within an organization which is split up on the basis of departments.

departmental budget A numerically specified and agreed plan (a BUDGET) as relating to one particular department within an organization.

depletion The physical using up of assets, particularly WASTING ASSETS such as mineral ores.

depletion accounting A method of charging the cost of a WASTING ASSET, such as mineral ores, against income in proportion to the rate of use or extraction.

depository receipt A certificate issued by a bank or other institution acknowledging that certain items (particularly a number of shares) have been deposited with them.

deposits in transit Cash receipts that have been recorded as leaving one company or bank but not yet recorded as arriving in another. Adjustments for this will therefore need to be made when making BANK RECONCILIATION STATEMENTS.

depreciable amount The amount to be charged as DEPRECIATION over an ASSET's useful life. This is the cost of an asset, or another amount substituted for cost in the FINANCIAL STATEMENTS, less its RESIDUAL VALUE.

depreciable asset An ASSET which is expected to be used during more than one accounting period and to have a limited useful life. Such assets include buildings, plant and machinery, vehicles and various INTANGIBLE ASSETS.

depreciated cost Usually the ORIGINAL COST of an ASSET less the DEPRECIATION charged so far against that. However, it could also mean the total amount of the COST that has been charged as depreciation.

depreciation The systematic allocation of the cost (or up-dated cost) of an ASSET over its USEFUL ECONOMIC LIFE. So, machinery and equipment, vehicles and buildings are depreciated, though land normally is not. The technique of depreciation means that accountants do not charge the whole cost of a FIXED ASSET against the PROFIT of the year of purchase, but they charge it gradually over the years of its use and wearing out. This fits with the ACCRUAL BASIS OF ACCOUNTING. The word 'AMORTIZATION' is also used, particularly in the context of INTANGIBLE ASSETS.

depreciation adjustment An adjustment to the expense of DEPRECIATION of FIXED ASSETS in the CURRENT COST ACCOUNTING system. Assuming that prices of a fixed asset are rising, the depreciation adjustment will be an extra EXPENSE, on top of the amount of depreciation related to the HISTORICAL COST of the asset, to take account of the fact that something more valuable than that is wearing out.

depreciation expense A charge against the profit of a period to represent the wearing out of FIXED ASSETS in that period. *See*, also, DEPRECIATION.

depreciation methods Arithmetical techniques for allocating the net cost of a FIXED ASSET over its useful life. These methods include STRAIGHT-LINE DEPRECIATION and REDUCING-BALANCE DEPRECIATION.

depreciation rate The percentage rate at which DEPRECIATION is charged under a particular method. The rate is applied to net cost under STRAIGHT-LINE DEPRECIATION or to the WRITTEN DOWN VALUE under REDUCING-BALANCE DEPRECIATION.

deprival value The amount by which a business would be worse off if it were deprived of a particular ASSET. This is sometimes referred to as its 'VALUE TO THE BUSINESS/OWNER'. When trying to arrive at a realistic and current value of individual assets in order to present a BALANCE SHEET, this method has much to commend it. It should be said at once, however, that deprival value is *not* the conventional valuation method for FINANCIAL STATEMENTS; instead, HISTORICAL COST ACCOUNTING is generally used.

Nevertheless, in the UK, Australia and New Zealand, deprival value has been a method used for SUPPLEMENTARY FINANCIAL STATEMENTS designed to take the changing prices of assets into account, e.g. as required for listed and large UK companies by STATEMENT OF STANDARD ACCOUNTING PRACTICE 16 of 1980 to 1985.

The deprival value of an asset depends upon the intentions of the business that owns it. If an asset would be replaced, its deprival value is its net CURRENT REPLACEMENT COST (CRC); this would be the normal case. However, for assets that would not be replaced, the deprival value would be NET REALIZABLE VALUE (NRV) if the asset was about to be sold, or ECONOMIC VALUE if it was to continue in use. An example of the latter would be an obsolete, but still used, cotton mill. It still produces worthwhile goods, it will perhaps not be replaced at all, but it is not to be sold (except for scrap when it falls to pieces). In such a case, the NRV might be very low and would not be relevant, and the CRC would be unrealistically high. Thus, the amount recoverable from its future use is what would be lost if the business were deprived of the asset.

depth of market The degree to which a market in SHARES, COMMODITIES, EXCHANGE RATES, etc. has sufficient volume that it can absorb even large transactions without a significant change in price.

derecognize To remove an ASSET or LIABILITY, or a portion of an asset or liability, from an enterprise's BALANCE SHEET.

de-registration The removal of an enterprise or person from an official list of members. For example, in the UK, a company might de-register for VALUE ADDED TAX because it falls below a certain level of sales; or in the USA, a company might be de-registered by the SECURITIES AND EXCHANGE COMMISSION.

deregulation The removal of, or reduction in, the rules imposed by law or other authorities.

derivative financial instrument A contract that has the effect of transferring between the parties to the instrument one or more of the financial risks inherent in an underlying item. Examples are financial options, futures and forwards, INTEREST RATE SWAPS and currency swaps.

detection risk In the context of an AUDIT, the risk that an auditor will not detect a material error or misstatement.

Deutsches Rechnungslegungs Standards Committee (DRSC) The private sector standard setting committee founded in Germany in 1998. The fact that the German for 'standards committee' is 'Standards Committee' shows how foreign the concept of non-governmental regulation was in that country. The DRSC can make rules, with the approval of the Ministry of Justice, relating to CONSOLIDATED FINANCIAL STATEMENTS.

devaluation A reduction in the value of a currency as measured in terms of another important currency or basket of currencies.

development costs Costs that are directly attributable to development activities or that can be allocated to them on a reasonable basis. Development activities are the application of research to a plan for the production of new or substantially improved products, processes or services before commercial production. Under certain circumstances, such costs can be (under UK rules) or should be (under INTERNATIONAL ACCOUNTING STANDARD rules) capitalized as INTANGIBLE ASSETS.

development expenditure *See* DEVELOPMENT COSTS.

development gains tax A former UK tax on gains arising on the sale of land available for development.

devise A gift of (or to give) real property (e.g. land) by means of a will.

differential analysis A detailed numerical comparison of the COSTS and REVENUES related to two or more proposed courses of action, as part of management decision making.

differential cost The INCREMENTAL COSTS associated with making a particular decision.

differential income This term can mean either DIFFERENTIAL REVENUE or DIFFERENTIAL PROFIT.

differential pricing The establishment of two or more prices for the same product at the same time when there are two or more identifiable types of customer or market.

differential profit The incremental profit associated with making a particular decision.

differential revenue The incremental revenues associated with making a particular decision.

dilapidations As a technical term, the costs of repairing LEASEHOLD buildings.

diluted earnings per share The NET PROFIT for the period attributable to ordinary shareholders divided by the weighted average number of ORDINARY SHARES outstanding during the period, both adjusted for the effects of all DILUTIVE POTENTIAL ORDINARY SHARES. This number is required to be disclosed by LISTED COMPANIES as a warning to investors that EARNINGS PER SHARE could get worse even if the company's operations continue at the same level of profit.

dilutive potential ordinary shares POTENTIAL ORDINARY SHARES whose conversion to ORDINARY SHARES would decrease NET PROFIT per share or increase loss per share.

diminishing-balance method *See* REDUCING-BALANCE DEPRECIATION.

direct costing US term for MARGINAL COSTING or variable costing.

direct cost of sales The costs of the goods that have been sold in the period, excluding OVERHEAD COSTS.

direct costs Costs which can be identified with the production of particular units or types of product.

direct debit system A banking system which enables a customer's DEBTS to be paid periodically from the customer's bank account at the instigation of a seller rather than the customer.

direct foreign investment The purchase of an overseas ASSET or enterprise which is to be controlled or influenced rather than being held at arm's length.

Directive In the context of the EU, a series of requirements accompanied by an instruction to the governments of the member states to turn them into law. Generally, the Directives contain options for member states and for the persons or companies who will be subject to the resulting laws. For financial reporting, *see* particularly, FOURTH DIRECTIVE and EIGHTH DIRECTIVE.

direct labour The employees (or the hours of those employees) that can be clearly linked to production.

direct labour cost *See* DIRECT WAGES.

direct labour efficiency variance The difference between the actual DIRECT LABOUR costs (at standard rate per hour) and the STANDARD COSTING allowed.

direct labour hour rate *See* LABOUR HOUR RATE.

direct labour rate variance The difference between the actual DIRECT LABOUR wages paid and the actual hours worked at the standard rate per hour.

direct labour total cost variance The difference between the ACTUAL COST of DIRECT LABOUR and the STANDARD costs. It is the total of the direct LABOUR EFFICIENCY and LABOUR RATE VARIANCE.

direct materials The materials whose usage can be clearly linked to production.

direct materials cost The expense in a period caused by the using up of materials whose usage can be clearly linked to production.

direct materials mix variance The difference (at standard prices) between the actual DIRECT MATERIALS used and the materials that would have been used at STANDARD proportions.

direct materials price variance The difference between the ACTUAL COST of the DIRECT MATERIALS used and the actual materials used at STANDARD PRICES.

direct materials total cost variance The difference between the ACTUAL COST of DIRECT MATERIALS and the STANDARD cost. It is the total of the DIRECT MATERIALS PRICE VARIANCE and DIRECT MATERIAL USAGE VARIANCES.

direct materials usage variance The difference between the ACTUAL COST of DIRECT MATERIALS used (at standard prices) and the STANDARD cost of direct materials. This is the total of the DIRECT MATERIALS MIX VARIANCE and DIRECT MATERIALS YIELD VARIANCES.

direct materials yield variance The difference between the cost of the actual material used (at standard proportions and prices) and the STANDARD cost.

direct method of reporting cash flows A method of calculating and reporting CASH FLOWS from operating activities which discloses major classes of gross cash receipts and gross cash payments. The method is unlike the INDIRECT

METHOD in that it takes information directly from accounting records or adjusts sales and cost of sales rather than adjusting NET PROFIT or OPERATING PROFIT.

director A person recognized in law as responsible (with other directors) for the management of a company. The directors are appointed by a company's shareholders. It is the directors' responsibility to prepare the annual FINANCIAL STATEMENTS.

directors' emoluments *See* DIRECTORS' REMUNERATION.

directors' interests The holdings of directors in the SHARES and other SECURITIES of a company.

directors' remuneration Amounts paid by a company to its directors in their capacity as officers or employees of the company. This includes salaries, fees, pensions and any compensation for loss of office.

directors' report A part of the contents of the ANNUAL REPORT of a UK company. By law it must contain such detailed disclosures as directors' shareholdings, charitable and political donations, a review of the past year and discussion of future plans and many other matters.

The directors' report must be examined by the company's auditors to ensure that it is 'consistent with' the FINANCIAL STATEMENTS.

In the USA, there is no direct equivalent. However, similar information is to be found in the Form 10-K which SECURITIES AND EXCHANGE COMMISSION-registered companies must prepare.

direct tax A tax assessed on those who are intended to bear the burden of it e.g. INCOME TAX and CORPORATION TAX. In the case of most employees in the UK, income tax is collected from the employer but is assessed on the employee, who also suffers its impact.

direct wages The LABOUR COSTS of employees that can be clearly linked to production.

dirty surplus The profit or loss of an enterprise in those cases where certain gains and losses are not included in the PROFIT AND LOSS ACCOUNT but are taken to RESERVES.

disaggregated financial statements The presentation of financial information by parts of the whole reporting entity. *See* SEGMENTAL REPORTING.

disbursement A payment made on behalf of a client by a professional adviser, such as a solicitor.

disclaimer of opinion In the context of an AUDIT REPORT, an inability of the auditor to give an opinion on whether FINANCIAL STATEMENTS have been properly prepared and give a TRUE AND FAIR VIEW. The problem will be caused perhaps by poor record keeping by the company or by large and unquantifiable uncertainties.

disclosure In the context of financial reporting, the provision of information somewhere in the documents published by an enterprise, particularly in the NOTES TO THE ACCOUNTS.

disclosure requirements Generally, the instructions in law or ACCOUNTING STANDARDS, for certain items of information to be included in the FINANCIAL STATEMENTS (including the NOTES).

discontinued operation In the context of UK rules, an operation that has discontinued or whose nature and focus has materially changed. Information about this must be disclosed in the PROFIT AND LOSS ACCOUNT in order to improve the prediction of future profits.

discontinuing operation In the context of financial reporting under INTERNATIONAL ACCOUNTING STANDARDS COMMITTEE rules, a separately identifiable major part of an enterprise's operations that is being discontinued by sale or abandonment, or by piecemeal sale as part of a single plan. A number of disclosures about this are required as soon as the enterprise announces the discontinuance or makes a binding sale contract. This information is designed to enable better prediction of future cash flows, INCOME and ASSETS from continuing operations.

discount A reduction in the size of an amount of a DEBT (e.g. a trade debt or a bond) below its legally denominated amount. The reason for the discount is often something to do with the length of period before payment.

discount allowed From a supplier's point of view, a reduction in the amount of a customer's bill, perhaps for early payment or to recognize an imperfection in goods supplied.

discounted cash flow Future cash flows, adjusted downwards to take account of their expected timing. Such discounted cash flows are used when making investment choices between competing projects. The most reliable method of deciding which project is best and whether any particular one is worth doing is to work out each project's NET PRESENT VALUE (NPV) by adding up all the discounted expected NET CASH FLOWS. The NPV calculation will include the outflow of the initial investment. A project with a positive NPV is worth doing; the project with the highest NPV is the best.

discounted value The worth of a stream of predicted cash flows once the timing of them has been taken into account. Another term for this is 'PRESENT VALUE'.

discount factor A number which, when used as a multiplier of a future amount, expresses that amount as a PRESENT VALUE, i.e. takes account of the TIME VALUE OF MONEY.

discounting The process of reducing the value of a future amount by taking account of the length of time until receipt or payment.

discount rate Either the relevant yearly rate for discounting future inflows or outflows of cash, for a particular person or business so that the amounts are expressed in terms of PRESENT VALUE (*see* DISCOUNTED CASH FLOW) or, as a UK banking term, the rate at which discount houses or other banks can borrow from the CENTRAL BANK.

discount received From a customer's point of view, a reduction in the amount of a bill for the purchase of goods or services, perhaps for early payment or to recognize an imperfection in the goods or services.

discretionary costs Costs whose amount varies, within a particular time frame, as a result of decisions by managers. Such costs include advertising and research expenditures.

discretionary trust A legal entity controlled by persons (TRUSTEES), who are not the beneficiaries, of the ASSETS or INCOME of the trust, in cases where the TRUSTEES alone have the choice of how much benefit to pass to each beneficiary.

discussion memorandum In the context of ACCOUNTING STANDARDS, a document which precedes an EXPOSURE DRAFT, and is designed to air alternative proposals for comment by interested parties.

dishonour In the context of CHEQUES or BILLS OF EXCHANGE (and as a verb), this word means to fail to accept or to pay.

disposable income The INCOME available for use (i.e. for consumption or investment) after essential payments, such as tax, have been made.

disposals account An ACCOUNT used to record the sale of a FIXED ASSET. The account records the cost, any ACCUMULATED DEPRECIATION, and the sale proceeds. The balance is the gain or loss on disposal.

disposal value The amount expected to be obtained from a FIXED ASSET when it is sold at the end of its useful economic life to an enterprise. The amount is measured at prices ruling when the asset was bought or subsequently revalued.

dissimilar activities In the context of preparing GROUP ACCOUNTS, the business of a subsidiary enterprise that is so different from the rest of the group that the subsidiary should not be consolidated because the resulting accounts would not give a TRUE AND FAIR VIEW. In the UK, this state of affairs would be regarded as most unusual. Under INTERNATIONAL ACCOUNTING STANDARDS COMMITTEE rules, such exclusion is not allowed.

dissolution The cessation of a business, particularly a PARTNERSHIP.

distributable profits An amount of a company's profit which is legally available to be paid out as a dividend. It is added to DISTRIBUTABLE RESERVES.

distributable reserves In general, the profits of this year, plus previous years' undistributed profits, which are legally available for payment as dividends. Whether they *are* so distributed will depend upon the company's need for investment funds, its available cash resources, and so on.

In the UK, there is an apparently simple definition for all companies: accumulated realized profits, less accumulated realized losses (but *see* REALIZED PROFITS). The law makes it clear that this is to be interpreted in the context of strict HISTORICAL COST ACCOUNTING. If, for example, any FIXED ASSETS have been revalued, with subsequent extra depreciation charges, the legally distributable profit will be different from that in the BALANCE SHEET. For PUBLIC COMPANIES, there is a slightly more restrictive definition, based on the sufficiency of NET ASSETS compared to DISTRIBUTABLE PROFITS.

In the USA, depending upon in which state a company is incorporated, the legally distributable profits (unrestricted earnings) will depend upon an 'earned surplus' or a 'net assets' rule (or both) similar to those above.

distributed profit An amount of PROFIT paid out by an enterprise to its owners.

distribution costs The legal term in a UK PROFIT AND LOSS ACCOUNT for the costs (such as postage, packing and insurance) of delivering products to customers.

distribution overhead The same as DISTRIBUTION COSTS but seen in the context of cost accounting rather than financial reporting.

distribution to owners The payment of amounts to shareholders in the form of a CASH DIVIDEND or sometimes in the form of other ASSETS or shares.

diversification The spreading of investments or operations over several areas so as to avoid the risk of having all one's eggs in one basket.

divestment The selling off of SHARES, other ASSETS or operations.

dividend The return to shareholders, the owners of companies. Dividends are usually paid in CASH, but could be paid in other ASSETS or in extra SHARES. In the UK, it is common for companies to pay an INTERIM DIVIDEND part way through the year, and a FINAL DIVIDEND after the end of the year.

Unlike INTEREST, which is a return to lenders, dividends do not have to be paid; they can be forgone for many years if the company deems this suitable for liquidity, expansion, tax saving or other reasons. Further, dividends are not at a fixed percentage, except for PREFERENCE SHARES. If a company does very well, the shareholders probably benefit by higher dividends, sooner or later.

Dividends, being a return to the owners, or an 'APPROPRIATION' rather than an EXPENSE, are not charged in the calculation of profit, nor are they tax deductible for the paying company.

dividend control Regulations from the government limiting the size of dividend payments. Such regulations have sometimes been brought into force in times of high inflation when prices are also controlled.

dividend cover The number of times that the most recent annual dividend could have been paid out of the most recent profit. It gives an indication of how secure the future dividend payments are; a high cover suggests room for contingencies.

dividend-growth model An algebraic specification of a company's assumptions about the future levels of dividend payments. The model is needed as part of the estimation of the company's COST OF CAPITAL.

dividend in specie A dividend paid other than in cash.

dividend policy The stance of a particular company on the amount or proportion of its profit that it should pay out as dividends, as opposed to retaining it for investment. Generally, companies try to avoid reducing the level of dividends from a previous year, as this gives a bad signal to the investors.

dividends in arrears Dividends to which the holders of CUMULATIVE PREFERENCE SHARES are entitled but which have not been paid.

dividends payable Dividends that a company has declared (and, in the UK, those proposed) but has not yet paid. These amounts are shown in a balance sheet as a CURRENT LIABILITY.

dividends per share The amount of a company's dividends for the year on ORDINARY SHARES divided by the number of ordinary shares.

dividend waiver The choice of a shareholder not to accept an entitlement to dividends.

dividend warrant A document issued by a company to a shareholder containing a cheque for the dividend and, in the UK, a TAX CREDIT to be set off against the shareholder's liability for INCOME TAX.

dividend yield The most recent total annual dividend per share (generally grossed up with the TAX CREDIT) divided by the market price. This is an indication of the cash return that can be expected by buying a particular share. However, one should remember that the shareholders also benefit from UNDISTRIBUTED PROFITS, since these increase the value of their company, and will lead to future dividends or CAPITAL GAINS.

division A significant part of a large organization which is granted a degree of autonomy over management decisions.

divisionalization The splitting up of a large group into a number of fairly autonomous divisions. This may involve the adding together of smaller units (e.g. SUBSIDIARIES) into these larger divisions.

divisional performance measurement The assessment of the success of divisions within a large organization by examining them as separate businesses from the point of view of such measures as RETURN ON CAPITAL EMPLOYED or PROFIT on SALES.

dollar value LIFO A US device for enabling retail businesses to pay reduced tax (by recording less income) in times of rising inventory prices, whereby INVEN-TORIES are valued at base-year prices using price indices. *See*, also, LIFO.

domicile In the context of tax law, the country to which a person belongs by birth or long-run relationship. This is often the same as, but may be different from, the country of residence.

dominant influence In the context of determining whether an enterprise is the parent of another, the power to govern the financial and operating policies of the other enterprise. This would normally be achieved by owning shares containing the majority of the voting rights over the subsidiary company but could be obtained despite the lack of this.

donated asset An asset received as a gift, generally by a charity. It therefore has a zero cost but should be recognized by a charity at its FAIR VALUE.

donated capital In the US, the account (equivalent to a part of STOCK-HOLDERS' EQUITY) where the value of donated assets is recorded.

dormant company A UK legal term for a company with no significant transactions in an accounting period. Such a company need not appoint an AUDITOR.

double account system A former UK method of presenting the FINANCIAL STATEMENTS of public utilities and railway companies. The basic feature of the system was the clear separation of the capital base from the operating assets and liabilities.

double declining balance method A US version of the DECLINING (OR REDUCING-BALANCE) DEPRECIATION METHOD for the calculation of DEPRECIATION of FIXED ASSETS.

double-entry bookkeeping A system of bookkeeping that records two aspects of every transaction. It is an Italian invention, that gradually became fully developed in the northern city states in the fourteenth century, probably in response to substantial increases in the complexity of business, particularly the extensive trading on credit, foreign branches and joint venture trading. Systems of single entry had been used for millennia. They involved the recording of cash amounts, and of debts to and from persons outside the business. An entry of DEBIT meant 'he owes', and an entry of CREDIT meant 'he trusts' (i.e. we owe him). Gradually, it became clear that every transaction could be seen to have two effects, that might both be recorded, by a debit and a credit each time. For example, the creation of an asset (a debit) might be the result of income (a credit) or the reduction of another asset.

The system has been expanded to include all possible transactions. This enables the complete recording of sales, cash, purchases, debts, various categories of expenses, etc. Each type of transaction is recorded on a separate ACCOUNT. Each account conventionally has debits on the left and credits on the right. If the BOOKKEEPING has been done correctly, at the end of the period the total debits in the system will equal the total credits. The system is self-balancing and makes the search for errors easier. Further, a balance can be struck on an account at any time, in order to see, for example, how much cash should be present, how much any debtor owes, or how many sales there have been.

For very numerous types of transactions, like sales, there are usually 'books of original entry' (e.g. a sales DAY BOOK or a JOURNAL) that record the daily transactions, and put a summary through to the main double-entry records.

At the end of an accounting period, a TRIAL BALANCE is prepared. This is a listing of all the balances on the accounts (having netted off debits against credits in each particular account). This should show equality of the total debits and total credits. The balances can then be used to prepare the FINANCIAL STATEMENTS. The balances for REVENUES and EXPENSES are taken to a PROFIT AND LOSS ACCOUNT (UK)/INCOME STATEMENT (US); the balances for ASSETS, LIABILITIES and CAPITAL go to the BALANCE SHEET.

double taxation agreement A treaty between two countries concerning the treatment of amounts of income (or other taxable item) that are subject to tax in both countries. Generally, some form of relief is available for the taxpayer from having to pay full taxation twice.

double taxation relief In the context of an agreement between two countries, a reduction in tax compared to full taxation under the tax laws of both countries.

doubtful debts Amounts legally due from customers but about which there is doubt concerning collectability. Such debts would not be written off but should not be shown at their full legal value in a BALANCE SHEET. They would be reduced by an allowance or PROVISION FOR BAD DEBTS.

Dow Jones Industrial Average *See* SHARE PRICE INDICES.

downstream transactions Sales of ASSETS (or other transactions) from an INVESTOR to an INVESTEE, e.g. sales from a company to its SUBSIDIARY. Such transactions within a group should be eliminated on consolidation. For transactions with associates and joint ventures, profits should be eliminated in proportion to the investor's interest unless the items have been sold on (realized) beyond the group's influence.

Dr Abbreviation for DEBIT (in DOUBLE-ENTRY BOOKKEEPING).

draft In the context of ACCOUNTING STANDARDS, a preliminary version, although a formal draft for public comment would normally be called an 'EXPOSURE DRAFT'. In the context of banking, an order in writing to pay a particular sum from one person to another.

dragon bond Colloquial term for a bond denominated in US dollars but issued in a Far Eastern market.

drawee The person or institution named on a CHEQUE or BILL OF EXCHANGE who must pay the amount shown.

drawer The person who signs a CHEQUE or BILL OF EXCHANGE.

drawings Amounts of money or other assets withdrawn from unincorporated businesses (such as SOLE TRADERS or PARTNERSHIPS) by the owners. The equivalent for companies is DIVIDENDS.

DRSC Abbreviation for the DEUTSCHES RECHNUNGSLEGUNGS STANDARDS COMMITTEE (of Germany).

dual capacity system A method of trading on most stock exchanges whereby traders (brokers) can buy and sell on their own account (as wholesalers) as well as acting as agents for others (as retailers).

dual pricing In the context of management accounting, a method of setting prices for the transfer of goods between divisions of an organization whereby the buyer is deemed to pay a lower price than the seller is deemed to receive. This encourages managers to buy from within the group.

due diligence An examination of the FINANCIAL POSITION of a company before the FLOTATION of its shares on a stock exchange or before the purchase of the whole or a large part of its shares by one investor. In the former case, independent accountants are appointed. In the latter case, the investor might conduct the examination but might also appoint accountants to act.

EAA Abbreviation for the EUROPEAN ACCOUNTING ASSOCIATION.

earned income In the context of taxation, income accruing to labour rather than to capital. For example, wages are considered to be EARNED INCOME, whereas dividend receipts are UNEARNED (or investment) INCOME.

earnings A technical accounting term, meaning the amount of profit (normally for a year) available to the ordinary shareholders. That is, it is the profit after all operating expenses, interest charges, taxes and dividends on preference shares. In the UK, 'earnings' as defined by ACCOUNTING STANDARDS includes EXTRA-ORDINARY ITEMS. However, investment analysts and the *Financial Times* use an alternative calculation called 'HEADLINE EARNINGS' which excludes various expenses and revenues that are not deemed to be part of the sustainable profit for shareholders.

earnings available for ordinary shareholders Same as EARNINGS.

earnings basis In the context of taxation, the use of the ACCRUAL BASIS OF ACCOUNTING rather than the CASH BASIS OF ACCOUNTING.

earnings before interest and tax The PROFIT of a company for a financial year but calculated without the deduction of interest or tax expense.

earnings per share Exactly what its name suggests: the most recent year's total EARNINGS divided by the number of ORDINARY SHARES. The earnings figure is the PROFIT available for ordinary shareholders; and the number of ordinary shares is calculated as the average number outstanding during the year. This is the description of BASIC EARNINGS PER SHARE, a number that must be disclosed by listed companies. There must also be disclosure of DILUTED EARNINGS PER SHARE.

earnings yield The EARNINGS PER SHARE divided by the MARKET PRICE. The reciprocal of this is the PRICE–EARNINGS RATIO. Such a figure will indicate the return that might be expected from an investment in the share.

earn-out agreement An element of a CONTRACT to acquire a company whereby the consideration increases if specific future levels of EARNINGS are achieved.

EBIT Abbreviation for EARNINGS BEFORE INTEREST AND TAX.

EBITDA Abbreviation for 'earnings before interest, tax, depreciation and amortization'. Analysts like to calculate this figure (among others) because it excludes the subjective expense of depreciation.

EC Abbreviation for the European Community.

ECGD Abbreviation for the Export Credits Guarantee Department; a UK government agency whose task is self-explanatory and is designed to aid exporters.

economic appraisal A method of choosing between competing investment projects which uses the techniques of DISCOUNTED CASH FLOW but adjusts the flows for such items as subsidies and taxes. It is a method used by governments for the appraisal of public sector projects such as the building of motorways.

economic batch quantity A refinement of the ECONOMIC ORDER QUANTITY in order to take account of the fact that the goods are produced in batches, not individually.

economic consequences In the context of the setting of ACCOUNTING STANDARDS, the possible real economic effects of particular accounting rules. Consideration of these is a relatively recent development, and so far mainly in the USA, and mainly by commentators rather than by standard setters.

economic exposure The degree to which an enterprise is exposed to real changes in worth (as opposed to being exposed to changes recorded in FINANCIAL STATEMENTS; (*see*, also, ACCOUNTING EXPOSURE) as a result of possible changes in foreign currency exchange rates.

economic life The period over which an ASSET is expected to be economically usable. The life could also be measured in units of production. Assets are depreciated over useful economic life to the current holder.

economic order quantity The optimum order size for the purchasing (or manufacturing) of INVENTORIES. This is the size which holds in balance the total ordering costs and the total holding costs.

economic rent The payment to a factor of production (e.g. labour or capital) beyond what is necessary to keep it in its present use.

economic substance *See* COMMERCIAL SUBSTANCE.

economic value A way of valuing ASSETS at the expected future NET CASH FLOWS from them, discounted to the present. The 'discounting' is designed to adjust for the fact that present money is more valuable than the same nominal amount of future money (*see* DISCOUNTED CASH FLOW).

There can be little doubt that this is in some sense the 'correct' way of valuing but, like many of the concepts of economics, it is strong on theory but weak on practicality. As a general basis for valuing assets in a BALANCE SHEET, it is a non-starter, because values reported to outsiders (such as shareholders) need to be reliable, objective and auditable. The economic value of an asset rests upon the prediction of all the future cash flows coming from it, and upon an estimation of the appropriate DISCOUNT RATE. This is far too subjective for financial reporting purposes, though the concept does appear in the context of IMPAIR-MENT and as part of the DEPRIVAL VALUE concept used in special cases, and often without discounting, in systems of CURRENT COST ACCOUNTING.

A further problem with economic value is that it will probably be practically impossible to estimate the cash flows *from any particular asset*, since groups of assets work together to produce products and cash flows. The value of the output of a machine depends upon other machines around it, and upon the factory that it works in.

However, for *internal* investment appraisal purposes, when one has to deal with the future and with subjectivity, economic value or NET PRESENT VALUE is of great use.

economies of scale Reductions in the average unit costs of production as the scale of production increases.

ECSAFA Abbreviation for the Eastern, Central and Southern Africa Federation of Accountants; a self-descriptive private sector organization of ACCOUNTANCY BODIES.

ECU Abbreviation for European currency unit.

ED Abbreviation for EXPOSURE DRAFT.

EDP Abbreviation for electronic data processing.

EEA Abbreviation for the EUROPEAN ECONOMIC AREA.

effective annual rate The year's total amount of interest on a loan as a proportion of the amount of the loan outstanding at the beginning of the year.

effective yield The pre-tax INTERNAL RATE OF RETURN on a bond bought at a particular price and date and held to maturity.

efficiency In economic terms, the optimal use or allocation of resources.

efficiency ratio The STANDARD HOURS allowed for production divided by the actual number of hours taken.

efficiency variances Measures of the actual quantities of items used compared to standard or budgeted amounts. *See*, for example, DIRECT LABOUR EFFICIENCY VARIANCE.

efficient market hypothesis An elegant and important theory, usually applied to the price of shares on large stock exchanges. One version of the hypothesis is that all publicly available information is immediately taken into account in the price of shares. In markets such as the New York or London stock exchanges there are many buyers and sellers of shares, the prices are well known, and much other information is freely available. In such cases, one would expect that any new and relevant information about a company would very rapidly affect its price.

There is considerable evidence, especially from the USA, that large stock exchanges *are* fairly efficient markets in the above sense. However, very few companies, investors, brokers, etc. behave as if they are. Of course, the efficiency of the market depends upon buyers and sellers behaving as if it were *not* efficient! Efficiency depends upon all the information being produced and all the analysis being done.

efficient portfolio The combination of investments which maximizes the expected return for a given risk, or minimizes the risk for a given return.

EFRAG Abbreviation for the EUROPEAN FINANCIAL REPORTING ADVISORY GROUP.

EFT Abbreviation for electronic funds transfer.

EFTPOS Abbreviation for electronic funds transfer at the point of sale.

EGM Abbreviation for an EXTRAORDINARY GENERAL MEETING.

Eighth Directive A document sent in 1984 from the EU to the governments of its member states requiring laws to be passed on the subject of audits and AUDITORS of the FINANCIAL STATEMENTS of limited companies. Strictly speaking, it is the Eighth Directive on Company Law, because there are many other series of Directives.

EITF Abbreviation for the EMERGING ISSUES TASK FORCE.

elective resolution A special type of proposal relating to certain matters to be decided at the ANNUAL GENERAL MEETING of a UK private limited company.

elements of cost In the context of COST ACCOUNTING, the three categories of production cost: materials, labour and other expenses.

elements of the financial statements The building blocks of the FINANCIAL STATEMENTS that result from the DOUBLE-ENTRY BOOKKEEPING system. The five main elements are ASSETS, LIABILITIES, EQUITY, REVENUES and EXPENSES. However, these could be divided up further. Also, if CASH FLOW STATEMENTS were added into consideration, various categories of cash flow could be considered as further elements.

eligible paper In the context of UK banking, those securities acceptable to banks for the purposes of DISCOUNTING.

eliminating entry In the context of the preparation of CONSOLIDATED FINANCIAL STATEMENTS, an adjustment designed to eliminate the effects of a transaction between enterprises within the group.

embedded audit facility The insertion of computer programs and data by an AUDITOR into a client enterprise's computerized accounting system in order to enhance the continuous review of the system.

embedded derivative A DERIVATIVE FINANCIAL INSTRUMENT that is a component of a hybrid FINANCIAL INSTRUMENT.

emergency tax code In the context of the UK taxation of personal income, a temporary code used for the calculation by an employer of an employee's INCOME TAX when the details of an employee's TAX ALLOWANCES are not yet available.

Emerging Issues Task Force US committee established in 1984 by the FINANCIAL ACCOUNTING STANDARDS BOARD and designed to create and publish consensuses for the treatment of new issues or on the interpretation in more detail of existing standards.

emoluments Remuneration for carrying out the duties of an office, e.g. the payments to the directors of a company.

emphasis of matter The drawing of attention to particularly important issues by auditors in their AUDIT REPORT on an enterprise's FINANCIAL STATEMENTS. The issue will already have been properly treated in the financial statements, and the emphasis of matter does not mean that there is a QUALIFIED AUDIT REPORT.

employee benefit obligations LIABILITIES that arise in an enterprise in connection with EMPLOYEE BENEFITS such as pensions. The obligations are the gross amount of the liabilities before any deduction of a fund set up to assist in the future payment of them.

employee benefit plan An arrangement for providing PENSIONS or other benefits to employees at or after their retirement.

employee benefits All forms of consideration given by an enterprise to employees in exchange for service rendered. This would include wages, pensions and medical benefits (both during and after employment).

employee reporting Telling the employees how the company is performing, with the aid of specially designed reports.

employee share ownership plan (or trust) An arrangement whereby an independent trust is set up for the purpose of owning a company's shares for distribution to the company's employees.

employment contract A written agreement between an employer and an employee concerning the conditions of the employment and its termination.

employment costs Those expenses of an enterprise related to employees, such as wages, salaries, employers' pension contributions and national insurance payments.

employment report A document published by a company concerning various aspects of its employees and the company's relationship with them. *See* CORPORATE SOCIAL REPORTING.

EMS Abbreviation for the EUROPEAN MONETARY SYSTEM.

ending inventory US term for CLOSING STOCK.

endorsement The process of writing on a document (literally, on the back of it) in order to vary its terms.

engagement letter *See* LETTER OF ENGAGEMENT.

engineered cost A cost (such as DIRECT LABOUR) that has a specified relationship to a measure of the level of activity.

enterprise The term generally used in INTERNATIONAL ACCOUNTING STANDARDS COMMITTEE rules to refer to a business organization. The term includes a company but also unincorporated businesses.

entity convention/view The entity convention is to view the business as separate from its owners. This is standard for accounting and, for many businesses, it is also the legal position. It enables accountants to prepare BALANCE SHEETS that balance, because amounts contributed by, and earned for, the owners can be shown as capital, with the liabilities owed to non-owners.

The 'entity view' is an extension of this, and can be contrasted to the PRO-PRIETARY VIEW. The entity view would see the business's viewpoint; the proprietary view sees things from the point of view of the owners.

entry A record of a transaction in an ACCOUNT.

entry value The amount recorded for an ASSET at prices in the market when acquired. The actual original entry value is the historical cost. The entry value at today's prices is the CURRENT REPLACEMENT COST. Compare to EXIT VALUE.

environmental accounting/reporting Disclosures by an enterprise that quantify and/or discuss the costs and benefits of the enterprise's effects on its environment.

environmental audit An assessment of the effects of an organization on its environment. The audit might also check that there are suitable policies in this area, and that these are being complied with.

EOQ Abbreviation for ECONOMIC ORDER QUANTITY.

EPS Abbreviation for EARNINGS PER SHARE.

equal-instalment depreciation Synonym for STRAIGHT-LINE DEPRECIATION.

equity As an element of a BALANCE SHEET, the interest of the owners of an enterprise, which is equal to the total of the ASSETS less the total of the LIABILITIES. The word can also mean an owner's beneficial interest in a particular asset. *See*, also, EQUITY INSTRUMENT.

equity accounting A method for including an investment in another enterprise in the financial statements of its investor, whereby the investment is included in the investor's balance sheet as a single line valued at the size of the investee's NET ASSETS. In the investor's income statement, the share of the investee's net income is included. This method is particularly used for the inclusion of an ASSOCIATE in the CONSOLIDATED FINANCIAL STATEMENTS of an investing group.

equity compensation benefits EMPLOYEE BENEFITS whereby employees are entitled to receive EQUITY INSTRUMENTS of the enterprise or amounts that depend on the future price of such instruments.

equity compensation plans Arrangements whereby an enterprise provides EQUITY COMPENSATION BENEFITS for employees.

equity dilution A reduction in an investor's proportion of the shares of a company caused by the issue of extra shares by that company.

equity finance Long-term capital of a company provided by EQUITY INSTRUMENTS rather than by loans.

equity gearing *See* GEARING.

equity instrument A contract that gives a right to a residual interest in the ASSETS of an enterprise after deducting all of its liabilities. An example is an ORDINARY SHARE.

equity method *See* EQUITY ACCOUNTING.

equity share UK technical expression for a share that is not redeemable and does not have any restricting characteristics, such as limited rights to dividends.

equity share capital UK term for the total of the issued EQUITY SHARES of a company.

equivalent units In the context of cost-accounting, unfinished units of production at a period end, expressed as notional whole completed units.

ERM Abbreviation for the EXCHANGE RATE MECHANISM.

ESOP Abbreviation for an EMPLOYEE SHARE OWNERSHIP PLAN.

estate duty Former UK tax on the value of a deceased person's assets.

EstG Abbreviation for the *Einkommensteuergesetz*; the general German income tax law.

estimated assessment In the UK, an estimate by the Inland Revenue of the amount of tax that will be due, based on the previous year's figures.

ethical investment A holding of securities in a company that is regarded as socially, politically or environmentally desirable. Depending on the views of the investor, this might rule out shares in companies producing, for example, tobacco products or armaments.

eurobond A bond issued in Europe (generally in London) and denominated in a currency other than that of the country of issue.

eurocurrency A currency held in a country (originally a European country) outside the currency's country of origin.

eurodollars US dollars deposited in financial institutions outside the USA (originally in Europe but now anywhere).

European Accounting Advisory Forum A body established by the Commission of the European Communities in 1990, including setters of ACCOUNTING STANDARDS within the EU, to advise on accounting matters, such as amendments to the DIRECTIVES on company law. It was closed down in 2001.

European Accounting Association A body for the advancement of the study of accounting formed in 1978. It is the main European grouping of academic accountants.

european company A proposed legal entity which would enable PUBLIC LIMITED COMPANIES to operate throughout the EU as though it were a single jurisdiction. The idea is the subject of a draft REGULATION from the EU Commission.

european currency unit A medium of account created in 1979 in what is now the EU. Its value is calculated on the basis of a basket of currencies.

European Economic Area The EU plus a number of other states, the largest of which is Norway.

european economic interest grouping A legal structure for the operation of multinational joint ventures within the EU. It was created by a REGULATION in 1985.

European Financial Reporting Advisory Group A private sector body set up in 2001, and based in Brussels, that liaises with the INTERNATIONAL ACCOUNTING STANDARDS BOARD and advises the ACCOUNTING REGULATORY COMMITTEE on whether an internatioinal standard is acceptable for adoption in the European Union.

European Monetary System A mechanism for stabilizing the exchange rates between currencies of countries of the EU. This is not now relevant for countries that have adopted the single currency, the euro.

european option A contract concerning the right to buy or sell something (commodities, securities, currencies, etc), in cases where the option can only be exercised on the date of its expiry. *See*, also, AMERICAN OPTION.

EV Abbreviation for ECONOMIC VALUE.

evasion of tax The illegal manipulation of a taxpayer's affairs or documents in order to reduce tax liabilities. Compare to AVOIDANCE OF TAX.

events occurring after the balance sheet date *See* POST BALANCE SHEET EVENTS.

except for In the context of an AUDIT REPORT, a qualification by the auditor on the degree to which FINANCIAL STATEMENTS comply with legal requirements and give a TRUE AND FAIR VIEW. However, the problem is not so fundamental as to lead to a DISCLAIMER OF OPINION.

exceptional items A UK expression for those items in a PROFIT AND LOSS ACCOUNT that are within the ordinary activities of the business, but are of unusual size or incidence. The treatment for these, as laid down in FINANCIAL REPORTING STANDARD 3, is to disclose them separately in the profit and loss account or in the notes to it. Items that must be disclosed on the face of the account include gains and losses on disposal of FIXED ASSETS and investments. Exceptional items are to be distinguished from EXTRAORDINARY ITEMS.

excess burden of taxation The loss of economic welfare resulting from economic behaviour caused by a tax rather than by consumers' or producers' preferences.

exchange difference The difference resulting from reporting an amount of foreign currency in the REPORTING CURRENCY at different EXCHANGE RATES.

exchange gain or loss *See* EXCHANGE DIFFERENCE.

exchange rate The ratio for exchange of two currencies.

Exchange Rate Mechanism The part of the EUROPEAN MONETARY SYSTEM under which countries commit themselves to maintaining the value of their currencies within narrow bands. This is not now relevant for countries that have adopted the single currency, the euro.

excise duty A tax on certain goods produced in or entering the country. For example, in the UK, excise duties are levied on tobacco, wine and hydrocarbons.

exclusion of subsidiaries from consolidation Depending on the rules being followed, a SUBSIDIARY is excluded from CONSOLIDATION for various reasons, e.g. if it is immaterial, acquired and held for resale, not properly controlled because of severe restrictions on the management of it, or so dissimilar from the rest of the group that its inclusion would not enable a TRUE AND FAIR VIEW to be given.

ex dividend Without dividend. A share is 'ex div.', if sales of it would not entitle the purchaser to the forthcoming dividend. So, if you buy a share in the period leading up to a dividend payment it will usually be 'ex div.'. For most of the time, a share is the opposite of this, namely 'cum div.'.

executive director A DIRECTOR of a company who is involved, usually full-time, in the day-to-day running of the company.

executive share option scheme An arrangement whereby a class of employees (including the directors) of a company have rights to purchase the company's shares under certain conditions and at specified prices. In the UK, if the scheme is approved by the tax authorities, there is no INCOME TAX on the grant or exercise of the shares, only on CAPITAL GAINS at sale.

executor A person named in a will as the one who will give effect to it.

executorship The process of carrying out the instructions recorded in a deceased person's will.

executorship accounts The accounting records and statements related to the affairs of a deceased person.

executory contract A legally binding agreement that is unperformed (or equi-proportionally unperformed) by both parties to the agreement. For example, suppose that a company signs a contract to have a building built, and will pay on completion. If the building has not yet been started, the contract is mutually unperformed. Although the company might be thought to have a LIABILITY and an ASSET (the right to receive a building), conventional accounting does not account for these.

exempt private company A former (until 1967) legal category of companies in the UK that was exempt from filing (making public) its FINANCIAL STATEMENTS.

exempt supplies In the context of the UK's VALUE ADDED TAX, supplies of goods or services on which the tax is not levied and for which no reclaim can be made on inputs. For contrast, *see* ZERO-RATED SUPPLIES.

exempt transfers In the context of the UK's INHERITANCE TAX, transfers (such as gifts to a spouse or other gifts up to a certain size) that are not subject to the tax.

exercise price The price at which the right to buy something (an option) can be used.

ex gratia Latin term for payments made 'out of grace' rather than because of a contractual or other legal requirement.

existing use value The price at which a sale of a property could be completed assuming that the property can be used for the foreseeable future only for its existing use.

exit value The value of an ASSET in terms of what it could be sold for, less costs to completion and costs of sale. The current exit value is the same as the NET

REALIZABLE VALUE but, in principle, exit values of the past or the future could be referred to. Compare to ENTRY VALUE.

expanded equity method A way of accounting for a JOINT VENTURE whereby a venturer's interest in the NET ASSETS of the joint venture is shown on a line-by-line basis, but not aggregated with those of enterprises in the investor's group. For contrasts, *see* EQUITY ACCOUNTING and PROPORTIONAL CONSOLIDATION.

expectations gap The difference between the public's perception of the duties or the level of performance of AUDITORS (or financial reporting in general) and their actual duties or performance.

expected deviations rate The level of non-compliance with procedures anticipated by AUDITORS when sampling.

expected error The level of errors anticipated by AUDITORS when sampling a population of transactions.

expected value (or expected monetary value) The value of an ASSET or a LIABILITY calculated by summing the estimated possible outcomes, having taken account of the probability of each outcome. Each possible outcome, measured in monetary terms, is multiplied by the probability that it will occur.

expenditure The costs of an enterprise in a period, but not restricted to those used up in the period. Consequently, there can be capital expenditure (which benefits the future, and possibly also the current period) and revenue (or current) expenditure. The word 'expenditure' should be contrasted to 'EXPENSE'.

expenditure code A numerical (or alphanumerical) label given to a particular category of cost in a bookkeeping system.

expenditure tax A tax based on the amount of a taxpayer's consumption in a period rather than the taxpayer's income. It would be a current DIRECT TAX.

expenditure variance Within a STANDARD COSTING system, the difference between the actual overhead expenditure incurred and the budgeted allowance for it.

expense When used by accountants, this is a technical term traditionally meaning a payment, whenever physically made, that *relates* to the period in question. For example, a business may pay its electricity account after the end of the year in which the electricity was used: or it may pay its rent in advance. Such amounts are ACCRUED EXPENSES and prepayments, respectively. Accountants would treat both as expenses of the year to which they relate, showing the accruals or prepayments in a BALANCE SHEET.

This practice is part of the ACCRUAL BASIS OF ACCOUNTING, and is designed to lead to a fairer presentation of profit for a period. Profit is calculated by deducting the 'expenses' from the REVENUES of the period.

Fairly recently, accounting has been moving to a balance sheet basis. In this case, expenses of an accounting period are defined as decreases in economic benefits during the period due to decreases in ASSETS or increases in LIABILITIES

expense account In the context of a DOUBLE-ENTRY BOOKKEEPING system, one of many ACCOUNTS which record a particular type of expenses. In the context of spending by an employee of an enterprise, the amount of money allowed to be spent by the employee on individual expenses relating to the business, such as travel or entertaining.

experience adjustments In the context of accounting for DEFINED BENEFIT EMPLOYEE OBLIGATIONS, the effect of differences between previous ACTUARIAL ASSUMPTIONS and what has actually occurred.

expert comptable Nearest equivalent in France to a professionally qualified accountant in the Anglo-American sense. Most *experts comptables* are auditors of French companies. The *Ordre des Experts Comptables* is a self-regulating professional body. However, most of the rules for accounting come from government-controlled institutions, and there is also a government-controlled auditing body to which many *experts comptables* belong.

exposure draft A document that precedes the issue of ACCOUNTING STANDARDS. It is intended to attract response from companies, auditors, academics, investment analysts, financial institutions, etc.

expropriation The confiscation of property by a government. This is one of the risks that multinational companies face in certain foreign countries where they have subsidiaries. Under INTERNATIONAL ACCOUNTING STANDARDS COMMITTEE (but not UK) rules, a loss due to expropriation would probably be treated as an EXTRAORDINARY ITEM.

ex rights Without the right to purchase shares involved in a RIGHTS ISSUE. Shares may be sold while a rights issue is in progress either with or without the ability to take part in the issue.

extended trial balance A listing (a trial balance) of all the balances in a DOUBLE-ENTRY BOOKKEEPING system at the end of a period, extended by columns showing various period-end adjustments and then the adjusted amounts to be shown in the FINANCIAL STATEMENTS.

external audit An AUDIT of an enterprise (particularly of its published FINANCIAL STATEMENTS) carried out by auditors who are independent of the owners and managers of the enterprise.

externalities COSTS or benefits created by an enterprise but not borne or received by the enterprise. For example, if a company's factory pollutes a river, the costs are borne downstream, unless some mechanism is introduced (perhaps by the government or through courts of law) to re-allocate the costs.

extraordinary general meeting A meeting of the shareholders of a company which is not the ANNUAL GENERAL MEETING. An EGM, as its name suggests, does not happen very often in any particular company. It will be held, within the rules laid down by company law and the company's own BYLAWS (US)/ARTICLES OF ASSOCIATION (UK), when certain unusual events require it. For example, a certain proportion of the shareholders may demand an EGM in order to question their directors on alleged improprieties or to deal with a takeover. An EGM may also be held when the company has SOLVENCY problems.

extraordinary items GAINS or LOSSES which are outside the ORDINARY ACTIVITIES of the business, are of material size, and are not expected to recur. In the UK, the definition of 'ordinary' in FINANCIAL REPORTING STANDARD 3 is so wide that the recognition of an extraordinary item is unlikely. However, in some other countries, the definition is wider, and could include such items as gains on the sale of FIXED ASSETS.

extraordinary resolution In the context of a meeting of the shareholders of a UK company, a proposal that needs a particular notice period and a 75 per cent majority for it to be passed.

extra-statutory concession In the context of the UK taxation system, a relaxation of the rules by the Inland Revenue in favour of a taxpayer (or small group of taxpayers) which is not strictly allowed by the legislation but seems reasonable and reduces argument.

F

face value The amount stated on a FINANCIAL INSTRUMENT such as a share or bond.

factoring The selling of trade DEBTORS to a financial institution in return for a proportion of the legal value. This is a technique similar to borrowing. The discounted amount will be designed to include an implied rate of interest, the costs of collection and the possibility of default.

factors of production The resources needed for the operation of business. The factors include land, labour, loan capital and entrepreneurship. These each demand a return: rent, wages, interest and profit.

factory burden US term for factory overheads or PRODUCTION OVERHEAD.

factory costs/expenses Costs of manufacturing or production.

factory overhead *See* PRODUCTION OVERHEAD.

fair presentation The US requirement that FINANCIAL STATEMENTS should not be misleading. Financial statements in the USA that are fully audited and prepared in accordance with GENERALLY ACCEPTED ACCOUNTING PRINCIPLES (GAAP) are required to 'fairly present' the position and results of a company. To a large extent this means obeying the rules of GAAP, but the concept of fairness may transcend that, to include an assessment of the overall picture given by the financial statements. A connected doctrine is that financial statements should reflect SUBSTANCE OVER FORM.

fair value The amount for which an ASSET could be exchanged, or a LIABILITY settled, between knowledgeable and willing parties at arm's length. The fair value differs from NET REALIZABLE VALUE in that it is not net of any selling costs. Increasingly, investments and other assets that have a readily observable fair value are being valued at fair value. In a business combination accounted for as an ACQUISITION, the assets and liabilities of the new subsidiary are brought in to the CONSOLIDATED FINANCIAL STATEMENTS at fair values, not their previous book values. In this context, fair value often means CURRENT REPLACEMENT COST.

FAS Abbreviation for a US financial accounting standard (*see* FINANCIAL ACCOUNTING STANDARDS BOARD).

FASB Abbreviation for the FINANCIAL ACCOUNTING STANDARDS BOARD (of the USA).

favourable variance A difference between an actual expense, income, output, etc. and what was included as standard in a financial plan, in those cases where the difference is an improvement on the standard.

FCA Designatory letters for a fellow of the INSTITUTE OF CHARTERED ACCOUNTANTS IN ENGLAND AND WALES.

FCCA Designatory letters for a fellow of the ASSOCIATION OF CHARTERED CERTIFIED ACCOUNTANTS.

FCIS Designatory letters for a fellow of the INSTITUTE OF CHARTERED SECRETARIES AND ADMINISTRATORS.

FCMA Designatory letters for a fellow of the CHARTERED INSTITUTE OF MANAGEMENT ACCOUNTANTS.

Fédération des Experts Comptables Européens A European body of accountants, which began work in 1987, although it had predecessor bodies. Some of its committees specialize in advising the Commission of the European Communities on company law harmonization.

FEE Abbreviation for the FÉDÉRATION DES EXPERTS COMPTABLES EUROPÉENS.

fellow subsidiaries Enterprises which are not subsidiaries of each other but which share a parent.

fidelity bond An insurance contract which covers dishonest acts by senior employees.

fiduciary accounting Accounting for ASSETS held in TRUST.

FIFO (first in, first out) A common assumption for accounting purposes about the flow of items of raw materials or other STOCKS (inventories), whereby the oldest inventories still in stock are those deemed to be the first used for production or sale. The assumption need not correspond with physical reality to be made for accounting purposes. This means that the most recent units are deemed to be those left at the period end. When prices are rising, and assuming a reasonably constant purchasing of materials, FIFO leads to a fairly up-to-date closing inventory figure. However, it gives an out-of-date and therefore low figure for the COST OF SALES. This leads to what many argue is an overstatement of profit figures, when prices are rising.

FII Abbreviation for FRANKED INVESTMENT INCOME.

filing of accounts Depositing a company's ANNUAL REPORTS with the appropriate authorities; in the UK, the Registrar of Companies.

FIMBRA Abbreviation for the Financial Intermediaries, Managers and Brokers Regulatory Organisation: one of the UK's former self-regulatory bodies for financial institutions. Its functions were absorbed into the Personal Investment Authority and then into the FINANCIAL SERVICES AUTHORITY.

final dividend A second payment for a year to the shareholders of a company out of past profits. The first payment, made during the year, is the interim payment. The final payment is generally proposed by the company's directors and then approved by the shareholders at their ANNUAL GENERAL MEETING.

Finance Act UK name for the annual law that introduces tax changes and the new rates of tax. It follows the Finance Bill, which itself follows a Budget Statement by the Chancellor of the Exchequer.

finance charge An amount payable in return for the use of financial resources for a period.

finance house A type of financial institution that provides the financial resources for arrangements such as hire-purchase.

finance lease A lease which is treated by accountants as though the lessee had borrowed money and bought the leased ASSETS, i.e. the lease is capitalized. Generally, such leases are taken out for a large proportion of the life of the asset. The lessor treats the lease contract as a receivable. The US term is 'CAPITAL LEASE'. Leases that are not capitalized are called 'OPERATING LEASES'.

financial accounting A fairly vague term which covers BOOKKEEPING and the subsequent processing and analysis that leads to the preparation of FINANCIAL STATEMENTS for shareholders and others. It may be contrasted, for example, with MANAGEMENT ACCOUNTING which deals with the use of accounting data by managers inside a business to enable better planning and control.

Financial Accounting Foundation A US trust that raises the money to run, and appoints the members of, the FINANCIAL ACCOUNTING STANDARDS BOARD.

Financial Accounting Standards Advisory Council A US body that advises the FINANCIAL ACCOUNTING STANDARDS BOARD on its agenda and the content of proposed accounting standards.

Financial Accounting Standards Board (FASB) A body set up in the USA in 1973 to set ACCOUNTING STANDARDS on measurement, valuation and disclosure practices to be followed in the preparation of FINANCIAL STATEMENTS. In this task it is given 'substantial authoritative support' by a government body, the SECURITIES AND EXCHANGE COMMISSION (SEC). US companies that wish their securities to be publicly traded must be registered and file financial statements with the SEC, which will not accept those that disobey FASB standards. Thus, the standards have considerable power, for the minority of US companies that are SEC-registered.

The FASB has seven full-time board members and a substantial research staff. The board members are appointed by the independent Financial Accounting Foundation, which also raises the money for the FASB. The donations come from companies and accounting firms, presumably fearing the intervention of the SEC if no private body were capable of setting standards. Donations are limited for any one donor, in order to preserve independence.

The FASB works by 'due process' which includes prior research, wide circulation of EXPOSURE DRAFTS, and public hearings before a standard is issued.

financial adaptability The ability of an enterprise to survive shocks and to take advantage of unexpected opportunities by changing its CASH FLOWS.

financial analysis The assessment of the present position and future prospects of an enterprise based on a study of its FINANCIAL STATEMENTS and other related data.

financial appraisal The assessment of a series of alternative investments in assets or companies using financial data such as projected cash flows.

financial asset According to the INTERNATIONAL ACCOUNTING STANDARDS COMMITTEE (IASC), any ASSET that is either:

(a) cash;
(b) a contractual right to receive cash or another financial asset from another enterprise;
(c) a contractual right to exchange FINANCIAL INSTRUMENTS with another enterprise under conditions that are potentially favourable; or
(d) an EQUITY INSTRUMENT of another enterprise.

Under US and IASC rules, there are three categories: HELD TO MATURITY FINANCIAL ASSETS, AVAILABLE-FOR-SALE FINANCIAL ASSETS, and TRADING FINANCIAL ASSETS.

financial budget A document which quantifies the planned cash flows of an enterprise for a number of future periods.

financial capital maintenance concept The measurement of the profit of an enterprise as the increase in net resources of the enterprise after its CAPITAL measured in money terms has been kept at the same level as it was at the beginning of the period. The capital might be adjusted for changes in the value of money.

financial control The management of the costs and revenues of an organization.

financial engineering A colloquial term for the re-arrangement of the financial structure and financial operations of an enterprise in order to reduce interest expense, tax or other costs.

financial expense A cost of an enterprise connected to the raising of finance. Such expenses include INTEREST payments.

financial futures Contracts for the postponed sale and purchase of financial items such as foreign currencies.

financial highlights Key financial information, such as sales, earnings or dividends, as disclosed in summarized form in a company's ANNUAL REPORT.

financial institution An organization that deals primarily in money or investments. A financial institution obtains funds from individuals, companies or governments and then buys investments or lends the funds on to others. Examples of such institutions are banks and life assurance companies.

financial instrument A contract that creates a FINANCIAL ASSET of one enterprise and a FINANCIAL LIABILITY or EQUITY INSTRUMENT of another.

financial liability According to the INTERNATIONAL ACCOUNTING STANDARDS COMMITTEE, any liability that is a contractual obligation to deliver cash or another financial asset to another enterprise; or to exchange such financial instruments with another enterprise under conditions that are potentially unfavourable.

financial management *See* FINANCIAL CONTROL.

financial modelling The creation and use of mathematical representations of an enterprise's activities expressed in money terms, in order to assist in decision making.

financial period The period for which FINANCIAL STATEMENTS are prepared.

financial planning The establishment of detailed numerical plans for the financial aspects of an enterprise for several periods into the future. The initial forecasts will have revealed problems for which proposed corrective actions have been prepared, and all this is included in the financial planning.

financial position The status of an enterprise, as shown by its ASSETS, LIABILITIES and EQUITY as reported in its BALANCE SHEET.

financial ratio The relationship between two figures (or aggregates of figures) in an enterprise's FINANCIAL STATEMENTS. Typical financial ratios are RETURN ON CAPITAL EMPLOYED or EARNINGS PER SHARE.

financial reporting The presentation of financial information about an entity to potential users of such information. The term usually refers to reporting to users outside of the entity, i.e. not to the entity's management. The information may be numerical or non-numerical. The term is wider than ACCOUNTING and could include discussions by management of its plans.

Financial Reporting Council A UK body set up in 1990 to supervise the setting and use of ACCOUNTING STANDARDS. It appoints the members of the ACCOUNTING STANDARDS BOARD and the FINANCIAL REPORTING REVIEW PANEL, and it raises the funds for their operations.

Financial Reporting Exposure Draft UK term (abbreviated to FRED) for a document issued for public comment that precedes the preparation of an ACCOUNTING STANDARD.

Financial Reporting Release A document issued by the SECURITIES AND EXCHANGE COMMISSION on technical issues of financial reporting.

Financial Reporting Review Panel (FRRP) A UK body established in 1991 whose task is to investigate complaints against large companies that their FINANCIAL STATEMENTS are defective, such as that they do not give a TRUE AND FAIR VIEW. The FRRP can take companies to court on this issue. The court has various powers, such as to require a company's directors to withdraw and amend the financial statements.

Financial Reporting Standard An ACCOUNTING STANDARD as promulgated in the UK by the ACCOUNTING STANDARDS BOARD since 1990.

Financial Reporting Standard for Smaller Entities (FRSSE) An omnibus version of UK ACCOUNTING STANDARDS which have been abbreviated and simplified. The FRSSE may be used instead of the full standards by enterprises that would qualify as small under the Companies Act.

Financial Services Authority UK government agency that oversees stock markets and other financial matters.

financial statement analysis The use of an enterprise's FINANCIAL STATEMENTS in order to assess its present position and future prospects. Such analysis may be carried out by investors, creditors or their advisers, with the objective of making financial decisions such as the purchase or sale of shares or bonds. The analysis involves comparisons over time and between enterprises of such matters as PROFITABILITY, LIQUIDITY and GEARING.

financial statements As a technical term, those documents required to be prepared by an enterprise at least once a year in accordance with particular rules. For example, under UK law and standards, the financial statements (also called 'annual accounts') comprise the BALANCE SHEET, PROFIT AND LOSS ACCOUNT, STATEMENT OF TOTAL RECOGNIZED GAINS AND LOSSES, CASH FLOW STATEMENT and the notes to all these.

financial structure The arrangement of an organization's sources of funds. *See* CAPITAL STRUCTURE.

financial year Usual UK expression for the period for which the ANNUAL REPORT and accounts are prepared. The most popular dates for the year end are December 31 and March 31, the second of which coincides with the end of the tax year for companies. Some companies account for exactly 52 or 53 weeks, so their precise year end may vary by a day or two in each year. In the USA, the analogous expression is fiscal year.

financing activities Activities that lead to changes in the size and composition of the capital and borrowings of an enterprise. This is one of the categories to be found in CASH FLOW STATEMENTS.

finished goods Those stocks/INVENTORIES of an enterprise that are ready for sale to customers, unlike raw materials and work in progress.

firm commitment A binding agreement for the exchange of particular resources at a particular price and date.

first in, first out *See* FIFO.

first year allowance In the context of the UK tax system, an amount of depreciation or capital allowance (expressed as a percentage of cost) granted in the year of purchase of particular assets. For example, at the time of writing, many smaller companies are allowed to charge 40 per cent of the cost of plant and machinery in the calculation of taxable income of the year of purchase.

fiscal policy Governmental variation of its expenditures and revenues (mainly tax) for the purpose of boosting or dampening down the level of activity in the country's economy.

fiscal year US expression for the period for which a company prepares its annual financial statements. The majority of US companies use December 31 as the fiscal year end, which corresponds with the year end for tax purposes. As an accounting term it is a slight misnomer, because 'fiscal year' really means tax year, and it is by no means for all companies that the accounting and tax years co-terminate on December 31.

In the UK, the equivalent term is FINANCIAL YEAR or accounting year.

fixed asset Mainly a UK rather than an INTERNATIONAL ACCOUNTING STANDARDS COMMITTEE, or US, expression, meaning the ASSETS that are to continue to be used in the business, such as land, buildings and machines. The opposite are CURRENT ASSETS, such as cash or STOCKS (inventories). The COMPANIES ACT defines fixed assets as those 'intended for use on a continuing basis'. The equivalent US expression is usually 'Property, Plant and Equipment'.

It is normal for fixed assets to wear out due to use or the effluxion of time, i.e. to have limited useful lives. This is recognized by a charge against profit and a reduction in the holding value of the assets, called DEPRECIATION. Some fixed assets may not wear out, such as plots of land.

fixed asset investment A holding in the securities of another organization that is intended to continue rather than to be sold.

fixed assets register A document listing the tangible (and perhaps intangible) FIXED ASSETS of an enterprise, and showing their costs, dates of purchase, estimated lives, accumulated depreciation, and so on.

fixed budget A detailed numerical plan (a BUDGET) that is not expressed in such a way as to take account of possible changes in volume.

fixed capital A term used by economists rather than by accountants for the long-run assets of an organization.

fixed charge The right of a CREDITOR to the proceeds from the sale of specified ASSETS of a DEBTOR if the debtor does not pay amounts when due. Consequently, the debtor is not allowed to sell these assets without the permission of the creditor. *See*, also, FLOATING CHARGE.

fixed costs In economics, those costs of a business that cannot be altered in the short term. In a COST ACCOUNTING context, the term means those COSTS that do not vary with levels of output or sales in the short term such as factory rents or staff on contracts. Fixed costs will normally be OVERHEADS that relate to several product lines or jobs. For example, the chief executive's salary and the interest on loans will be FIXED OVERHEAD COSTS.

fixed exchange rate A ratio of exchange of one currency expressed in terms of others, when that ratio is fixed by the authorities of the country.

fixed overhead absorption rate The rate (in terms of cost per volume) at which the FIXED OVERHEAD COST is added to PRODUCTION COSTS. The rate is calculated as the budgeted fixed overhead cost divided by the budgeted hours or units.

fixed overhead cost The costs of an organization that cannot be directly related to particular units of product and do not vary (at least in the short term) with the volume of production. Such cost would include the rent on a factory or the salaries of administrators.

fixed price contract A contract for the production or supply of goods and services where the price is fixed at the beginning.

fixed production overhead Those elements of the FIXED OVERHEAD COST that relate specifically to manufacturing, such as the rent on a factory. Another way of putting this is that fixed production overhead is those indirect costs of production that remain fairly constant as the volume of production varies.

fixed rate loan A loan for which the rate of interest is settled at the beginning and does not change.

flexed budget A BUDGET that has been adjusted for the actual volume of activity.

flexed budget allowance The budgeted expenditure for a particular VARIABLE COST item after it has been adjusted for the actual volume of activity.

flexible budget A detailed numerical plan (a BUDGET) that is expressed in such a way as to take account of various volumes of activity.

float A relatively small amount of money held to enable small cash transactions, including giving change to customers.

floating assets Old-fashioned term for CURRENT ASSETS.

floating charge The right of a CREDITOR to the proceeds from the sale of all (or a class) of the ASSETS of a DEBTOR if the debtor does not pay amounts when due. The debtor is allowed to sell the individual assets until default, unlike the case of a FIXED CHARGE.

floating exchange rate A ratio of exchange of one currency expressed in terms of others, when that ratio moves in response to market pressures.

floating rate loan (or note) A loan whose interest rate moves in response to market pressures.

floor In the context of an OPTION, the minimum rate of interest payable.

flotation The process whereby a company issues publicly traded securities for the first time.

flotation costs The expenses (such as legal, marketing and accountancy) related to FLOTATION.

flow of funds accounts Financial statements recording for a national economy the financial and non-financial flows through different sectors of the economy. Compare to SOURCE AND APPLICATION OF FUNDS STATEMENTS.

folio In the context of DOUBLE-ENTRY BOOKKEEPING, a page in an account book.

forecasts In the context of financial reporting, projected data which are included in the reports on PROSPECTUSES of companies.

foreclosure A legal process whereby a mortgagee or other lender takes possession of an ASSET of a borrower who has not paid moneys when due.

foreign currency For financial reporting purposes, a currency other than the REPORTING CURRENCY of an enterprise.

foreign currency transaction A transaction which is legally denominated in or requires settlement in a FOREIGN CURRENCY. Foreign currency transactions are recorded in the REPORTING CURRENCY when they occur. After that, monetary balances are generally retranslated at the exchange rate ruling on the date of the BALANCE SHEET.

foreign currency translation The restatement of transactions, balances or whole FINANCIAL STATEMENTS into another currency. For example, the financial statements of a foreign subsidiary or branch are translated into the currency of the parent company (or other reporting currency) to enable the preparation of CONSOLIDATED FINANCIAL STATEMENTS. Translation can be distinguished from 'currency conversion' in that the latter involves the physical exchange of money from one currency to another. Translation is purely an accounting exercise, but a very complex and controversial one.

foreign emoluments In the context of UK taxation, certain earnings received from a non-resident employer.

foreign entity A technical term in INTERNATIONAL ACCOUNTING STANDARDS COMMITTEE literature, meaning a foreign operation, which is not an integral part of the reporting enterprise. In other words, such an operation is to be seen as operating somewhat independently. This may be the normal position for a foreign SUBSIDIARY.

foreign exchange Amounts of money denominated in the currency of another country.

foreign exchange exposure *See* CURRENCY EXPOSURE.

foreign exchange risk The chance of loss caused by exchange rate movements affecting ASSETS, LIABILITIES or operations denominated in foreign currencies.

foreign operation An operation (subsidiary, branch, joint venture, ASSOCIATE, etc.) whose activities are based in a country other than that of the reporting enterprise.

foreign subsidiary From the point of view of one enterprise (the parent), another enterprise which is controlled by the parent but operates in another country.

forensic accounting In the context of a court case, the use of accounting as part of determining the legality of various past actions.

forfaiting The purchase of financial ASSETS such as BILLS OF EXCHANGE (by a forfaiter) on a discounted basis because the forfaiter takes the risk of non-payment.

forfeited share A share in a company that has been legally taken away from a former shareholder by the company because that shareholder had not paid all the amounts called up by the company.

forgivable loans Loans the repayment of which the lender (perhaps a government) offers to waive under certain conditions.

Form 8-K A monthly document required to be filed with the SECURITIES AND EXCHANGE COMMISSION by any company registered with it when certain events occur in that month.

Form 10-K An annual document required to be filed with the SECURITIES AND EXCHANGE COMMISSION by all companies registered with it within 120 days of a company's financial year end. Form 10-K contains a great deal of information about the company, including its FINANCIAL STATEMENTS.

Form 10-Q A quarterly document required to be filed with the SECURITIES AND EXCHANGE COMMISSION by companies registered with it. Form 10-Q contains condensed FINANCIAL STATEMENTS relating to the quarter and the year so far.

Form 20-F A document required to be filed annually with the SECURITIES AND EXCHANGE COMMISSION by those non-US registrants who do not produce an annual report based on US rules.

formation expenses The costs of setting up a company. These must be treated as expenses under UK and INTERNATIONAL ACCOUNTING STANDARDS COMMITTEE rules, but can be treated as ASSETS in some continental European countries.

formats The allowed layouts of FINANCIAL STATEMENTS such as the BALANCE SHEET and the PROFIT AND LOSS ACCOUNT. In the UK, the Companies Act 1985 prescribes formats for those two statements.

forward exchange rate The price (expressed in another currency) at which a currency can be bought or sold for delivery at a specified future date.

forward market A market in which such items as foreign currencies are traded for exchange at a specified future date.

forward points The difference between the current EXCHANGE RATE between two currencies and a future rate.

forward rate The RATE OF EXCHANGE of a currency at some specified future date, as opposed to the SPOT RATE.

forward rate agreement A contract specifying an amount of currency to be exchanged at a particular rate and date.

founders' shares Shares issued to those who set up a company. Such shares may have advantageous rights to dividends when profits are above a certain level.

Fourth Directive A document comprising detailed instructions from the EU to its member states to enact laws concerning the financial reporting of limited companies. The Directive was adopted by the Council of Ministers in 1978. Strictly speaking, it is the Fourth Directive on company law, because there are many other series of Directives.

framework *See* CONCEPTUAL FRAMEWORK.

franked investment income Dividends received by one UK company from another. These are not chargeable to CORPORATION TAX because they have already borne corporation tax in the paying company. Such income is called 'franked investment income' because it has been franked, i.e. taxed or stamped.

franked payments Formerly, a company's dividend payments grossed up by the related ADVANCE CORPORATION TAX.

franked SORPs In the UK, those STATEMENTS OF RECOMMENDED PRACTICE that were not prepared by, but approved by, the ACCOUNTING STANDARDS COMMITTEE.

FRC Abbreviation for the FINANCIAL REPORTING COUNCIL (of the UK).

FRED Abbreviation for a FINANCIAL REPORTING EXPOSURE DRAFT (in the UK).

free asset ratio In the context of an insurance company, the market value of the company's assets divided by its liabilities.

freehold land and buildings Those items of land and buildings that are legally possessed by their owners with no limit on time. In contrast, LEASEHOLD property reverts back to the freehold owners at the end of the lease.

Friendly Society A type of UK NON-PROFIT association owned by its investors or policyholders.

fringe benefits Non-monetary benefits received by employees or perhaps shareholders. In the case of the employees, such benefits might include health care and the use of a company car.

front-end loading The practice of insurance companies or other financial institutions whereby the commission and administrative expenses related to a continuing series of investments are extracted from the initial receipts.

frozen assets ASSETS that, because of some regulatory or other constraint, cannot be used, exchanged or turned into cash.

frozen GAAP The GENERALLY ACCEPTED ACCOUNTING PRINCIPLES ruling when a CONTRACT is agreed, in those cases where future changes to the principles are to be ignored under the contract. The context is generally the specification of required ratios (e.g. a GEARING ratio) not to be exceeded by a lender.

FRR Abbreviation for a FINANCIAL REPORTING RELEASE (in the US).

FRRP Abbreviation for the FINANCIAL REPORTING REVIEW PANEL (of the UK).

FRS Abbreviation for a FINANCIAL REPORTING STANDARD (in the UK).

FRSSE Abbreviation for the FINANCIAL REPORTING STANDARD FOR SMALLER ENTITIES (in the UK).

frustration of contract The cessation of a contract because it cannot be fulfilled because it becomes illegal or impossible due to unforeseen circumstances.

FSA Abbreviation for the FINANCIAL SERVICES AUTHORITY (of the UK).

FTII Abbreviation for a fellow of the CHARTERED INSTITUTE OF TAXATION.

FTSE Abbreviation for the Financial Times Stock Exchange Index. *See* SHARE PRICE INDICES.

full accounts A legal term for FINANCIAL STATEMENTS that comply with the full provisions of law, rather than being SUMMARY FINANCIAL STATEMENTS.

full consolidation The normal treatment of subsidiaries when preparing CONSOLIDATED FINANCIAL STATEMENTS, whereby 100 per cent of all assets, liabilities, expenses and revenues are brought in, except for adjustments for intra-group items. This applies even if a subsidiary is not wholly owned.

full costing method The calculation of the cost of a product or service by including both DIRECT COSTS and INDIRECT COSTS.

full cost method In the context of accounting for oil and gas exploration costs, the capitalization of the costs related to both successful and unsuccessful efforts in a particular area of exploration.

full cost pricing The practice of setting selling prices such that they cover all costs, including an allocation of FIXED COSTS. A mark-up is added to the costs in order to fix the selling price.

fully diluted earnings per share A former term for DILUTED EARNINGS PER SHARE.

fully funded plan (or scheme) An EMPLOYEE BENEFIT PLAN for which the obligations are at least matched by resources available in a FUND.

fully paid share A share for which the shareholder has paid all the calls for payment and for which there can be no more calls (*see* CALLED-UP SHARE CAPITAL).

functional budget A detailed numerical plan (a BUDGET) drawn up for a part of an organization which has been divided up along functional lines, such as production, marketing and administration.

functional currency   From the point of view of a parent company preparing CONSOLIDATED FINANCIAL STATEMENTS, the currency in which a particular foreign subsidiary is deemed to operate. For an independently operating FOREIGN SUBSIDIARY, the functional currency is usually that of the subsidiary's country, but for a highly integrated subsidiary it may be the parent's currency.

function costing   The collection and presentation of costs by parts of an organization divided up along functional lines, such as production, marketing and administration.

fund   A pool of resources set aside for particular purposes. For example, a pension fund is a separate legal entity that contains investments and other resources designed to provide payments to pensioners. In the context of the public sector, the fund may be a separate accounting unit.

fund accounting   In the public sector, generally CASH-based accounting for units of government activity identified as funds.

fundamental accounting principles   In the context of UK company law, the principles of ACCRUALS, CONSISTENCY, GOING CONCERN, PRUDENCE and separate valuation.

fundamental analysis   The examination of FINANCIAL STATEMENTS and other information in order to establish what the value of a company should be, and thereby to identify those whose SHARES seem to be mis-priced on a stock exchange.

fundamental error   An error that is of such significance that the FINANCIAL STATEMENTS cannot be considered to have been reliable at the date of their issue. Such errors are generally corrected in the UK or the US by PRIOR-YEAR ADJUSTMENTS, i.e. the enterprise's opening BALANCE SHEET is corrected. An alternative approach allowed by INTERNATIONAL ACCOUNTING STANDARD is to absorb the errors into the current period's INCOME STATEMENT.

funded pension scheme   A PENSION SCHEME (or plan) for which the obligations are wholly or partly matched by resources available in a FUND.

funding   The process whereby contributions (generally cash) are transferred by an enterprise, and sometimes by its employees, into an entity (a FUND) that is legally separate from the reporting enterprise and from which EMPLOYEE BENEFITS are paid. Funding is common in the UK or the US but less normal in continental Europe. Funding of employee benefits should be distinguished from

PROVISION for employee benefits. The latter record the OBLIGATIONS, not the means to pay them.

funds flow statement *See* SOURCE AND APPLICATION OF FUNDS STATEMENTS.

fungible assets Assets that are interchangeable because they are indistinguishable from one another. For example, the ORDINARY SHARES in a LISTED COMPANY are homogeneous and therefore fungible. The same might apply to certain INVENTORIES.

fungible issue The creation and release by a company of further BONDS that are identical to those previously issued.

futures contract A binding agreement for the sale and purchase of a specified amount of a COMMODITY, FINANCIAL INSTRUMENT or currency at a specified price and future date.

futures market A locus for the trading of FUTURES CONTRACTS.

G

GAAP Abbreviation for GENERALLY ACCEPTED ACCOUNTING PRINCIPLES.

GAAS Abbreviation for GENERALLY ACCEPTED AUDITING STANDARDS.

gains Increases in economic benefits. Sometimes this term is used to denote those increases resulting from the rise in value (or the sale) of ASSETS other than INVENTORY.

Garner v Murray rule A legal precedent established under English law whereby, unless a PARTNERSHIP AGREEMENT specifies otherwise, the DEBIT BALANCE of an insolvent partner is shared among the other partners in proportion to their capital balances.

GASB Abbreviation for the GOVERNMENTAL ACCOUNTING STANDARDS BOARD (of the USA).

gearing A measurement of the degree to which a business is funded by loans rather than SHAREHOLDERS' EQUITY. The US expression is 'LEVERAGE'.

Different analysts of a company's financial position use different definitions of gearing. The main rule, as with other ratios, is to try to be consistent from year to year or company to company. Common measures of gearing are long-term loans divided by total capital, or long-term loans divided by shareholders' equity. The higher the proportion of loan finance, the higher is the gearing.

A further measure of the danger of INSOLVENCY is 'interest gearing', which measures the extent to which a company's pre-tax, pre-interest PROFIT is pre-empted by the need to pay interest. Higher interest gearing means greater danger.

gearing adjustment One of the several adjustments to PROFIT to be found in some systems of CURRENT COST ACCOUNTING that adjust profits to take account of changing prices. The main other adjustments are the DEPRECIATION ADJUSTMENT and COST OF SALES ADJUSTMENT, which are extra charges against profit when prices are rising. The gearing adjustment is designed to take account of the degree to which these deductions in a particular company are compensated for by the fact that the company is financed by loans, i.e. the degree to which it has high GEARING).

gearing ratios *See* GEARING.

General Commissioners A body of part-time unpaid persons appointed in the UK to consider appeals made by taxpayers against their assessments. *See*, also, SPECIAL COMMISSIONERS.

general expenses Expenses, also known as 'sundries', which do not fit into any other category.

general ledger *See* NOMINAL LEDGER.

generally accepted accounting principles (GAAP) A term originally used in the USA, where it includes the ACCOUNTING STANDARDS of the FINANCIAL ACCOUNTING STANDARDS BOARD and extant rules of predecessor bodies. Also included are some of the rules propounded by the SECURITIES AND EXCHANGE COMMISSION (SEC) as Accounting Series Releases and Financial Reporting Releases. These documents, and others, comprise written (or promulgated) GAAP but there are also unpromulgated GAAP comprising the practices of respected companies, AUDITORS or textbooks.

The SEC requires that companies registered with it prepare audited FINANCIAL STATEMENTS according to US GAAP.

In other countries, GAAP is a vaguer term, presumably including laws, standards and practices of respected companies.

generally accepted auditing standards A technical term, used in the USA, to include those rules that should be followed by auditors when carrying out a 'full' AUDIT on FINANCIAL STATEMENTS, particularly for SECURITIES AND EXCHANGE COMMISSION filing purposes.

general meeting A meeting that all members of a COMPANY, or other association, are allowed to attend. In the case of a company, such meetings would be the ANNUAL GENERAL MEETING or an EXTRAORDINARY GENERAL MEETING.

general partner A PARTNER whose LIABILITY for a PARTNERSHIP's debts is unlimited, in the context that some other partners have limited liability.

general price level adjusted US term for a system of financial reporting that takes account of changes in inflation. *See* CURRENT PURCHASING POWER ACCOUNTING.

general purchasing power approach US term for the ideas behind CURRENT PURCHASING POWER ACCOUNTING.

general purpose financial statements The normal FINANCIAL STATEMENTS of a company prepared under UK or INTERNATIONAL ACCOUNTING STANDARDS COMMITTEE rules. Such statements are presumed to be suitable for many purposes, although the needs of investors are largely the contexts foreseen by the makers of the laws or standards.

geographical segment A distinguishable component of an enterprise that provides products or services within a particular economic environment and is subject to risks and returns different from those of other components. If a geographical segment accounts for at least 10 per cent of sales, PROFITS or ASSETS of an enterprise, then its contribution needs to be disclosed as part of SEGMENT REPORTING.

Gesellschaft mit beschränkter Haftung An Austrian, German or Swiss PRIVATE COMPANY. It is abbreviated to GmbH.

gifts inter vivos In the context of INHERITANCE TAX, gifts made between living persons. Certain gifts made during a donor's lifetime are exempt from the tax.

gilt-edged security (gilt) UK expression for some loans made to the government. So secure are the interest payments and eventual repayment deemed to be, that this form of LOAN STOCK is seen to be almost risk-free or 'as good as gold', hence 'gilt-edged'. Another name for government securities is 'TREASURY BILLS'. This opens the door to the possibility of extreme confusion for UK accountants and businessmen when they meet the expression TREASURY STOCK in US BALANCE SHEETS. In the USA, 'treasury stock' means a company's own shares bought back and held in the corporate treasury. The UK expression for this is OWN SHARES.

global custody A full-scale service by a financial institution for the trading, registration, management and safekeeping of securities belonging to clients.

GmbH Abbreviation for an Austrian, German or Swiss private limited company, a *Gesellschaft mit beschränkter Haftung*.

GmbH & Co KG A type of German partnership in which one of the partners is a private limited liability company. The other partners may be persons who have limited liability for the PARTNERSHIP's debts.

goal congruence A state of affairs where two or more parties share the same objectives. The term might be used where individual managers and the organization as a whole have the same purpose.

GoB *Grundsätze ordnungsmässiger Buchführung*. A German phrase meaning 'orderly bookkeeping principles', although sometimes translated as 'generally accepted accounting principles'.

going concern An enterprise whose managers have neither the intention nor the necessity of liquidating it. It can then be assumed that the enterprise will continue for the foreseeable future.

going concern concept An important underlying concept in accounting practice. The assumption for most businesses is that they will continue for the foreseeable future. This means that, for most purposes, the break-up or forced-sale value of the ASSETS is not relevant. Particularly for FIXED ASSETS, what they could be sold for may be a severe underestimate of their value to a business in terms of REPLACEMENT COST or ECONOMIC VALUE. Thus, their NET REALIZABLE VALUE is ignored in most systems of accounting, including the conventional system, HISTORICAL COST ACCOUNTING.

Companies do not need to disclose that they are following the going concern convention. However, if there are doubts that a business is a going concern, the convention should be abandoned, with appropriate disclosures and with appropriate PROVISIONS and IMPAIRMENTS.

golden handcuffs Informal expression for financial incentives to persuade employees to remain with their employers.

golden handshake Informal expression for payments made by an employer to an employee at the end of an employment, particularly in compensation for termination of a contract before its end.

golden hello Informal expression for a payment at the beginning of an employment, offered as a financial inducement to prospective employees.

golden parachute Informal expression for a clause in an employment contract of a senior employee that provides for general financial compensation if the contract is terminated as a result, for example, of a TAKEOVER BID.

golden share A shareholding in a company that gives the holder a CONTROLLING INTEREST under certain circumstances. For example, a government might hold a golden share in a company in a strategic industry such as defence. The share could be used in the event of a TAKEOVER BID by a foreign company.

good output In the context of PROCESS COSTING, the flawless production from a process.

goods received note A form which is part of an organization's INVENTORY CONTROL system. The form records the date, type, quantity and order number relating to goods received.

goodwill The amount paid for a business in excess of the fair value of its identifiable NET ASSETS at the date of acquisition. It exists because a GOING CONCERN business is usually worth more than the sum of the values of its separable net assets. Goodwill may be looked upon as the ability to earn future PROFITS above those of a similar newly formed company, or it may be seen as the loyalty of customers, the established network of contacts, trained staff and skilled management.

If the business being bought is unincorporated (such as a PARTNERSHIP) it will be absorbed into the legal and accounting entity of the acquiring company. Any resulting purchased goodwill is shown in the BALANCE SHEET of the company. In the more usual cases, where a *company* is bought, the resulting goodwill in the CONSOLIDATED FINANCIAL STATEMENTS is called 'goodwill on consolidation'. ASSETS are brought into the consolidated financial statements at their fair value rather than their BOOK VALUE because the former is a better indication of the 'cost' to the group of the newly arrived assets. The exception to this practice is MERGER ACCOUNTING. In the UK, normal practice until 1998 was to write goodwill off against group RESERVES immediately on acquisition. However, goodwill purchased since then must be capitalized, and then amortized over its useful life, with a rebuttable presumption that the life will not exceed twenty years. If a life over twenty years is used, there must be annual IMPAIRMENT tests. INTERNATIONAL ACCOUNTING STANDARDS COMMITTEE requirements are similar.

Governmental Accounting Standards Board (GASB) US standard-setting body controlled by the FINANCIAL ACCOUNTING FOUNDATION which also controls the FINANCIAL ACCOUNTING STANDARDS BOARD. The GASB's task is to develop accounting standards for government-controlled enterprises.

government assistance Actions by government for the purpose of giving benefits to specific enterprises.

government grants Help for an enterprise from government in the form of transfers of resources (often cash) in return for compliance with conditions. This excludes transactions with government which cannot be distinguished from normal trading transactions. If these grants are related to the purchase of ASSETS, they are generally taken to INCOME over the life of the asset.

government stock Borrowings made by the government in order to finance its EXPENDITURES.

Gower Report A UK report of 1984 on investor protection. It led to the Financial Services Act 1986.

GPP *See* GENERAL PURCHASING POWER APPROACH.

grandfather clause A provision in a contract or a regulation which exempts events or transactions carried out before the rules came into force.

green audit *See* ENVIRONMENTAL AUDIT.

Greenbury Report A UK report of 1995 which carried further the recommendations of the CADBURY REPORT, particularly in the field of directors' remuneration.

greenmail A threat made to a company by a substantial shareholder to launch a HOSTILE TAKEOVER BID unless the shareholding is bought out at a high price.

green reporting *See* ENVIRONMENTAL ACCOUNTING.

grey market In the context of trading in shares, a market in shares that have not yet been issued or officially listed on a stock exchange.

gross dividend The amount of a DIVIDEND before any deduction of tax. In the UK, tax is not deducted from dividend payments, so the term 'gross dividend' is misleading. It is used to mean the dividend grossed up by the TAX CREDIT received by a shareholder.

gross dividend per share The total of the gross (i.e. grossed-up) dividends paid by a company relating to a particular year for each ORDINARY SHARE.

gross dividend yield The GROSS DIVIDEND PER SHARE of a company for the most recent year divided by the current price of its shares.

grossed-up dividend *See* GROSS DIVIDEND.

gross equity method A method required in the UK for the valuation and presentation of interests in JOINT VENTURES in CONSOLIDATED FINANCIAL STATEMENTS. In the CONSOLIDATED BALANCE SHEET, the venturer's proportion of the venture's gross ASSETS and gross LIABILITIES are shown, leading to the net assets being shown as the value of the investment.

gross income Income before the deduction of any expenses.

gross investment in a lease The aggregate of the MINIMUM LEASE PAYMENTS and any unguaranteed RESIDUAL VALUE accruing to a LESSOR.

gross margin A term sometimes used in a manufacturing company to mean the same as GROSS PROFIT.

gross margin ratio The GROSS PROFIT or gross margin expressed as a percentage of sales.

gross profit The difference between the value of an enterprise's sales for a period and the COST OF SALES. For a manufacturing company, the latter includes the purchases of RAW MATERIALS STOCK, adjusted for changes to STOCKS (inventories), and all the other costs of producing the goods that were sold in the period, such as factory wages. From the gross profit, one would then deduct non-manufacturing expenses, such as administration costs and interest charges, to arrive at NET PROFIT before tax.

gross profit percentage The GROSS PROFIT expressed as a percentage of sales.

gross redemption yield The pre-tax INTERNAL RATE OF RETURN on a bond bought at a particular price and date and held to maturity.

gross up To enlarge an amount by a percentage in order to calculate what it would have been before something (e.g. a tax) had been deducted.

group A parent and all its subsidiaries, i.e. the set of enterprises under common control. This suggests the exclusion of JOINT VENTURES and ASSOCIATES, although (unhelpfully) these are sometimes called 'group companies'.

group accounts *See* GROUP FINANCIAL STATEMENTS.

group company A company that is a parent or a subsidiary within the same group of companies.

Groupe d'Etudes des Experts Comptables de la CEE The EU Accountants' Study Group, which was set up at the request of the Commission of the European Communities. Its task was to respond to the Commission on matters concerning accountants, particularly draft DIRECTIVES. Its functions were absorbed into the FÉDÉRATION DES EXPERTS COMPTABLES EUROPÉENS at the end of 1986.

group financial statements The FINANCIAL STATEMENTS of a GROUP of companies (the parent company and its subsidiaries). This term has the same meaning as consolidated accounts or CONSOLIDATED FINANCIAL STATEMENTS.

group registration In the context of VALUE ADDED TAX in the UK, registration of companies as a group so that transfers between them are ignored for the tax. The definition of a group for this purpose is not the same as for financial reporting, e.g. it is restricted to UK companies.

group relief A system within a CORPORATION TAX for allowing connected companies to pass tax reductions (e.g. due to losses) from one company to another. For UK taxation, a parent and its 75 per cent (or greater) held subsidiaries constitute a group.

H

hard currency A currency that tends to rise against other currencies and is therefore widely accepted outside its own country.

harmonization The making of practices more compatible, though not necessarily exactly standardized. The word is commonly used in the context of the efforts of the Commission and Council of the European Communities to bring about compatibility of financial reporting and company law throughout the member states. Enforceability is achieved primarily by passing DIRECTIVES on company law, which have to be enacted and enforced by member states.

hash total A total of a set of numbers that are not all of the same denomination. This is done as part of a control procedure rather than to use the total for some other purpose.

head lease The lease that grants the use of an ASSET to a LESSOR from its owner, in the case where the lessor then leases the asset to someone else under a sub-lease.

headline earnings A measure of a company's earnings as calculated by a formula originally set out in the UK by the Institute of Investment Management and Research. This is the definition of earnings used by many analysts and newspapers. The definition removes from the earnings calculation certain items deemed to be non-recurring or non-operating, e.g. gains on the sale of fixed assets. Compare EARNINGS.

headline earnings per share The HEADLINE EARNINGS of a company for the most recent period divided by the average number of its ORDINARY SHARES outstanding in the period.

hedge accounting The offset of changes in value or cash flows of a HEDGED ITEM by those of a HEDGING INSTRUMENT. Such accounting is only allowed under certain conditions, including prior designation of the item and instrument.

hedged asset An asset that is exposed to risk of changes in value but is seen as being offset by a HEDGING INSTRUMENT.

hedged item An item (e.g. an ASSET, LIABILITY, or forecasted future transaction) that is exposed to the risk of changes in fair value or in future cash flows and that is seen as being offset by a HEDGING INSTRUMENT. For financial reporting purposes, this offset is only allowed under the conditions for HEDGE ACCOUNTING.

hedge effectiveness The degree to which a HEDGING INSTRUMENT achieves offsetting changes in the cash flows or fair value attributable to a HEDGED ITEM.

hedging Using one or more HEDGING INSTRUMENTS so that their change in fair value is an offset, in whole or in part, to the change in FAIR VALUE or CASH FLOWS of another item (the hedged item).

hedging instrument A FINANCIAL INSTRUMENT whose fair value or cash flows are expected to offset changes in the fair value or cash flows of a HEDGED ITEM.

held-to-maturity financial assets Financial ASSETS with fixed or determinable payments and maturity that an enterprise intends to hold to maturity. This is one of the categories of investment under US and INTERNATIONAL ACCOUNTING STANDARDS COMMITTEE rules. Such investments are valued on the basis of cost, with gains and losses in value being recognized only at sale.

herd basis In the context of UK taxation, the treatment of animals on a collective basis.

HGB Abbreviation for the *Handelsgesetzbuch*; the German Commercial Code.

Hicksian income concept The idea, named after the economist J R Hicks, that income for a period should be measured as the maximum amount that could be spent in the period while remaining as well off as at the beginning of the period.

hidden reserves *See* SECRET RESERVES.

higher-rate tax In the context of the UK's system of income tax, amounts of tax levied on income above a certain level at a rate higher than the basic rate. The higher rate for many years has been 40 per cent.

highlights Summaries of particularly important figures (such as sales or PROFITS) that are given prominence in the ANNUAL REPORT of a company.

high–low method An approximate technique for the prediction of costs or other quantities by fitting a straight line between the highest and lowest points on a graph.

hire purchase contract A contract for the hire of an ASSET which contains a provision giving the hirer an option to acquire title to the asset on the fulfilment of agreed conditions. These contracts are treated for accounting purposes like LEASES.

historical cost The original purchase price or PRODUCTION COST of an ASSET.

historical cost accounting The conventional system of accounting, widely established throughout the world except in some countries where inflation is endemic and high, and even in these cases historical cost records are maintained and subjected to simple indexation adjustments for the preparation of FINANCIAL STATEMENTS.

Under historical cost accounting, the purchases of ASSETS, such as land, buildings, machines and INVENTORY (stock), are recorded at their purchase price at the date of ACQUISITION. Generally that value is not subsequently changed except to write down the value below cost in order to recognize any loss in value or normal wearing out. The former is known as IMPAIRMENT, the latter as DEPRECIATION. Other balances, such as for a DEBTOR or various sorts of LIABILITIES are valued at what is expected to be received or paid in cash. Compare CURRENT COST ACCOUNTING.

historical summary The presentation in a company's ANNUAL REPORT of the key financial data relating to the company over the past five or ten years.

HKSA Abbreviation for the Hong Kong Society of Accountants.

holding company A company that controls other undertakings. In the narrow use of the expression, it implies that the company does not actively trade but operates through various SUBSIDIARIES. The similar term 'parent company' would not have this connotation. The accounting treatment for such parent–subsidiary relationships is to prepare CONSOLIDATED FINANCIAL STATEMENTS for the combined group.

holding gain A gain that results from holding rather than from operating activities. During periods of rising prices, the NET REALIZABLE VALUE of ASSETS will rise. When these assets are sold, part or all of the gain realized is not due to the normal trading operations of the business, but is a 'holding gain'.

Holding gains may also be unrealized but realizable, up to the point of the sale of the asset concerned. Conventional HISTORICAL COST ACCOUNTING ignores realizable holding gains, and records only the realized gains. Thus, PROFITS are distorted, particularly in the year of sale of significant assets. Most systems of INFLATION ACCOUNTING either deduct or separately identify some version of holding gains, in order to calculate 'OPERATING PROFIT'.

For a simple example relating to holding gains on INVENTORIES, *see* COST OF SALES ADJUSTMENT.

horizontal equity In the context of taxation, the principle that equal people in equal circumstances should be taxed equally.

horizontal format The presentation of a FINANCIAL STATEMENT in DOUBLE-

ENTRY BOOKEEPING form, with DEBITS on the left and CREDITS on the right. In the case of a BALANCE SHEET, ASSETS would be on the left, and EQUITY and LIABILITIES on the right. Such a format is used, for example, in France, Italy and Spain.

horizontal integration The joining together of several enterprises that carry out the same activities in order to gain ECONOMIES OF SCALE or to reduce competition.

hostile take-over bid A TAKE-OVER BID for a company opposed by its directors.

human assets RESOURCES such as loyal staff and skilled managers. It is clear that the total value of some businesses rests heavily on these. At the extreme, the value of 'owning' a football or basketball team may rest almost entirely on human ASSETS. In conventional accounting, such items have been ignored because of the difficulty of establishing an objective and auditable value. The future ECONOMIC VALUE of employees is obviously hard to determine with any accuracy and, even if one were to use HISTORICAL COST ACCOUNTING, it would not be clear exactly what was spent on creating the assets, nor how much of what was spent was wasted. Indeed, since the definition of 'asset' includes control over resources, it is not clear that staff are normally an asset, because their labour is rented, not bought, in advance.

Nevertheless, some schemes for the valuation of human assets have been worked out. They involve the accumulation of such costs as recruitment and training, with a reduction for staff who have left. Practical application has not followed these theoretical exercises; so, when purchased, human assets remain a part of the mysterious total of GOODWILL.

human resource accounting *See* HUMAN ASSETS.

hurdle rate A rate of return that a project must be expected to exceed if it is to be acceptable.

hybrid security A FINANCIAL INSTRUMENT involving characteristics of both equity and debt. *See* COMPOUND INSTRUMENT.

hyperinflation Under US accounting rules, a cumulative amount of inflation over three years in excess of 100 per cent. A similar definition exists in other sets of accounting rules.

hyperinflationary economy An economy experiencing HYPERINFLATION. Under INTERNATIONAL ACCOUNTANCY STANDARDS COMMITTEE rules, if an enterprise operates in such an economy, FINANCIAL STATEMENTS must be adjusted in CURRENT PURCHASING POWER ACCOUNTING terms.

IAPC Abbreviation for the INTERNATIONAL AUDITING PRACTICES COMMITTEE.

IAS Abbreviation for an INTERNATIONAL ACCOUNTING STANDARD.

IASB Abbreviation for the INTERNATIONAL ACCOUNTING STANDARDS BOARD.

IASC Abbreviation for the INTERNATIONAL ACCOUNTING STANDARDS COMMITTEE.

ICAA Abbreviation for the Institute of Chartered Accountants in Australia.

ICAEW Abbreviation for the INSTITUTE OF CHARTERED ACCOUNTANTS IN ENGLAND AND WALES.

ICAI Abbreviation for the INSTITUTE OF CHARTERED ACCOUNTANTS IN IRELAND.

ICAS Abbreviation for the INSTITUTE OF CHARTERED ACCOUNTANTS OF SCOTLAND.

ICCAP Abbreviation for the International Coordination Committee for the Accounting Profession, which preceded the INTERNATIONAL FEDERATION OF ACCOUNTANTS.

ICQ Abbreviation for INTERNAL CONTROL QUESTIONNAIRE.

ICSA Abbreviation for the INSTITUTE OF CHARTERED SECRETARIES AND ADMINISTRATORS (of the UK).

ideal standard cost The minimum cost obtainable for a particular activity under the best possible conditions. This is a standard sometimes set in a STANDARD COSTING system.

identifiable assets and liabilities The ASSETS and LIABILITIES of an enterprise that can be separately identified from each other and from the enterprise as a whole. In the context of the purchase of an enterprise, it is necessary to identify and estimate the FAIR VALUE of such items. Any excess above this paid for the enterprise is GOODWILL. Under UK standards, identifiable assets are defined as being separable (i.e. capable of being sold separately), but this condition does not apply under INTERNATIONAL ACCOUNTING STANDARDS COMMITTEE rules.

idle capacity That part of an organization's budgeted capacity for output or production that is unused. This is generally expressed in terms of hours.

idle capacity ratio The IDLE CAPACITY for a particular period expressed as a percentage of the capacity in the BUDGET.

idle capacity variance A measure of the gain or loss in a period, compared to a BUDGET, caused because the hours worked are larger or smaller than planned.

idle time The period (normally measured in hours) during which production cannot proceed because of shortages of input or mechanical failure.

IdW Abbreviation for the *Institut der Wirtschaftsprüfer* (German Institute of Auditors).

IFAC Abbreviation for the INTERNATIONAL FEDERATION OF ACCOUNTANTS.

IFRIC Abbreviation for the INTERNATIONAL FINANCIAL REPORTING INTERPRETATIONS COMMITTEE.

IFRS Abbreviation for an INTERNATIONAL FINANCIAL REPORTING STANDARD.

illiquid assets ASSETS that cannot easily and quickly be turned into cash

IMA Abbreviation for the INSTITUTE OF MANAGEMENT ACCOUNTANTS (of the US).

immaterial Sufficiently small, in the context of an enterprise's FINANCIAL STATEMENTS, that incorrect treatment would not affect interpretation of those statements.

immediate holding company The direct PARENT COMPANY of another enterprise, in those cases where that parent is itself owned by another enterprise. The top company in the structure is the 'ULTIMATE HOLDING COMPANY'.

impaired asset An ASSET whose carrying value has had to be reduced below DEPRECIATED COST because of an IMPAIRMENT.

impairment A loss in value of a FIXED ASSET below DEPRECIATED COST. The impairment might be caused by physical damage or by a fall in market value of the asset's output. An IMPAIRMENT LOSS is charged against INCOME.

impairment loss Under UK and INTERNATIONAL ACCOUNTING STANDARDS COMMITTEE rules, the amount by which the CARRYING AMOUNT of an asset exceeds its RECOVERABLE AMOUNT. In the USA, the impairment loss is measured as the difference between the carrying amount and the FAIR VALUE of an ASSET.

impairment review The process of calculating whether an ASSET has suffered an IMPAIRMENT loss. Under UK or INTERNATIONAL ACCOUNTING STANDARDS COMMITTEE rules, this involves comparing the carrying amount with the RECOVERABLE AMOUNT.

impersonal account A LEDGER account recording transactions other than those with persons. Such accounts might be 'real' (e.g. dealing with property) or 'nominal' (e.g. dealing with EXPENSES).

impersonal ledger A term sometimes used for NOMINAL LEDGER.

imprest account The record relating to all the transactions of a float of petty cash looked after by a particular person. When money is spent, VOUCHERS or receipts are collected which can be used to reclaim cash. At any moment, the total of cash plus vouchers should equal the original FLOAT.

imputation system A form of corporate income tax in which SHAREHOLDERS are given TAX CREDITS with their DIVIDEND receipts. The tax credits give back to the shareholders some of the tax suffered by their company. The credits can be used to help pay the shareholders' income tax liabilities.

imputed cost A deemed cost, measured in terms of sacrifice of income rather than actual expenditure. For example, if the owner of an enterprise provides the enterprise with a building free of rent, the calculation of the enterprise's costs (for decision-making purposes) might be more realistic if it included what it would have cost to pay RENT.

imputed interest The amount of interest that would have to be paid on the use of money by an enterprise if it had to borrow that amount of money rather than using its own spare cash resources.

IMRO Abbreviation for Investment Management Regulatory Organisation, a former UK self-regulating body for certain financial institutions. The FINANCIAL SERVICES AUTHORITY has taken over these functions.

inception of a lease A technical term meaning the earlier of the date of a LEASE agreement or of commitment by the parties to the provisions of the lease.

income Increases in economic benefits during a period. The words 'REVENUES', 'PROFIT', 'EARNINGS' and 'income' are used somewhat vaguely by accountants and businessmen, and usage in the UK and the USA is different.

In the UK, 'income' tends not to be used in connection with commercial businesses. Instead, the terms used include turnover (sales revenues), gross and net profits and earnings (in increasing order of the extraction of expenses). The word 'income' is associated more with NON-PROFIT organizations.

In the USA, 'income' tends to be used more widely in a commercial context, instead of 'profit'.

income and expenditure account A version of the PROFIT AND LOSS ACCOUNT for NON-PROFIT organizations. It retains the ACCRUAL BASIS OF ACCOUNTING and so includes revenues and expenses which relate to the period. (The alternative, RECEIPTS AND PAYMENTS ACCOUNT, concentrates on cash movements instead.) Thus, the income and expenditure account for a period leads to the surplus or deficit for the period.

income generating unit In the context of the measurement of IMPAIRMENT, the UK term for the smallest group of net assets for which the generation of income is largely independent.

income in kind Benefits received in terms of goods and services rather than as cash.

income smoothing Reducing the variation in yearly profit figures; a practice which is not generally acceptable in the UK or the USA. This can be done by charging high PROVISIONS for depreciation, risks or contingencies in successful years, and by reversing or reducing such provisions in poor years. In some countries these provision 'slush funds' can be so enormous that the real results of individual years are quite hidden in the final 'profit' announcements. Thus, someone used to UK or US accounting should take care in reading the FINANCIAL STATEMENTS of countries using quite different systems.

income standard In the context of a STANDARD COSTING system, the budgeted level of income expected to be generated.

income statement The usual US name for the PROFIT AND LOSS ACCOUNT.

income tax A tax on personal or corporate income. In the USA, persons and all forms of businesses pay income tax. In the UK, persons including the owners of unincorporated businesses pay income tax, but companies pay CORPORATION TAX.

Personal income tax is an annual tax on income adjusted by various allowances. In the USA, corporate income tax is paid on a quarterly prepayment system, using estimates based on the previous year's profits. The tax is calculated by applying a series of stepped, increasing marginal rates to taxable income, which is based on the net profit for accounting purposes but with some adjustments.

income tax allowances Deductions allowed from a taxpayer's income in the calculation of TAXABLE INCOME. For example, in the UK, there is a PERSONAL ALLOWANCE, originally designed to take out of taxable income enough for a person to pay for food, shelter and clothing.

income tax code *See* TAX CODE.

income tax schedules In the UK, divisions of INCOME which are separately assessed. For example, Schedule E applies to employment income, Schedule D to income from trades or professions, and Schedule F to dividend income.

incomplete records Partial accounting records. The full DOUBLE-ENTRY BOOK-KEEPING system may be found by small or poorly organized businesses to be somewhat complex, time-consuming and expensive. Instead, there may be only a CASH BOOK, a list of sales, or records on the backs of envelopes. These can be described by the broad term 'INCOMPLETE RECORDS'. The problem will also occur if the books are mislaid, stolen or burnt.

Accountants are good at taking incomplete records and reconstructing what must have happened, with the aid of BANK STATEMENTS, last year's BALANCE SHEET, and so on. This is necessary to calculate profits for the information of the owner and the tax authorities.

incorporated company A legal entity separate from its owners (*see* COMPANY).

incorporation The process by which a corporate body comes into existence as a legal entity. The normal route in the UK is by registration using the provisions of the Companies Act. However, incorporation can come about by other means, such as the granting of a royal charter.

incorporation of audit firms The transformation of a firm of auditors from a PARTNERSHIP into a LIMITED COMPANY. This was first allowed in the UK under the Companies Act 1989.

incremental analysis A technique for financial decision making that considers only those COSTS, REVENUES or CASH FLOWS that would alter as a result of the decision taken.

incremental budget A type of detailed numerical plan (a BUDGET) in which the amounts are determined by adjusting the previous period's budget or actual results. This approach is less likely to result in a budget adapted to the actual circumstances than is ZERO-BASE BUDGETING.

incremental cost The additional or differential COST that results from a particular action.

independence (of auditors) A prime professional requirement for EXTERNAL AUDIT, that the auditors should be able to form their judgements objectively without influence from the management or by other factors. For example, auditors are expected not to own shares in the company being audited and not to rely on one client for a large proportion of their fee income.

independent financial adviser As a technical term under the UK's Financial Services Act, a person who is not employed by, or committed to, the products of any financial institution.

independent projects A capital investment proposal whose acceptance or rejection does not depend on, and will not affect, the acceptance or rejection of other projects.

independent taxation In the context of the UK's system of personal INCOME TAX, the treatment of a husband and wife as two separate persons.

index The size of some variable at a particular date expressed as a percentage of its size at a base date. For example, a RETAIL PRICE INDEX refers to the comparative level of prices of a specified basket of goods, and a share price index refers to the comparative level of prices of a particular set of shares.

indexation The adjustment of monetary amounts to take account of the fall in value of money caused by a general rise in prices. The adjustment would generally use changes in a RETAIL PRICE INDEX. In inflationary times, this process might be applied by accountants to figures in FINANCIAL STATEMENTS. One such system is CURRENT PURCHASING POWER ACCOUNTING. The process might also be applied by governments to taxation, wages, pensions, etc.

indexation allowance In the context of the taxation of CAPITAL GAINS in the UK, a reduction in the taxable amount in order to take account of inflation between 1982 and 1998.

index-linked gilt A government BOND whose value, in terms of INTEREST payments and REDEMPTION amount, is adjusted over time in line with changes in the RETAIL PRICE INDEX.

indirect cost centre A unit within an organization for which costs are collected, in cases where the unit is not directly involved in production. The term 'SERVICE COST CENTRE' has the same meaning.

indirect costs Costs of a business that cannot be identified with the production of a particular unit or type of product. Examples are: (a) machines used for the production of a variety of products at different times of the day, (b) the supervising staff in a factory who look after several product lines, and (c) the heating and rental costs of a manufacturing unit that produces several products.

indirect labour Employees whose work cannot be directly identified with particular units of production. Examples include senior executives or maintenance staff.

indirect labour cost The total remuneration and other EXPENSES, such as social security costs, related to INDIRECT LABOUR.

indirect manufacturing costs Those costs of production that cannot be identified with units of output. *See* PRODUCTION OVERHEADS.

indirect materials Those materials used in an organization that cannot be identified with units of output.

indirect method (of reporting cash flows) In the context of a CASH FLOW STATEMENT, a method of reporting operating cash flow whereby the net profit or loss (or, in the UK, the operating profit) is adjusted for the effects of non-cash transactions, any deferrals or accruals of past or future operating cash receipts or payments, and items associated with cash flows from INVESTING ACTIVITIES or FINANCING ACTIVITIES.

indirect tax A tax assessed on someone other than the person intended to bear it. For example, VALUE ADDED TAX is assessed and paid by traders but, at first sight, borne by customers in terms of increased prices. Of course, this is too simple. For goods in elastic demand, the traders may have to bear some or all of the tax because customers will pay no more.

individual savings accounts A tax-exempt savings account in the UK.

industrial buildings In the context of CAPITAL ALLOWANCES in the UK, those factories and related buildings that qualify for such allowances.

industry ratios RATIOS (e.g. a GEARING RATIO) calculated as an average for all the companies in a particular industry.

industry segment *See* BUSINESS SEGMENT.

ineligible group In the context of the UK Companies Act, a group of companies that does not qualify for exemption from filing requirements because it contains, for example, a PUBLIC LIMITED COMPANY.

inflation accounting Various types of systems that might adjust or replace HISTORICAL COST ACCOUNTING to take account of changing prices. Many such systems are poorly described by the term, because they do not involve a recognition of general price level movements. Systems that do adjust for *inflation* are called CURRENT PURCHASING POWER ACCOUNTING in the UK or GENERAL PRICE LEVEL ADJUSTED accounting in the USA.

Alternatives that adjust for the specific price changes affecting the ASSETS and operations of a business are CURRENT COST ACCOUNTING, REPLACEMENT COST ACCOUNTING, and systems that rely on NET REALIZABLE VALUES and ECONOMIC VALUES.

In nearly all systems of 'inflation accounting' there are adjustments of BALANCE SHEET assets each year, and also adjustments to profit for DEPRECIATION and COST OF SALES. In some systems there are also adjustments for monetary items, including a GEARING ADJUSTMENT.

In practice, most countries have continued to use accounting based on historical cost for the main FINANCIAL STATEMENTS of businesses. However, in some South American countries with very high rates of inflation, general price level adjusted accounting has been adopted. In The Netherlands, some companies use replacement cost accounting, and others provide notes on this basis.

information intermediaries Such professionals as financial analysts who collect and analyse FINANCIAL STATEMENTS and other information about companies in order to produce advice for investors.

information overload A state of affairs in which the recipients of information get so much of it that they cannot usefully process it all. For example, unsophisticated shareholders may find that a company's full ANNUAL REPORT contains more data than can be absorbed.

inherent goodwill The excess of a company's MARKET VALUE at a particular date over the value of its NET ASSETS. Since this is not an official term, there is no agreed definition. The net assets could be measured at BOOK VALUES or at FAIR VALUES. *See*, also, INTERNALLY GENERATED GOODWILL.

inheritance tax A UK tax on the transfer of property from a person during life or at death. Certain transfers are exempt, and there are lower tax rates for lifetime transfers.

initial accounts FINANCIAL STATEMENTS required from a public limited company in the UK when it wishes to pay a dividend before the end of its first accounting period.

initial allowance In the context of the UK's CAPITAL ALLOWANCES, an amount granted in the first year of the purchase of an ASSET.

initial disclosure event In the context of DISCLOSURES required by INTER-NATIONAL ACCOUNTING STANDARDS concerning DISCONTINUING OPER-ATIONS, the date of the earlier of a binding sale agreement and an announcement of a detailed plan for discontinuance. Once this event has occurred, disclosures must begin.

initial public offering In the USA, the flotation of a company on a stock market by the first offer to the public of shares in it.

Inland Revenue The UK government body responsible for the assessment and collection of most DIRECT TAXES, such as INCOME TAX, CORPORATION TAX and CAPITAL GAINS TAX.

input tax In the context of the UK's VALUE ADDED TAX, the amount of that tax included in the prices paid by a business on its purchases. The amount of INPUT TAX is used to reduce the payments of tax levied on outputs.

insider dealing The use of information, that is not publicly available, to make decisions about buying or selling publicly traded shares. Such dealing is prohibited in the UK and the USA.

insolvency A state of affairs in which a business or person is unable to pay DEBTS as they fall due.

insolvency administration order In the UK, an order of a court for the administration of the estate of a deceased BANKRUPT debtor.

insolvency practitioner In the UK, a person authorized to act as a liquidator or other appointee in INSOLVENCY administration.

inspector of taxes In the context of the administration of certain taxes in the UK, an employee of the Inland Revenue responsible for the assessment, but not the collection, of tax.

instalment method of accounting A method of recognizing REVENUE on a sale paid by instalments in line with the proportion of the selling price received in a period.

instalment sale In the USA, a sale for which payments are made by the customer in instalments.

Institute of Chartered Accountants in England and Wales The largest body of accountants in the UK. Its earliest predecessor was founded in 1870, and it was granted a royal charter in 1880.

Institute of Chartered Accountants in Ireland An accountancy body recognized in the Republic of Ireland and in the UK, which was granted a royal charter in 1888.

Institute of Chartered Accountants of Scotland The world's oldest private sector accountancy body, its oldest predecessor being granted a royal charter in 1854. The present body was formed by amalgamation in 1951.

Institute of Chartered Secretaries and Administrators A UK body of COMPANY SECRETARIES and administrators, founded in 1891.

Institute of Internal Auditors A body of practitioners of INTERNAL AUDIT, originally established in the USA but with a corresponding UK body.

Institute of Management Accountants A US professional body of company accountants, rather than AUDITORS, founded in 1919.

institutional investor A financial institution, such as a life assurance company or a pension fund, that holds securities. In the UK, such investors are the largest shareholders.

in-substance defeasance US term for the placing of monetary ASSETS in TRUST solely to pay off a DEBT. Under certain conditions, the accounting practice is then to remove the debt and the related monetary assets from the BALANCE SHEET.

intangible asset A non-monetary ASSET that is not physical or tangible. Intangible assets that may be shown on a BALANCE SHEET include PATENTS, licences, TRADE MARKS and GOODWILL. The last of these is an unidentifiable asset, and the others are identifiable. When purchased separately or as part of a business combination, identifiable assets should generally be separately recognized. The conditions for recognizing internally generated intangibles are stricter. Under UK and INTERNATIONAL ACCOUNTING STANDARDS COMMITTEE rules, internally generated GOODWILL, RESEARCH costs and BRAND names must not be recognized as assets.

integrated accounts An ACCOUNTING SYSTEM in which the same records are used to generate FINANCIAL ACCOUNTING and COST ACCOUNTING statements.

integrated test facility A test inserted into a client enterprise's computer-based accounting system by an AUDITOR. The test comprises a fictitious customer, supplier or other entity coupled with test transactions to see how the system deals with them.

intellectual capital An enterprise's knowledge-based assets (both those recognized on a BALANCE SHEET and those not) including human resources, INTELLECTUAL PROPERTY and RESEARCH AND DEVELOPMENT.

intellectual property A term used to describe certain INTANGIBLE ASSETS over which an enterprise has registered legal rights. Intellectual property would include PATENTS, licences and copyrights.

Inter-American Accounting Association A regional grouping of private sector accountancy bodies in the Americas.

inter-company profits Profits generated in an enterprise as a result of sales to other members of the same group of commonly controlled enterprises. Such profits are eliminated in the preparation of CONSOLIDATED FINANCIAL STATEMENTS.

inter-company transactions Sales, purchases or other transactions between enterprises within the same group of commonly controlled enterprises. Such transactions are eliminated in the preparation of CONSOLIDATED FINANCIAL STATEMENTS.

interest The payment made by borrowers to lenders as a return on money lent. It may be contrasted to the payments to shareholders, who receive DIVIDENDS. Interest is usually a contractual payment, so an unpaid lender can take legal action against the defaulting borrower. Interest may be paid at a fixed rate or at one which varies with prevailing rates (a floating rate). It is part of the EXPENSES of a business, and is generally tax-deductible.

interest cover The degree to which an enterprise's interest expense for a period is exceeded by the profit available. This can be measured as the number of times that the interest could be paid out of the profit before interest and tax.

interest rate implicit in a lease The DISCOUNT RATE that would cause the sum of the PRESENT VALUE of the MINIMUM LEASE PAYMENTS and the UNGUARANTEED RESIDUAL VALUE to equal the FAIR VALUE of a leased ASSET.

interest rate risk The risk that the value of a FINANCIAL INSTRUMENT will change because of changes in market interest rates. Disclosures concerning interest rate risk are now required in ANNUAL REPORTS.

interest rate swap A contract whereby two parties agree to pay each other different patterns of interest payments.

inter-firm comparison The pooling of financial data by several enterprises, perhaps privately by a trade association, so that each enterprise can compare its performance with the average for the industry.

interim accounts *See* INTERIM REPORT.

interim audit The elements of an AUDIT carried out during the year rather than at, or after, the end of the year.

interim dividend A dividend paid during a company's year and relating to the year. It will normally be less than half of the total DIVIDEND for the whole year; the larger part being the FINAL DIVIDEND which is paid after the year end.

interim financial statements *See* INTERIM REPORT.

interim period A financial reporting period shorter than a FINANCIAL YEAR. In the UK, half-yearly reporting is required for LISTED COMPANIES by the London Stock Exchange. In the USA, quarterly reporting is required by the SECURITIES AND EXCHANGE COMMISSION.

interim report A half-yearly report by a company listed on the London Stock Exchange. Such reports must be published, but they need not be audited and are not as detailed as an ANNUAL REPORT. These reports are required in order to inform SHAREHOLDERS of a company's progress and to allow share prices to adjust more smoothly during the year.
   In the USA, quarterly interim reports are required from companies registered with the SECURITIES AND EXCHANGE COMMISSION.

interlocking accounts An accounting system that keeps separate records for FINANCIAL ACCOUNTING and COST ACCOUNTING purposes, but regularly reconciles the two sets of information. This can be contrasted with INTEGRATED ACCOUNTS.

intermediate holding company A PARENT company which is itself a subsidiary of another company.

internal audit The examination of the systems of control and the accuracy of records of an enterprise by its own staff. This may be distinguished from external auditing which involves the checking, *by* or *for* the owners of resources or companies, *on* the stewards or managers of those resources. This is called 'EXTERNAL AUDIT', because it is done by professional accountants who are not day-to-day employees of the company.
   To some extent, internal audit may duplicate or pre-empt the work of external auditors, and may reduce the work and fees of the latter. However, internal audit tends also to be actively concerned with the discovery and prevention of fraud and with the design and effectiveness of systems of internal control.

internal auditor A person who carries out an INTERNAL AUDIT.

internal check One part of INTERNAL CONTROL: office systems designed to make error and fraud difficult. Internal check rests on the separation of duties achieved when two or more employees are involved in control processes. At its simplest, this suggests that at least two people should have to sign or be involved in the completion of cheques or the distribution of cash wages. Good internal check also involves the rotation of duties and insistence on holidays for employees. This ensures that certain elaborate frauds involving the falsification of records cannot be covered up indefinitely.

internal control All those management systems controlling the administration of an organization. This will include INTERNAL AUDIT, INTERNAL CHECK and BUDGETS. Good internal control will make error and fraud more difficult, and will also make accounting records more reliable.

internal control questionnaire A document containing a standardized set of questions as used by an AUDITOR in order to check the quality of an organization's INTERNAL CONTROL.

internal control risk That element of AUDIT RISK that is caused because a company's INTERNAL CONTROL system does not prevent or discover material errors or fraud.

internal control system *See* INTERNAL CONTROL.

internally generated goodwill The amount by which the worth of an enterprise has increased due to the creation (rather than purchase) by the company of such advantages as loyal customers and skilled staff. Since this goodwill has not been purchased and there is therefore no past transaction, it is not recognized as an ASSET for accounting purposes. *See*, also, INHERENT GOODWILL.

internally generated intangible assets Those INTANGIBLE ASSETS of an enterprise that have not been purchased by it but created. Generally, such assets are not recognized in BALANCE SHEETS, although under certain circumstances development expenditure and some other costs can be capitalized.

internal rate of return The annual percentage profitability on the initial investment in a project, taking into account the fact that money received later is worth less than money received earlier. The rate calculated can be compared to the assumed interest cost for the capital used in the project. The interest cost will depend upon the enterprise's individual sources and uses of finance. Projects with higher internal rates of return will be preferred to those with lower; and all projects carried out should have internal rates of return that exceed the cost of the capital.

The NET PRESENT VALUE method involves similar calculations but is regarded as a more reliable means of discriminating between projects.

internal revenue code The regulations governing the operations of the federal income tax in the USA.

Internal Revenue Service The US federal governmental body concerned with the assessment and collection of personal and corporate income taxes and some other federal taxes.

International Accounting Standards The standards of the INTERNATIONAL ACCOUNTING STANDARDS COMMITTEE.

International Accounting Standards Board The standard setting board of the INTERNATIONAL ACCOUNTING STANDARDS COMMITTEE. This term was first officially used when a newly constituted board, of twelve full-time and two part-time members, met in 2001.

International Accounting Standards Committee (IASC) An organization, formed in 1973, whose purpose is to devise and promulgate international standards in order to reduce the variation of practices in financial reporting throughout the world. The Standards are generally similar to US and UK practices. From 1973 to 2000, the IASC was controlled by the world's accountancy bodies. However, from 2001, an independent structure comprising trustees and a board was established.

International Auditing Practices Committee A committee of the INTERNATIONAL FEDERATION OF ACCOUNTANTS whose task is to prepare and publish international standards on AUDITING procedures.

International Congresses of Accountants Meetings of accountants held now on a quinquennial basis in different cities around the world. The first meeting was in 1904 in St Louis, USA.

International Federation of Accountants A body comprising representatives from the accountancy professions of many countries. It was formed in 1977, and is based in New York. One of its committees sets international auditing standards, but it leaves accounting standards to the INTERNATIONAL ACCOUNTING STANDARDS COMMITTEE.

International Financial Reporting Interpretations Committee A body set up by the INTERNATIONAL ACCOUNTING STANDARDS BOARD to issue interpretations of international standards. It replaced the STANDING INTERPRETATIONS COMMITTEE.

International Financial Reporting Standard A standard issued by the INTERNATIONAL ACCOUNTING STANDARDS BOARD. Former standards (International Accounting Standards) are still also in force until withdrawn.

International Organization of Securities Commissions (IOSCO) An international body of governmental regulators of stock exchanges, such as the SECURITIES AND EXCHANGE COMMISSION of the USA. From the late 1980s, IOSCO began to collaborate with the INTERNATIONAL ACCOUNTING STANDARDS COMMITTEE (IASC) on the creation of a high-quality set of core accounting standards for use on all the world's stock markets. In 2000, IOSCO endorsed the IASC's standards and recommended their members to accept FINANCIAL STATEMENTS prepared using those standards.

International Securities Market Association The international association of bond dealers and other traders.

International Standards on Auditing The standards published by the INTERNATIONAL AUDITING PRACTICES COMMITTEE.

interperiod tax allocation Another way of referring to accounting for DEFERRED TAX.

in-the-money option A contract that gives the holder the right to buy a security in those cases where the current market price of the security exceeds the price at which the right can be exercised.

intra-group profit *See* INTER-COMPANY PROFIT.

intra-group transactions *See* INTER-COMPANY TRANSACTIONS.

introduction In the context of the shares of companies listed on the London Stock Exchange, the selling of shares without marketing arrangements.

inventoriable costs US term for costs that should be added into the BALANCE SHEET value of STOCKS.

inventories Normal US term for raw materials, WORK IN PROGRESS and goods ready for sale. In the UK, the word 'STOCKS' is generally used instead.

inventory accounting A term used to describe at least the financial reporting aspects of accounting for inventories or STOCKS, i.e. the counting of inventory, the use of the lower of cost and market valuation, and the choice of a flow assumption such as FIFO, The term might also cover the recording system for ordering, receipt and usage of materials.

inventory control *See* STOCK CONTROL.

inventory turnover *See* STOCK TURNOVER.

inventory valuation *See* STOCK VALUATION.

investee A company in which another party has an investment. For example, a SUBSIDIARY is an investee of its parent.

investing activities In the context of CASH FLOW STATEMENTS, those activities involving the acquisition and disposal of long-term ASSETS and other investments not included in CASH or CASH EQUIVALENTS. Under US and INTERNATIONAL ACCOUNTING STANDARDS COMMITTEE rules, cash flows are divided into 'operating', 'investing' and 'financing'.

investment analysis The process of estimating the future returns and values of securities and other potential investments in order to assist those who make investment decisions. Fundamental analysis uses financial reporting and other information to predict future earnings, cash flows and values. Technical analysis uses a study of past price movements to predict future prices.

investment analyst A person, usually working for a financial institution, who conducts INVESTMENT ANALYSIS.

investment appraisal The assessment of potential CAPITAL INVESTMENT projects to decide which should be selected as uses of scarce funds. It is generally agreed that the best procedure is to isolate all the expected differential CASH FLOWS that would result from proceeding with a particular investment project. These cash flows are then analysed by methods such as the PAYBACK PERIOD, INTERNAL RATE OF RETURN or NET PRESENT VALUE. The first of these is the easiest to understand and the most popular, but (unlike the latter two) it does not take account of the timing of cash flows or the size of cash flows after the payback period.

investment bank A financial institution which advises its clients on mergers and acquisitions and assists in the financial aspects of such deals.

investment business In the context of the UK's Financial Services Act dealing in, and advising on, investments in securities.

investment company *See* INVESTMENT TRUST.

investment expenditure *See* CAPITAL EXPENDITURE.

investment grants *See* GOVERNMENT GRANTS.

investment property A property held by a business for investment potential or rental income, rather than for its own occupation. Thus, investment properties may be owned by businesses other than property companies. The UK accounting standard for investment properties (STATEMENT OF STANDARD ACCOUNTING PRACTICE 19) requires such properties to be revalued annually and not to be subjected to DEPRECIATION. This is allowed by the equivalent INTERNATIONAL ACCOUNTING STANDARD but not by the US standard.

investments Financial ASSETS, other than CASH or RECEIVABLES, held by an enterprise. In the UK, such assets must be classified as FIXED ASSETS or CURRENT ASSETS on the basis of whether or not they are intended for continuing use in the business.

investment securities A financial institution's investments other than those for trading.

investment tax credit A former US tax incentive for the purchase of capital equipment, whereby a percentage of the cost of such assets was set against tax payable.

investment trust A COMPANY whose main purpose is to use the FUNDS contributed by SHAREHOLDERS to own and manage profitably a PORTFOLIO of STOCKS and SHARES. Unlike UNIT TRUSTS, these are 'CLOSE-ENDED FUNDS' in that there are no extra regular contributions from participants. If a shareholder wishes to extract his or her funds, he or she must sell the shares to another investor. This would have no direct effect on the trust.

invisible earnings In the context of the measurement of a country's balance of payments, the profits for international transactions involving services such as accountancy, banking, insurance and tourism.

invoice A document sent by an enterprise to a customer giving details of the goods or services supplied, the total payment due and the expected method of payment.

IOSCO Abbreviation for the INTERNATIONAL ORGANIZATION OF SECURITIES COMMISSIONS.

IPO Abbreviation for an INITIAL PUBLIC OFFERING.

IRR Abbreviation for an INTERNAL RATE OF RETURN.

irrecoverable advance corporation tax A former element of the UK's CORPORATION TAX system whereby certain amounts of ADVANCE CORPORATION TAX could not be set off against other amounts of tax to be paid in the future.

irrecoverable input VAT Amounts of VALUE ADDED TAX paid by an enterprise on its purchases but which cannot be set off against amounts of the tax that the enterprise must pay relating to its SALES. This is because its sales are EXEMPT SUPPLIES.

irredeemable debentures Securities are 'irredeemable' if there is no provision for their holders to be paid back by the issuing company. Normally, loans are redeemable but SHARES are not. However, there are exceptions to both these rules; and in the UK there are loans called 'IRREDEEMABLE DEBENTURES'.

irrevocable letter of credit A LETTER OF CREDIT that cannot be cancelled without agreement from its beneficiary.

IRS Abbreviation for the INTERNAL REVENUE SERVICE of the USA.

ISA Abbreviation for an INTERNATIONAL STANDARD ON AUDITING or an INDIVIDUAL SAVINGS ACCOUNT.

ISMA Abbreviation for the INTERNATIONAL SECURITIES MARKET ASSOCIATION.

issue by tender *See* SALE BY TENDER.

issued share A SHARE in a company that has been sold by that company.

issued share capital The amount of SHARE CAPITAL of a company, at NOMINAL VALUE, that has been issued to the SHAREHOLDERS. Sometimes, not all of this is yet CALLED-UP SHARE CAPITAL. The MEMORANDUM OF ASSOCIATION of a company specifies the maximum share capital that is authorized for a company, although this can be changed by the shareholders. Often, a company will not have issued as many shares as are authorized. The ISSUED SHARE CAPITAL will be shown in the BALANCE SHEET, and the AUTHORIZED SHARE CAPITAL will be shown in the NOTES TO THE ACCOUNTS.

All shares in the UK, and most shares in the USA, have a NOMINAL VALUE or par value. Normally, shares will be sold by a company at a price above the par value. In the FINANCIAL STATEMENTS, such shares are recorded 'at par' under the heading of share capital, COMMON STOCK (USA), etc. The excess contributed above the par value is shown as SHARE PREMIUM (UK) or capital surplus/PAID-IN SURPLUS (USA).

issue price The price at which a SECURITY is sold by the issuing company.

J

JICPA Abbreviation for the Japanese Institute of Certified Public Accountants.

JIT techniques *See* JUST-IN-TIME.

job In the context of COST ACCOUNTING, a discretely identifiable operation within an organization.

job card A card (or perhaps, now, a computer printout) on which are found instructions for carrying out a particular production JOB.

job cost The costs that can be directly or indirectly associated with a particular production JOB.

job costing A version of COST ACCOUNTING sometimes used in an organization whose activities can be split up into discretely identifiable operations (JOBS). PRODUCT COSTS can then be accumulated on this basis rather than in some other way, e.g. by different processes.

joint and several liability A typical feature of PARTNERSHIP AGREEMENTS, whereby a whole group (in this case, all the partners) is liable one by one and in total for DEBTS incurred in the name of the group. If one member does not pay, any or all of the others must.

joint audit An AUDIT carried out by two or more AUDITORS who jointly sign the AUDIT REPORT.

joint control The contractually agreed sharing of control over an enterprise or a group of ASSETS. The existence of joint control is the key aspect of a JOINT VENTURE.

joint costs The common costs of two or more linked products where those products cannot be identified separately from each other until a certain stage of production. The joint costs are those up to the SPLIT-OFF POINT after which the costs of the products can be separately recorded.

Joint Disciplinary Scheme A mechanism established by several of the UK accountancy bodies for investigating alleged professional misconduct of their members.

jointly controlled assets Assets used for JOINT VENTURE purposes in cases where those ASSETS are jointly owned or controlled by the VENTURES rather than being the assets of a separate joint venture entity. The venturers account for their shares of the assets.

jointly controlled entity Another way of saying JOINT VENTURE ENTITY.

jointly controlled operations Activities of JOINT VENTURERS in cases where ASSETS are contributed by the venturers without there being a separate JOINT VENTURE ENTITY. The venturers continue to account for the assets as their own.

joint products The outputs of a production process in cases where there is more than one output of significance.

joint stock company A legal entity with CAPITAL contributed by the owners and divided into SHARES of fixed amount. Such a company can be registered with limited liability under the Companies Act 1985 as a PRIVATE LIMITED COMPANY or a PUBLIC LIMITED COMPANY.

joint venture A co-operative exercise between two or more businesses, often set up for a specific purpose and a limited time. A joint venture involves a legal CONTRACT between the parties concerning their rights and duties with respect to the venture.

joint venture entity A JOINT VENTURE which is constituted as a separate entity rather than being the joint use of ASSETS. In the CONSOLIDATED FINANCIAL STATEMENTS of a UK VENTURER, its investment in the joint venture is accounted for by using the GROSS EQUITY METHOD. In the US, the EQUITY METHOD is used. Under INTERNATIONAL ACCOUNTING STANDARDS COMMITTEE a venturer may use either the equity method or PROPORTIONAL CONSOLIDATION.

journal A business will usually have very many transactions each day. The DOUBLE-ENTRY BOOKKEEPING system has to record all these. However, there is a danger that the main BOOKS of account would get swamped with information if each one were recorded separately in them. Thus, for some very frequent events, such as SALES, there are special DAY BOOKS. The 'journal' or 'general journal', as its name suggests, is also a day book; it contains a record of the creation of double entries for those types of item that are not sufficiently frequent to have their own specialized day book, such as year-end entries and the correction of errors. Every DEBIT or CREDIT that is recorded will have gone through a day book. Thus, all entries can be traced back to their source, where a description and date can be found.

journal entry A record made in a JOURNAL.

judgemental sampling In the context of an AUDIT, the selection of a sample of transactions, balances, etc. on the basis of the AUDITOR's judgement rather than using statistical techniques.

junk bond A contract acknowledging indebtedness, in cases where there is an unusually high risk of non-payment by the borrower. As a result, the interest rate is high. The bond may be backed by specific claims on the assets of the borrowing company.

just-in-time The production or purchasing of materials in such a way that INVENTORIES are kept to a minimum. Production is driven by demand; and purchasing is designed to match receipt and usage as exactly as possible.

K

KapAEG Abbreviation for the *Kapitalaufnahmeerleichterungsgesetz*. A German law of 1998 designed to enable listed companies to depart from normal German rules in order to comply with international standards for their consolidated statements.

KG Abbreviation for a *Kommanditgesellschaft* (German limited partnership).

KGaA Abbreviation for a *Kommanditgesellschaft auf Aktien* (German PUBLIC COMPANY with personally liable shareholders).

KICPA Abbreviation for the (South) Korean Institute of Certified Public Accountants.

KK Abbreviation for a *Kabushiki Kaisha* (Japanese PUBLIC COMPANY).

know-how Skills or knowledge of use in manufacturing or other processes. In the context of the UK's CAPITAL ALLOWANCES system, expenditure on such items attracts tax deductions.

KonTraG Abbreviation for the *Gesetz zur Kontrolle und Transparenz im Unternehmensbereich*, a German law of 1998 which, among other things, set up the DEUTSCHES RECHNUNGSLEGUNGS STANDARDS COMMITTEE.

L

labour costs The COSTS to an enterprise of its employees. This would include wages, pension contributions and taxes. The expression 'labour cost' could be restricted to those employees engaged directly or indirectly in production.

labour efficiency variance The difference between the actual LABOUR COSTS (at the standard rate per hour) and the standard labour cost allowed.

labour hour rate As part of a STANDARD COSTING system, an established overhead rate based on the number of direct labour hours used for particular activities.

labour intensive A process or enterprise for which the use of labour is more important than the use of capital equipment.

labour rate variance The difference between the actual wages paid and the actual hours worked at the standard rate per hour.

lapping US term for TEEMING AND LADING.

lapsed option An OPTION that has expired unused.

last in, first out *See* LIFO.

LAUTRO Abbreviation for one of the former UK self-regulatory organizations: the Life Assurance and Unit Trust Organisation. Its functions were absorbed into the Personal Investment Authority and then into the FINANCIAL SERVICES AUTHORITY.

lead bankers/managers Banks that are in charge of a launch of a new issue of SHARES.

leading and lagging Arrangements to improve an enterprise's cash position, particularly just before its BALANCE SHEET date e.g. collection of DEBTS from customers more quickly (leading) or the payment of LIABILITIES more slowly (lagging).

lease A lease is a contract whereby a person or a company (the LESSEE) is granted the exclusive right to the use of an asset owned by another (the LESSOR). In return, the lessee makes periodic payments throughout the agreed term of the lease.

For a lease that lasts for most of the expected useful life of the ASSET or that transfers most of the risks and rewards to the lessee, the act of leasing is very similar to a purchase made with a loan from the lessor. In this case, accountants treat the lease as a finance or capital base, i.e. they record the plant as an asset and the liabilities as if they were loans, despite the fact that the assets are not owned by the lessee. This is an example of the application of the principle of SUBSTANCE OVER FORM, because the assets are controlled by the lessee and the lessee has OBLIGATIONS.

lease accounting The treatment of a LEASE as either a FINANCE LEASE or an OPERATING LEASE.

leaseback *See* SALE AND LEASEBACK.

leasehold The legal right to use property (land or buildings) for a specified period and under particular conditions, including usually the payment of a ground rent.

lease term The non-cancellable period for which a lessee has contracted to LEASE an ASSET plus any further periods for which the lessee has the option to continue to lease which it is reasonably certain that the lessee will exercise.

ledger *See* BOOKS OF ACCOUNT.

ledger account A particular account in a DOUBLE-ENTRY BOOKKEEPING system which records all the transactions relating to a specified person or item.

legal merger A merger between two companies in which the ASSETS and LIABILITIES of company A are transferred to company B, and company A is dissolved or the assets and liabilities of both companies are transferred to a new company and both A and B are dissolved. Such combinations are fairly common in continental Europe, e.g. in France, they are called *fusions*.

legal obligation A legally enforceable requirement to pay an amount of money (or in some other way pass over benefits) as a result of a CONTRACT or a law. This can be distinguished from a CONSTRUCTIVE OBLIGATION. Either way, such obligations should be accounted for as LIABILITIES if they will probably lead to payment and they can be reliably measured.

legal reserves Undistributable RESERVES required to be set up by companies in certain countries for the protection of CREDITORS. For example, in Germany and France, such reserves must be built up to the extent of 10 per cent of ISSUED SHARE CAPITAL. Such reserves are not required in the UK or the USA.

legal right of set-off A DEBTOR's legal right, by CONTRACT or otherwise, to settle or otherwise eliminate all or a portion of an amount due to a CREDITOR by applying against that amount an amount due from the creditor.

legal tender Money that must, by law, be accepted as payment in the settlement of DEBT.

lessee A party to a CONTRACT who gains the use of ASSETS for a particular period under a LEASE.

lessor A party to a contract who grants the use of ASSETS for a particular period under a LEASE.

letter of allotment A notification from a company to a person to whom SHARES have been allocated. The letter specifies the number of shares allotted and the procedure for payment.

letter of comfort *See* COMFORT LETTER.

letter of consent *See* CONSENT LETTER.

letter of credit A document sent from one bank to another (particularly internationally) authorizing the payment of specified amounts to specified persons.

letter of engagement A document sent by an AUDITOR to a new client setting out the agreed scope of the audit and the fees to be charged.

letter of representation A document from the directors of a company to its AUDITORS but generally drafted by the auditors) recording confirmations of facts asserted by the directors but of which the auditors have no independent confirmation.

letters of administration A document sent by a court of law to empower an administrator of the estate of an intestate deceased person.

leverage The US term for GEARING.

leveraged buyout The purchase of a company, perhaps by its management, using borrowed money.

leveraged lease A LEASE for which the LESSOR has borrowed money to purchase the ASSET to be leased to the LESSEE.

leverage ratios *See* GEARING.

liability An OBLIGATION, arising from past events, to transfer resources to another party. Many liabilities are of known amount and date of due payment. They include long-term loans, bank overdrafts and amounts owed to suppliers. These may be current or non-current liabilities: the former are expected to be paid within a year from the date of the BALANCE SHEET on which they appear. The difference between the CURRENT ASSETS and the CURRENT LIABILITIES is described as NET CURRENT ASSETS.

Liabilities are valued at the amounts expected to be paid at the expected MATURITY DATE. In some cases, amounts that are not quite certain will be included as PROVISIONS for liabilities; they will be valued at the best estimate available. In some cases, liabilities are shown at a DISCOUNTED VALUE.

LIBOR Abbreviation for the London inter-bank offered rate, an internationally referenced rate of interest on borrowed money.

lien A legal right over ASSETS belonging to another person. The holder of the lien would have the right to receive the assets if their owner did not pay a DEBT.

life-cycle costing The profiling of costs over the whole life of a product or an asset in order to improve decisions.

LIFFE Abbreviation for the London International Financial Futures and Options Exchange.

LIFO (last in, first out) One of the methods available for the calculation of the cost of STOCKS (inventory), in those frequent cases where it is difficult or impossible to determine which specific items remain and which have been used. When prices are rising, LIFO will lead to more up-to-date costs for the inventory used (COST OF SALES) and, thus, lower profits than would be shown by other methods, such as FIFO. Therefore, it is popular with many companies in the USA, where it is allowed for tax purposes (as long as it is also used in the INCOME STATEMENT).

However, the inventory value shown in the BALANCE SHEET may be seriously misleading as it will be based on very old prices. Thus, the method is discouraged by the appropriate ACCOUNTING STANDARD (STATEMENT OF STANDARD ACCOUNTING PRACTICE 9) in the UK, and is rarely found. Nevertheless, it is allowed by the COMPANIES ACT; though it is not accepted for tax purposes.

limitation of scope In the context of an AUDIT, a restriction on the evidence available to the auditor that would lead to a qualification of the audit report.

limited company/liability *See* LIMITED LIABILITY COMPANY.

limited liability company A company whose owners have LIMITED LIABILITY for the DEBTS of their business. The owners of PARTNERSHIPS and SOLE TRADER businesses are fully liable in law for the debts of those businesses. Therefore, the providers of ownership finance for such businesses tend to be few in number, and restricted to those who are able and willing to become managers of the business in order to protect their interests.

For really large businesses with thousands of owners another legal form is necessary, so that the owners (or SHAREHOLDERS) may have limited liability for the debts of their business, and therefore be prepared to delegate management to DIRECTORS. In 1855 in the UK a Companies Act introduced the possibility of registration of companies in limited liability form.

For most companies, the liability of shareholders is limited to their SHARE CAPITAL. However, another type of company is one where liability is limited to amounts guaranteed by the shareholders. Of course, these limitations may damage the interests of lenders. Thus, companies are generally not allowed to pay back capital to shareholders, and have to notify lenders of their status by putting after their names some such warnings as Ltd or plc. For equivalent names in some other countries, *see* Table 1 in COMPANY (page 69).

limited liability partnership A legal form of business organization, found extensively among AUDIT firms in the USA and, from 2000, in the UK, whereby certain PARTNERS have LIMITED LIABILITY for the DEBTS of the PARTNERSHIP under certain circumstances.

limited partner A co-owner of a PARTNERSHIP business who has LIMITED LIABILITY for the DEBTS of the partnership.

limited partnership A PARTNERSHIP business in which some but not all of the PARTNERS have LIMITED LIABILITY for the DEBTS of the partnership. There must be at least one general partner who is responsible for the debts. Such partnerships are more common in continental Europe than in the UK. *See*, also, LIMITED LIABILITY PARTNERSHIP.

limited recourse financing Borrowings for which the lender has rights over the ASSETS of the borrower only under certain circumstances or conditions.

limiting factor In the context of production, a CONSTRAINT caused by shortage of a particular input.

linear cost function A pattern of behaviour of COSTS which stays the same as activity increases. For example, total FIXED COSTS and VARIABLE COST per unit may both behave in this way because they stay the same as volume increases (within certain limits). However, total variable cost may also be linear because it rises steadily with volume.

linear depreciation Generally, a synonym for STRAIGHT-LINE DEPRECIATION, i.e. depreciation charges which, when plotted on a graph over time, show a straight line.

linear programming A problem-solving technique whereby a problem can be expressed as a series of equations which include the existence of CONSTRAINTS.

linked presentation In the context of a UK BALANCE SHEET, the showing of an ASSET and the related financing together. The asset is shown gross with the finance deducted from it, leading to a net amount. Such a presentation is allowed under certain conditions, such as that the financing will be repaid from the sale of the asset.

liquid assets A somewhat vague term referring to CASH and other CURRENT ASSETS that can readily be turned into cash.

liquidation The legal process of closing down a company involving the sale of its ASSETS and distribution of the proceeds to CREDITORS and SHAREHOLDERS. The expression 'winding up' has the same meaning.

liquidator In the UK, a person appointed by a COMPANY, its CREDITORS or a court of law to manage the LIQUIDATION of a company.

liquidity An expression denoting the cash or near-cash resources of a business. Thus, a COMPANY with ample cash may be said to have good liquidity. Poor liquidity may lead to difficulties in paying DEBTS as they fall due, and to inability to undertake profitable projects due to lack of funds. Of course, it may be possible to solve this in the long run by being profitable, or in the short run by selling assets or issuing more SHARES or long-term loan stock.

One measure of liquidity is formed by the NET CURRENT ASSETS or working capital of a business, which is the CURRENT ASSETS less the CURRENT LIABILITIES. Other measures include the liquidity ratios: the CURRENT RATIO and the QUICK RATIO (ACID TEST). However, all these measures are most useful when seen in the context of similar companies and when one can look at a trend for a particular company.

liquidity crisis A state of affairs in which there is a significant danger that an enterprise may not be able to pay its DEBTS as they fall due.

liquidity management The operational management of an enterprise's finances with the objective of constantly maintaining the optimal liquidity position. An enterprise must not run out of liquid resources but it would not want to leave funds idle.

liquidity ratios Measures of LIQUIDITY, such as the QUICK RATIO and the CURRENT RATIO.

liquidity risk In the context of FINANCIAL INSTRUMENTS, the risk that an enterprise will have difficulty in raising funds to meet commitments associated with the instruments. Such risk should be disclosed in notes to the FINANCIAL STATEMENTS.

liquid ratio *See* QUICK RATIO.

listed company A company whose SHARES are listed or quoted on a STOCK EXCHANGE. This means that there is an organized and substantial market in its shares, such that one can always buy or sell them. Stock exchanges have 'listing requirements' concerning behaviour and the financial disclosures that listed companies must make.

In order to be listed, a company must be a PUBLIC LIMITED COMPANY (plc) in the UK, or registered with the SECURITIES AND EXCHANGE COMMISSION in the USA. In most countries, there are many public limited companies (or equivalents, such as an SA in France or an AG in Germany) that are not listed.

listed security Any FINANCIAL INSTRUMENT of a company whose price is listed on a stock exchange.

Listing Agreement In the UK, the document that sets out the responsibilities of a company that is listed on the London Stock Exchange. This is now controlled by the FINANCIAL SERVICES AUTHORITY.

listing requirements The conditions, found in the Listing Agreement, that companies listed on the London Stock Exchange must satisfy.

list price The price of a good or service as set out in the seller's documentation.

little GAAP Informal expression for the financial reporting requirements relating to smaller or non-listed companies. In the case of the UK, there is a special simplified accounting standard (the FINANCIAL REPORTING STANDARD FOR SMALLER ENTITIES) for certain small enterprises.

LLP Abbreviation for a LIMITED LIABILITY PARTNERSHIP.

loan capital One of the many expressions for long-term loans with a similar meaning to DEBT CAPITAL, LOAN STOCK, DEBENTURES or fixed interest capital. Loans may be made by private persons, other businesses or banks. In many cases, there is a market in loan securities, so that they can be sold to other investors by the original lender. The loans will usually have a fixed repayment, REDEMPTION or MATURITY DATE, and a fixed interest entitlement until that date.

loan covenant A clause in a contract covering a loan whereby the borrower promises to obey certain conditions.

loan creditor A person who is owed money as a result of a loan rather than for other reasons, such as being a supplier.

loan stock Securities issued by a company as acknowledgement that it has borrowed money.

local currency The currency of the country in which an enterprise operates.

local taxation Taxation of profits or other TAX BASES which is levied locally rather than nationally.

LOCOM US informal abbreviation for LOWER OF COST AND MARKET.

long-form report A detailed, private report sent to the management of a company by its AUDITORS. This deals with items in the FINANCIAL STATEMENTS or with control issues.

long lease In the context of UK company law, a LEASE on property that has 50 years or more to run.

long position A state of affairs in which holdings of and agreements to purchase SECURITIES or COMMODITIES exceed agreements to sell. A trader might establish a LONG POSITION if prices are expected to rise.

long-term contract A contract to supply goods or services to a customer that is unfinished at the end of an accounting period. If the outcome of the contract can be estimated reliably, the enterprise should recognize an appropriate proportion of REVENUES and COSTS for each period during which the contract runs. This is called 'the PERCENTAGE-OF-COMPLETION METHOD'. Where outcomes cannot be reliably estimated, revenues and PROFIT should be taken on completion. In any case, anticipated losses on the contract should be accounted for immediately.

long-term debt A vague term for loans to be repaid by an enterprise after the short term. This could mean after twelve months, or a longer horizon might be intended.

long-term debtors A vague term for amounts receivable (or the persons who must pay those amounts) beyond the short term, perhaps beyond twelve months from a BALANCE SHEET date.

long-term investment A holding of securities not intended for sale in the near future. A similar term is 'FIXED ASSET INVESTMENT'.

long-term liability Loans and other LIABILITIES to be paid after the short-term. If a cut-off point of twelve months is intended, a more precise term is NON-CURRENT LIABILITIES.

losses Decreases in economic benefits. Sometimes this term is used to denote those decreases resulting from the fall in value (or the sale) of ASSETS other than INVENTORIES.

loss on manufacture In the context of COST ACCOUNTING, a loss generated within an organization's accounting system when manufactured items are transferred from production units at a price below the cost of manufacture.

loss reliefs In the context of the taxation of corporate income, various arrangements within the tax rules whereby losses can be used to reduce the taxation to be paid on profits. For example, in the UK's CORPORATION TAX system, trading losses can be carried back one year and forward without limit.

lowballing The quotation by an AUDITOR of an unreasonably low price for a prospective AUDIT engagement. The objective is to win the engagement and then to make profit from non-audit fees from the client.

lower of cost and market A well-established rule for the valuation of CURRENT ASSETS, particularly STOCKS (inventories), whereby the assets are measured at whichever of COST and a MARKET VALUE is the lower. In conventional accounting, 'cost' means the historical purchase price of the stock, plus the costs of work done on it. In the UK, 'market value' means NET REALIZABLE VALUE (NRV), which is what the stock could be sold for in the normal course of business when ready for sale (less any expected costs involved in finishing and selling it).

The reason for this rule is PRUDENCE. This suggests that, since the business intends to sell the stock fairly soon, its value should not be held above its expected selling price. On the other hand, it should also not be held above its cost since this would be to anticipate profits. Normally, in a successful business and particularly if prices are rising, cost will be used, because it will be below NRV. However, certain items of slow-moving or damaged stock will be reduced to NRV.

In the USA, the market value generally means the current cost of replacement of the inventories.

lower of cost and net realizable value rule *See* LOWER OF COST AND MARKET.

lower rate of income tax In the UK's system of the taxation of personal income, a rate of tax applying to a small band of taxable income of each individual. Amounts of taxable income beyond this are taxed at the BASIC RATE and then the higher rate.

Ltd Abbreviation for 'limited' (the designation of a PRIVATE LIMITED COMPANY in the UK and Ireland).

machine hour A unit of usage of productive equipment. A process or product can have OVERHEAD COSTS absorbed on the basis of how many MACHINE HOURS it uses.

machine hour rate An established rate at which OVERHEAD COSTS of a COST CENTRE are absorbed into production. The rate is equal to the budgeted overheads of the cost centre divided by the budgeted machine hours.

mainstream corporation tax (MCT) An element of the UK tax system from 1973 to 1999; MCT was the amount of the corporation tax liability (CTL) for a year that had not already been paid as the ADVANCE CORPORATION TAX (ACT) connected to a dividend payment. Thus, MCT is CTL minus ACT. The MCT was paid nine months after a company's year end. MCT was not allowed to fall below zero.

maintenance expense The costs to an organization of keeping FIXED ASSETS in working order. As a technical term within COST ACCOUNTING, the term could mean something more precise, such as the costs of keeping the fixed assets at the normal level of CAPACITY.

make or buy decision The choice by an organization of whether to manufacture a component of a product or to purchase it from an outside supplier.

malpractice insurance The US term for insurance cover taken out by a firm of accountants against the possibility of loss from litigation connected to the firm's professional services.

managed costs *See* DISCRETIONARY COSTS.

management accounting Activity that may be distinguished from other work done by accountants, such as AUDITING or FINANCIAL ACCOUNTING, in that it is designed specifically to serve the needs of the managers of a business. Financial accounting and reporting are required by law (for SHAREHOLDERS and CREDITORS) or to satisfy the needs of other outside parties such as customers or suppliers.

Thus, it has to obey many rules and has to strive for objectivity. Management accounting, on the other hand, can be tailor-made for a particular company and will be designed to help managers make decisions. It may involve many estimates and FORECASTS. It includes such activities as BUDGETARY CONTROL and COST ACCOUNTING.

management audit An independent investigation of the efficiency of the management of an organization in all its aspects.

management board In the context of companies with two tiers of board members, the board of full-time executive directors who are in charge of day-to-day operations of an organization. They are appointed and overseen by a SUPERVISORY BOARD. Such a structure is required for PUBLIC COMPANIES in Germany and for certain large companies in The Netherlands.

management buy-out The purchase of a company, as a GOING CONCERN, by members of its management.

management by exception The operation of control on the basis that areas that are running smoothly need no attention, so that efforts can be put into those areas that are not running according to plan or BUDGET.

management by objectives A system of management of an organization whereby a manager's goals and targets are set (in numerical terms wherever possible) by that manager in consultation with the immediately superior manager. The managers at each level are then assessed according to those objectives.

management information system An integrated system for the provision of financial information to all levels of management within an organization.

management letter A letter from the AUDITORS of a company to its directors or senior managers concerning audit findings, including the adequacy of control systems, the application of accounting principles, organizational efficiency, etc.

management's discussion and analysis A report that must be filed annually with the SECURITIES AND EXCHANGE COMMISSION of the USA by a company registered with it. The report (generally abbreviated to MD & A) explains the company's financial condition and results, concentrating on changes and new developments. The UK equivalent is the voluntary OPERATING AND FINANCIAL REVIEW.

mandatory liquid assets In the context of a UK bank, the amounts required by the Bank of England to be deposited with it.

manufacturing account A document, used internally by an organization, that shows the COSTS (both direct and indirect) of the goods manufactured during the accounting period.

manufacturing costs The COSTS (both direct and indirect) of producing goods during a period.

manufacturing overhead *See* PRODUCTION OVERHEAD.

manufacturing profit The excess of the value at which goods are transferred from manufacturing over the PRODUCTION COST of those goods.

manufacturing statement *See* MANUFACTURING ACCOUNT.

margin The difference between a sale price and a cost. *See*, also, GROSS MARGIN.

marginal cost The extra cost that would result from producing one extra unit of a product (strictly, an infinitesimally small amount extra). For the purpose of calculating marginal cost, all the FIXED COSTS should be ignored; only those extra costs that are strictly related to the small production increase should be measured. For decision-making purposes, it is often useful to compare the marginal cost of extra production with the MARGINAL REVENUE that would result.

marginal cost pricing The setting of prices by a producer by reference to MARGINAL COSTS of production rather than to the full costs.

marginal costing A method of COST ACCOUNTING used for internal decision making in an organization whereby only MARGINAL COSTS are charged to a product. The FIXED COSTS are instead charged each period against the total contributions (i.e. the REVENUES minus marginal costs) of all the products.

marginal rate of tax The rate of tax that would apply to a small increase in a taxpayer's TAX BASE, e.g. TAXABLE INCOME. In a PROGRESSIVE TAX system, the marginal rate rises as income increases, and the marginal rate exceeds the average rate.

marginal relief In the context of the CORPORATION TAX in the UK as applied to certain companies with small profits, the reduction in taxation when companies fall between an upper and a lower limit of a particular measure of TAXABLE INCOME.

marginal revenue The extra revenue that would result from selling one extra unit of a product.

margin of safety In the context of BREAKEVEN ANALYSIS, the excess of some measure of activity (e.g. sales or units) over the level needed to break even.

margin of safety ratio The MARGIN OF SAFETY as a percentage of the achieved level of activity.

marketable securities Investments for which there is an ACTIVE MARKET from which a market value can be observed or for which there is some indicator that enables a market value to be calculated. Increasingly, such assets are valued at FAIR VALUE.

market beta That part of the risk relating to a particular security that is related to the market as a whole. *See* CAPITAL ASSET PRICING MODEL.

market capitalization The total value of the SHARES of a company at a particular moment, as found by multiplying the number of its shares by the market price. In some newspapers, market capitalization is published, next to share prices.

marketing costs Part of the distribution costs of an organization, including the wages of sales staff and advertising expenses.

marketing cost variance The difference between actual MARKETING COST of a period and the amount budgeted for.

market maker A dealer in traded securities who holds inventories of the securities and announces buying and selling prices.

market price The price of a good or service in an open market, assuming arm's length dealing.

market risk In the context of FINANCIAL INSTRUMENTS, the risk that the value of an instrument will change because of changes in market prices. Such risk should be disclosed in the notes to the FINANCIAL STATEMENTS.

market value The price of a good or service in an open market, assuming arm's length dealing.

marking to market Accounting for investments or commodities by constantly up-dating their values to the current market value in BALANCE SHEETS and taking any resulting gains or losses to income immediately.

mark-up The amount (or percentage of the COST) by which the sale price of a good or service exceeds its cost.

master budget A detailed numerical summary of all the BUDGETS of the elements of an organization. The master budget also contains the CASH BUDGET and the budgeted PROFIT AND LOSS ACCOUNT.

master netting arrangement An agreement whereby an enterprise that undertakes several FINANCIAL INSTRUMENT transactions with a single other party will make a single net settlement of all the instruments covered by the agreement if there is a default on, or termination of, any one contract.

matching concept The convention that the expenses that should be recognized in the PROFIT AND LOSS ACCOUNT for a period are those COSTS that can be associated with items of revenue that have been recognized in that period. For example, the costs of sales are recognized at the same time as the related sales revenue. The matching concept is part of the ACCRUAL BASIS OF ACCOUNTING.

material Sufficiently important that omission or mistreatment of an item would alter a reader's assessment of the FINANCIAL STATEMENTS. As a rule of thumb, this might be expressed as a few per cent of TURNOVER or PROFIT.

materiality A very strong concept which means that DISCLOSURES are not necessary for, and rules need not be strictly applied to, unimportant amounts. For example, some companies may have very small amounts of a particular REVENUE, EXPENSE, ASSET or LIABILITY; if such an amount would normally be separately disclosed in the FINANCIAL STATEMENTS, this need not be done if it is immaterial in size. This will help to make the statements clearer, by omission of trivial amounts. Materiality is also to be seen at work in the extensive rounding of numbers in financial statements. Similarly, approximate measurement or valuation methods may be used if the end result is close to that which would be arrived at by stricter practices.

materials control account An ACCOUNT recording the total of the materials purchased and the total used in production, and therefore the balance that there should be.

materials cost The total expenditure by an organization on materials, both DIRECT COSTS and INDIRECT COSTS.

materials requisition *See* STORES REQUISITION.

materials returns note *See* STORES RETURNS NOTE.

materials variances Differences between actual and standard costs for various aspects of materials. *See*, for example, DIRECT MATERIALS PRICE VARIANCE.

matrix accounting The use of arrays of rows and columns of figures (a matrix) to record transactions rather than the use of traditional ACCOUNTS.

maturity date The date on which the requirements of a contract to satisfy an

OBLIGATION to transfer resources must be fulfilled. For certain securities, this is also known as the 'redemption date'.

maximum stock level The highest planned level of INVENTORIES of a particular type.

MCT Abbreviation for MAINSTREAM CORPORATION TAX.

MD & A Abbreviation for MANAGEMENT'S DISCUSSION AND ANALYSIS.

measurement The process of determining the monetary amounts at which ASSETS, LIABILITIES and REVENUES EXPENSES, are to be recognized in the BALANCE SHEET and INCOME STATEMENT. To take the example of an asset: the first stage is to ask if an item is an asset; the second stage is to ask if it meets the RECOGNITION criteria; and the third stage is measurement.

medium of exchange An item, such as money, which acts as an intermediary for the exchange of goods or services even though it may have little intrinsic value.

medium-sized company In the context of the UK COMPANIES ACTS, a company below two out of three size thresholds: 250 employees and specified levels (which are raised from time to time) of TURNOVER and TOTAL ASSETS. Such companies are exempted from some filing requirements.

medium-sized group A GROUP of companies that in total would meet the criteria to be a MEDIUM-SIZED COMPANY. The size criteria for TURNOVER and TOTAL ASSETS are measured after consolidation adjustments (i.e. net) but slightly larger thresholds are available in gross terms.
   A parent company is not required to prepare CONSOLIDATED FINANCIAL STATEMENTS for a medium-sized group.

member of a company Anyone whose name is listed in the company's register of members. For a company limited by SHARES, its members are the SHAREHOLDERS.

members' voluntary liquidation The WINDING-UP of a company by a SPECIAL RESOLUTION of its members, in circumstances where its directors have declared that it is solvent.

memorandum entry An ACCOUNTING RECORD which does not form part of a DOUBLE-ENTRY BOOKKEEPING system.

memorandum of association A legal document drawn up as part of the registration of a company in the UK. The memorandum includes a record of the company's name, its registered office, its purposes and its AUTHORIZED SHARE CAPITAL.

The other document drawn up at the birth of a company is the ARTICLES OF ASSOCIATION. These are rules concerning the relationships of the company to the SHAREHOLDERS, the shareholders to each other, and so on.

merger As a non-technical term, this means a mutually agreed coming together of two or more enterprises in order to create a new combined enterprise. As a technical accounting term, it may mean the type of business combination required to use MERGER ACCOUNTING.

merger accounting A method of accounting for a BUSINESS COMBINATION. In the USA it was in fairly frequent use until 2001, under the name of POOLING OF INTERESTS. In the UK, merger accounting is rarely used and only became legal in 1981, so it has been normal to use the ACQUISITION method for business combinations and the subsequent preparation of CONSOLIDATED FINANCIAL STATEMENTS. In the UK, according to FINANCIAL REPORTING STANDARD 6, merger accounting can only be used when no acquirer can be identified. No FAIR VALUE exercise is carried out when accounting for a business combination by merger accounting, and no GOODWILL is recognized.

merger relief In the context of UK COMPANY LAW, the permission for a company not to record a SHARE PREMIUM when issuing SHARES for the purpose of obtaining the shares of another company. The relief is necessary in order to carry out MERGER ACCOUNTING for a BUSINESS COMBINATION but may also be used in other cases.

merger reserve A RESERVE created in the context of MERGER RELIEF which takes the place of a SHARE PREMIUM ACCOUNT but can subsequently be used for more purposes than share premium.

mezzanine finance Long-term monetary resources provided to a company in exchange for CAPITAL INSTRUMENTS that have features of both EQUITY and DEBT.

middle price The average of the buying and selling prices of a SECURITY listed on a stock exchange.

minimum lease payments Usually, the payments that a LESSEE must make over the LEASE term, plus any amounts guaranteed by the lessee or by a party related to the lessee.

minimum subscription The minimum amount that must be raised before a new share issue will proceed. This amount is stated in the PROSPECTUS for the issue.

minority interest The amount, that arises in CONSOLIDATED FINANCIAL STATEMENTS when a SUBSIDIARY is not wholly owned, which represents the capital provided by, and earned for, group SHAREHOLDERS who are not parent company shareholders. Even if a subsidiary is partly owned by 'MINORITY SHAREHOLDERS', accountants bring in 100 per cent of all its ASSETS, LIABILITIES, EXPENSES and REVENUES when preparing the consolidated statements. In such statements, the proportions of these attributable to the minority shareholders is separately recognized as 'MINORITY INTERESTS'.

minority shareholders SHAREHOLDERS in subsidiary companies other than the parent or other members of its group.

MIRAS Abbreviation for MORTGAGE INTEREST RELIEF AT SOURCE.

mixed cost *See* SEMI-VARIABLE COST.

mix variance A difference between actual and standard cost caused by the fact that the actual mix of materials used or goods sold is different from the standard mix.

MMC Abbreviation for the MONOPOLIES AND MERGERS COMMISSION (of the UK).

MNM Abbreviation for the MONETARY/NON-MONETARY METHOD of currency translation.

modern equivalent asset In the context of estimating the CURRENT REPLACEMENT COST of a TANGIBLE FIXED ASSET, the closest available potential replacement asset for an existing ASSET. The modern equivalent asset should be able to replace the services of the existing asset as closely as possible. The replacement cost of the existing asset would be estimated by adjusting the cost of a modern equivalent for any differences in productive potential.

modified accounts A former UK legal term for ABBREVIATED ACCOUNTS.

modified historical cost convention A UK term for the use of a mixture of HISTORICAL COST and other valuation bases. For example, some UK companies value most ASSETS at COST (or DEPRECIATED COST) but land and buildings at current revaluations.

monetary assets Those assets that are denominated in money terms or have a 'FACE VALUE'. Cash or DEBTORS (UK)/ACCOUNTS RECEIVABLE (US) are examples of monetary assets. NON-MONETARY ASSETS include land, buildings and equipment. The distinction between monetary and non-monetary assets is important for some systems of FOREIGN CURRENCY TRANSLATION and of INFLATION ACCOUNTING.

monetary items Items (either ASSETS or LIABILITIES) that have fixed or determinable monetary values.

monetary measurement convention The inevitable convention that transactions and BALANCES can only be recorded and then summarized in FINANCIAL STATEMENTS if they can be put into money terms.

monetary/non-monetary method One of the theoretically possible methods of translating the FINANCIAL STATEMENTS of FOREIGN SUBSIDIARIES into their group's REPORTING CURRENCY. This method translates MONETARY ITEMS in a BALANCE SHEET at closing rates of exchange, and non-monetary items at historical rates. The method was used in the USA in the 1960s. It is somewhat similar to the TEMPORAL METHOD.

monetary working capital adjustment One of the adjustments made to HISTORICAL COST ACCOUNTING profit in certain systems of CURRENT COST ACCOUNTING (CCA) in order to take account of changing prices. It is designed to adjust for the extra money tied up in trade DEBTORS (net of trade CREDITORS) as a result of the rise in price of STOCKS.

money capital The size of an enterprise's NET ASSETS (or EQUITY) measured in monetary units that are not adjusted for price changes. *See* CAPITAL MAINTENANCE CONCEPT.

money measurement convention *See* MONETARY MEASUREMENT CONVENTION.

Monopolies and Mergers Commission A former UK body that investigated cases referred to it by the Secretary of State for Trade and Industry. It made recommendations, for example, on whether proposed BUSINESS COMBINATIONS are in the public interest.

mortgage A legal interest in a property given as security for a loan from the owner of the property (the mortgagor) to a lender (the mortgagee).

mortgage bond A US term for a debt secured on real property, e.g. on land and buildings.

mortgagee *See* MORTGAGE.

mortgage interest relief at source A former UK arrangement for giving tax relief on the interest paid by a MORTGAGOR. It was abolished in 2000.

mortgagor *See* MORTAGE.

multi-column reporting The presentation, in FINANCIAL STATEMENTS, of information on more than one basis in a series of columns. For example, a BALANCE SHEET might present its items on both HISTORICAL COST and CURRENT COST bases.

multi-employer plans An EMPLOYEE BENEFIT plan that is not run by the State but that pools the ASSETS contributed by several employing enterprises for the purposes of providing benefits to the employees of the enterprises.

mutual funds US name for financial institutions that use money provided by investors to own and manage a PORTFOLIO of investment in other stocks and shares. The UK equivalents are UNIT TRUSTS.

mutually exclusive projects In the context of CAPITAL INVESTMENT APPRAISAL, projects of which only one can be carried out because they all call for the use of a unique resource.

MWCA Abbreviation for MONETARY WORKING CAPITAL ADJUSTMENT.

N

NAA Abbreviation for the NATIONAL ASSOCIATION OF ACCOUNTANTS (of the US).

Naamloze Vennootschap *See* NV.

NAO Abbreviation for the NATIONAL AUDIT OFFICE (of the UK).

NASDAQ The second largest stock market in the USA, specializing in the shares of high-tech companies. The initials stand for National Association of Securities Dealers Automated Quotations System.

National Association of Accountants The former name of the US accountancy body that is now called the INSTITUTE OF MANAGEMENT ACCOUNTANTS.

National Association of Securities Dealers Automated Quotations System *See* NASDAQ.

National Audit Office A UK body established in 1983 and headed by the Comptroller and Auditor General. It reports to a parliamentary committee on the accounts of government departments and on the efficiency of those departments.

national income accounting The process of calculating the production, distribution and consumption of a national economy, leading to the preparation and presentation of national income and expenditure accounts.

National Insurance contributions A UK tax on employers and employees which can be seen as part of the INCOME TAX system.

NBV Abbreviation for NET BOOK VALUE.

NCSC Abbreviation for the former National Companies and Securities Commission of Australia.

near money ASSETS that are not as liquid as banknotes or deposits in bank current accounts but which can be turned into money very quickly.

negative goodwill An excess of the FAIR VALUE of the identifiable NET ASSETS of an acquired enterprise over the cost of buying it. Negative goodwill might result from a bargain purchase or from the purchase of future losses. Under UK and INTERNATIONAL ACCOUNTING STANDARDS COMMITTEE rules, negative goodwill should be deducted from the BALANCE SHEET figure of GOODWILL.

negative income tax A proposed system of personal income tax whereby if an individual's income fell below a certain level, amounts would be paid to the individual.

negotiable instrument A document whose ownership passes from one person to another by delivery and ENDORSEMENT. Negotiable instruments include cheques and other bills of exchange.

net assets The worth of a business in accounting terms, as measured from its BALANCE SHEET, i.e. it is the total of all the ASSETS, less the LIABILITIES that are owed to outsiders. Naturally, this total equals the SHAREHOLDERS' EQUITY.
  However, in reality, a business is nearly always worth more than its net assets, because accountants use HISTORICAL COST ACCOUNTING as a measurement basis, and because important assets, such as the loyalty of customers, are excluded due to CONSERVATISM and the MONEY MEASUREMENT CONVENTION. Thus, the MARKET CAPITALIZATION of a company will nearly always be greater than its accounting net assets.

net asset value In the context of estimating the value of a share in a company, the NET ASSETS of a company, generally divided by the number of SHARES outstanding.

net basis A former UK basis of calculating EARNINGS PER SHARE.

net book value The amount at which an ASSET is stated in the BALANCE SHEET of a business. This will depend upon the system of accounting being used, and is unlikely to be directly related to what the asset could be sold for. Conventional accounting measures most assets at their net HISTORICAL COST of purchase or production. The reason for the word 'net' is that most FIXED ASSETS are gradually written off over their useful lives by amounts of DEPRECIATION. Thus, the NBV is usually the historical cost less accumulated depreciation.

net cash flow The difference between the inward cash flows and the outward cash flows for an enterprise or a project for a period.

net cash investment in a lease In the context of accounting for the FINANCE

LEASES of a LESSOR, the amount invested by the lessor in the leased ASSET after taking account of government grants and taxation effects. In the UK, the lessor's income is calculated by reference to this rather than to the NET INVESTMENT IN A LEASE.

net current assets The net current assets or working capital of a business is the excess of the CURRENT ASSETS (such as CASH, DEBTORS and STOCKS) over the CURRENT LIABILITIES (such as trade creditors and overdrafts).

This is one measure of the liquidity of the business. However, the movement of the total from year to year, or of the CURRENT RATIO (of CURRENT ASSETS to CURRENT LIABILITIES) might be more useful information.

net dividend A dividend after any deduction of tax in the paying company and before adding any TAX CREDIT. In the UK, the term 'NET DIVIDEND' is used to mean the amount of cash paid by a company and received by the SHAREHOLDERS.

net income Normal US expression for NET PROFIT in UK terminology.

net investment concept An idea behind the CLOSING RATE (or current rate) method of FOREIGN CURRENCY TRANSLATION, whereby a foreign subsidiary is seen as a stand-alone entity in which the group holds a net investment rather than holding all the subsidiary's individual assets and liabilities.

net investment in a foreign entity The reporting enterprise's share in the NET ASSETS of a FOREIGN ENTITY.

net investment in a lease The GROSS INVESTMENT IN A LEASE less UNEARNED INCOME. On this basis, under INTERNATIONAL ACCOUNTING STANDARDS COMMITTEE requirements, a LESSOR calculates income on a FINANCE LEASE.

net margin The GROSS MARGIN after deduction of all other expenses.

net present value (NPV) The value now of a stream of future cash inflows and outflows from an ASSET or a project. The term is normally used in the context of the NPV method of INVESTMENT APPRAISAL, which compares projects (or judges the likely success of one project) by estimating all the future cash flows (in and out) that would result from them, including the initial investment as an outflow and any investment incentives as inflows. These flows are 'discounted' to take account of the fact that money *now* is worth more than money *later*. Thus, the method involves estimation of a DISCOUNT RATE and of many years' worth of future cash inflows and outflows.

net profit The excess of all the REVENUES over all the EXPENSES of a business for a period. The PROFIT AND LOSS ACCOUNT (or income statement) of a business will show the NET PROFIT both before and after tax and the net profit after

EXTRAORDINARY ITEMS. In the case of an individual legal entity, this profit is then available for distribution as dividends (assuming that there is sufficient cash and that no past losses have to be covered first) or for transfer to various RESERVES. For a group, after any MINORITY INTERESTS and dividends on PREFERENCE SHARES have been deducted, the figure may be called EARNINGS.

net profit ratio An enterprise's NET PROFIT for a period expressed in terms of its sales of the period.

net realizable value (NRV) The amount that could be raised by selling an ASSET, less the costs of the sale. NRV implies a sale in the normal course of trade; thus, there would also be a deduction for any costs to bring the asset into a saleable state.

The normal rule for the valuation of CURRENT ASSETS, such as STOCKS, is to use the 'lower of cost and market', where the latter means the NRV (except that, in the USA, it can mean the replacement cost, where lower).

net selling price The amount obtainable from the sale of an ASSET between knowledgeable and willing parties at arm's length, less the COSTS OF DISPOSAL. This can differ from NET REALIZABLE VALUE because the latter is also net of costs of completion.

netting In the context of FOREIGN EXCHANGE transactions, the bilateral or multilateral setting off of payments and receipts.

netting off The setting off of an ASSET balance against a LIABILITY balance or of an EXPENSE against a REVENUE. The accounting rules restrict this process.

net worth *See* NET ASSETS.

neutrality Freedom from bias. In the context of financial reporting, the CONCEPTUAL FRAMEWORK of the INTERNATIONAL ACCOUNTING STANDARDS COMMITTEE imposes a requirement for neutrality. This suggests that deliberate overstatement or understatement of the ELEMENTS OF FINANCIAL STATEMENTS is not allowed. Nevertheless, there may still be some room for PRUDENCE.

next-in, first-out In the context of INVENTORY valuation, the measurement of the cost of materials used on the basis that the next materials bought will be the first to be used. This amounts to using a REPLACEMENT COST.

NIC Abbreviation for NATIONAL INSURANCE CONTRIBUTIONS.

nil basis A former UK method of calculating EARNINGS PER SHARE.

nil paid shares Shares on which no payment has yet been made from the SHAREHOLDER to the issuing company.

NIVRA Abbreviation for [*Koninklijk*] *Nederlands Instituut van Registeraccountants*, the [Royal] Dutch Institute of Auditors.

NL Abbreviation used to designate a NO LIABILITY COMPANY.

no liability company A type of Australian company, found particularly in the mining industry, which does not have the right to recover money not paid by SHAREHOLDERS when the SHARES are called up.

nominal account An account in the DOUBLE-ENTRY BOOKKEEPING system which does not relate to persons or to other ASSETS and LIABILITIES, but to EXPENSES or REVENUES.

nominal capital *See* AUTHORIZED SHARE CAPITAL.

nominal ledger An expression that tends to be used now to mean the main BOOKS OF ACCOUNT in which are stored the DOUBLE-ENTRY BOOKKEEPING records of the business. It could also be called the 'GENERAL LEDGER'. Originally, the only records kept would have related to amounts owed to, or by, persons. These would have been recorded on pieces of paper in a 'PERSONAL LEDGER'. Later, there would have been records of land and property in the 'REAL LEDGER'; and of things that were 'accounts' in name only, like interest or electricity expenses, in the nominal ledger. However, the term 'NOMINAL LEDGER' has now supplanted the others in the UK, and it remains in use even where all the information is actually on a computer tape rather than in the traditional big black book.

nominal rate of interest A rate of interest expressed in terms of the FACE VALUE of a loan.

nominal share capital *See* AUTHORIZED SHARE CAPITAL.

nominal value The face value of a SECURITY. All SHARES in the UK have a NOMINAL VALUE or par value. This is usually little more than a label to distinguish a share from any other type of security issued by the same company. However, it does denote the extent of a SHAREHOLDER's liability in the event of LIQUIDATION. Normally, the shares will be currently exchanged at above the nominal value, and the company will consequently issue any new shares at approximately the market price, leading to the recording of a SHARE PREMIUM ACCOUNT.
   Dividends are expressed as a percentage of nominal value; and SHARE CAPITAL is recorded at nominal value, any excess being recorded as SHARE PREMIUM (UK)/ PAID-IN SURPLUS (US).

nominee A person named by another to act on the former's behalf.

nominee shareholding A holding of SHARES in a company where the legal registered owner (e.g. a bank) holds the shares on behalf of the BENEFICIAL OWNER.

non-adjusting events Events after the BALANCE SHEET date that do not lead to a change to the ASSETS and LIABILITIES recognized in the balance sheet, but might lead to note disclosures (*see*, POST BALANCE SHEET EVENTS).

non-cancellable lease A LEASE that cannot be terminated by the LESSEE except by permission of the LESSOR or on some remote contingency or by payment of a prohibitive amount.

non-cash transactions Transactions, such as a swap of one ASSET for another, that do not involve the receipt or payment of cash.

non-contributory pension scheme A PENSION SCHEME which does not involve contributions from the persons who will receive the pensions.

non-controllable costs *See* UNCONTROLLABLE COSTS.

non-cumulative preference share A PREFERENCE SHARE for which dividends unpaid in one period are not carried forward to be paid in the next.

non-current liabilities In the context of the laws of EU member states, those LIABILITIES that must be paid within twelve months of the balance sheet date. An alternative meaning, which could be used elsewhere, is the liabilities that are not expected to be settled in the course of an enterprise's operating cycle.

non-equity share UK expression for SHARES that are redeemable or have restrictions on their rights to dividends or to participation in a SURPLUS on the WINDING-UP of a company.

non-executive director A DIRECTOR of a company who is not involved in the day-to-day running of it.

non-monetary assets ASSETS of an enterprise that do not have fixed or determinable monetary values.

non-participating preference shares PREFERENCE SHARES whose owners are not entitled to DIVIDENDS beyond a fixed level.

non-performing loans Loans on which the borrower is not paying interest as it falls legally due.

non-profit Description applied to an organization whose main aims are not commercial, e.g. a university or a charity. Depending on the legal structure of such bodies, they may not be subject to normal accounting rules, though they may well be subject to other special rules.

Such an organization will usually prepare a BALANCE SHEET, but will not prepare a PROFIT AND LOSS ACCOUNT. It may instead prepare an INCOME AND EXPENDITURE ACCOUNT which still uses the MATCHING CONCEPT and other normal accounting rules, but arrives at a SURPLUS or DEFICIT rather than a PROFIT or loss. Alternatively, it may abandon the matching convention in favour of cash accounting, when it will prepare a RECEIPTS AND PAYMENTS ACCOUNT.

non-purchased goodwill GOODWILL inherent in an enterprise in the sense that the total market value of its shares exceeds its NET ASSETS. Such goodwill is not recognized in BALANCE SHEETS.

non-recourse finance Loans whose lenders are entitled to interest only to the extent that this can be paid from the returns on the project that they finance.

non-resident In the context of tax regulations, a person or organization based outside a country.

non-voting ordinary shares ORDINARY SHARES whose owners are not allowed to vote at meetings of SHAREHOLDERS. In the UK, these are called 'A shares' and are rare.

no par value stock In the US, shares without a par value or NOMINAL VALUE.

normal capacity The production expected from an ASSET on average over a number of periods under normal circumstances, taking into account any loss of capacity resulting from planned maintenance.

normal loss The amount of loss in a production process that would be regarded as expected under efficient operations. This is therefore part of the PRODUCTION COST.

normal shrinkage A part of NORMAL LOSS.

normal spoilage A part of NORMAL LOSS.

normal volume Generally the budgeted volume of production for a period. It is used to calculate OVERHEAD ABSORPTION RATES.

normal waste A part of NORMAL LOSS.

normative theories of accounting Theories, based on deductive reasoning, which suggest the best ways to carry out financial reporting.

nostro account An account (literally, from Italian, 'our' account) held by a bank with a bank in another country.

notes payable US term for money to be paid by an enterprise to suppliers or others, as evidenced by BILLS OF EXCHANGE written by the enterprise.

notes receivable US term for money to be received by an enterprise from customers or others, as evidenced by BILLS OF EXCHANGE written by those debtors.

notes to the accounts The explanatory notes to such statements as the BALANCE SHEET, giving more details concerning the items shown on the face of the FINANCIAL STATEMENTS. Many such notes are required by law or by ACCOUNTING STANDARDS. The notes are regarded as an integral part of the financial statements.

notes to the financial statements *See* NOTES TO THE ACCOUNTS.

not-for-profit organization US term for NON-PROFIT organization.

notice of coding In the context of the UK's system of INCOME TAX, a document sent by an Inspector of Taxes to a taxpayer and to the taxpayer's employer explaining the taxpayer's TAX CODE for the year.

NPV Abbreviation for NET PRESENT VALUE.

NRV Abbreviation for NET REALIZABLE VALUE.

NV Abbreviation for a *Naamloze Vennootschap*, a Dutch or Belgian PUBLIC LIMITED COMPANY.

NYSE Abbreviation for the New York Stock Exchange.

O

objectives of financial statements As recorded in a CONCEPTUAL FRAME-WORK, the purposes (including the expected users and uses) of FINANCIAL STATE-MENTS. According to UK, US and INTERNATIONAL ACCOUNTING STANDARDS COMMITTEE thinking, the objective is primarily to give useful information to investors so that they can make financial decisions.

objectivity An accounting measurement is said to be 'objective' if it is reasonably independent of the judgement of accountants. There is much to be said for objectivity in accounting, because this reduces the time taken to arrive at figures, and the time taken to check them. It also means that the readers of FINANCIAL STATEMENTS can be more easily reassured that the figures contained are not arbitrary. This is connected to the RELIABILITY of the information.

The most obvious result of this desire for a simple, checkable system is the conventional use of HISTORICAL COST ACCOUNTING. The original purchase price of an ASSET is much more objective than its current selling price, REPLACEMENT COST or the value of future benefits expected to flow from it. However, such techniques as DEPRECIATION and PROVISIONS FOR BAD DEBTS do add subjectivity, even to historical cost accounting.

The main problem with greater objectivity is the possible sacrifice of relevance. The price of a machine eight years ago is objective, but irrelevant for a knowledge about how much the machine is worth or a decision about what to do with it.

A well-known saying in accounting is that it may be better to be approximately right than precisely wrong. Nevertheless, at present, most of the world settles for a system that might be said to be not even precisely wrong.

objects clause A clause in a company's MEMORANDUM OF ASSOCIATION which sets out the objectives of the company, so that it is clear what is beyond its powers (*ultra vires*). Generally, now, objects clauses are drafted very widely.

obligating event In the context of establishing whether an enterprise has a LIABILITY, an event that creates a LEGAL or CONSTRUCTIVE OBLIGATION that the enterprise has no realistic alternative but to settle.

obligation A requirement to perform in a certain way. Obligations may be legally enforceable as a consequence of a CONTRACT. However, they may also arise because of a statutory requirement, e.g. for an oil company to clean up after it has finished an exploration. Also, a CONSTRUCTIVE OBLIGATION may arise from expectations created by a company's past behaviour.

obsolescence The decline in usefulness of an ASSET caused by technological or fashion changes. This is one of the causes of the wearing out of an asset that means that DEPRECIATION must be recognized.

occupational pension scheme A PENSION SCHEME run by an employer for the benefit of its employees.

OEC Abbreviation for the *Ordre des Experts Comptables*, the French professional accountancy body.

OECD Abbreviation for the Organisation for Economic Co-operation and Development, a Paris-based institution representing the interests of the world's most developed nations. In the accounting area, it makes recommendations on the DISCLOSURES to be required of multinational companies.

off-balance sheet finance Obligations of an enterprise that are not recognized as LIABILITIES on its BALANCE SHEET. One example of off-balance sheet finance is the existence of finance LEASES that are not treated as ASSETS and liabilities (capitalized). In the UK and the USA, it is now necessary for 'CAPITAL' or 'FINANCE' LEASES to be capitalized as though owned, and for an equal liability to be created. This adjusts for the otherwise misleading off-balance sheet finance. It expresses SUBSTANCE OVER FORM and is an attempt to achieve FAIR PRESENTATION.
   A further example of off-balance sheet finance would be the non-consolidation of the liabilities of controlled companies that are technically not SUBSIDIARIES.

offer by prospectus In the context of an issue of shares, an offer to the public of a new type of shares by means of a PROSPECTUS.

offer for sale In the context of an issue of shares, an offer to the public of more of a company's shares of a type already traded. The offer is made by a financial institution on the company's behalf.

offer price The price at which a security is offered for sale. Compare to BID PRICE.

officers of a company A UK legal term for a company's DIRECTORS and its secretary.

official discount rate The rate at which a central bank discounts (i.e. buys at a price below face value) BILLS OF EXCHANGE for financial institutions.

Official List The London Stock Exchange's list of the securities traded on its main market.

official receivers Government officials appointed to act in BANKRUPTCIES and WINDINGS-UP.

offsetting The netting of an ASSET and LIABILITY or of an INCOME and EXPENSE. Generally, offsetting is not allowed for financial reporting, although offsetting of assets and liabilities is allowed under conditions such as that a LEGAL RIGHT OF SET-OFF exists.

offshore company A company registered in a different country from that of its owners or its transactions. This will usually be for tax or exchange control reasons.

OFR Abbreviation for the OPERATING AND FINANCIAL REVIEW.

OHG Abbreviation for an *offene Handelsgesellschaft*, a German general partnership.

oil and gas accounting Financial reporting for the specialist activities of oil and gas companies. In the UK, the rules for accounting for oil and gas exploration costs are to be found in STATEMENTS OF RECOMMENDED PRACTICE written by the oil industry. These are largely consistent with US requirements, in that the SUCCESSFUL EFFORTS METHOD and the FULL COST METHOD are allowed.

on-cost The additional COST caused by a particular activity. The term can also be used to mean OVERHEAD.

one-line consolidation A US term for the EQUITY METHOD.

onerous contract A contract where the unavoidable costs of meeting the OBLIGATIONS exceed the benefits expected. Such contracts amount to a LIABILITY for which a PROVISION should be made.

opening balance In an ACCOUNT, the debit or credit balance at the beginning of a period.

opening entries In a DOUBLE-ENTRY BOOKKEEPING system, the entries necessary to open up a set of books.

opening stock The STOCK (INVENTORIES) at the beginning of an ACCOUNTING PERIOD.

open market value In the context of property, the expected selling price between willing buyers and sellers, not restricted to the property's existing use.

open outcry In the context of an organized market for commodities or securities, the shouting of bids and offers between traders.

operating activities The principal revenue-producing activities of an enterprise. This is a rather vague concept. For CASH FLOW STATEMENTS under INTERNATIONAL ACCOUNTING STANDARDS COMMITTEE or US rules, operating activities are those that are not INVESTING ACTIVITIES or FINANCING ACTIVITIES.

operating and financial review (OFR) A statement which UK directors are encouraged to produce as part of a company's ANNUAL REPORT. The OFR examines and explains important features of the company's financial position and results. The US equivalent is 'MANAGEMENT'S DISCUSSION AND ANALYSIS' (MD&A).

operating budget The part of an organization's overall BUDGET that deals with its main operations, such as sales, production and administration.

operating cycle The period between the purchase of materials entering into a process and their realization in CASH, RECEIVABLES or instruments that are readily convertible into cash.

operating expenses and revenues Although there is no clear definition, the term could be used to mean those EXPENSES and REVENUES related to an enterprise's ordinary activities, possibly excluding financial items.

operating lease A lease which is treated by accountants as a rental rather than as a FINANCE LEASE.

operating performance ratios Generally, those RATIOS that are concerned with sales figures.

operating profit (or loss) 'Operating profit' means different things in different contexts. In conventional HISTORICAL COST ACCOUNTING it usually means the profit before the deduction of interest and tax and before EXTRAORDINARY ITEMS, and possibly excluding gains from the letting of property or the sale of used machines. However, in the context of INFLATION ACCOUNTING, 'operating profit' may mean something more complicated, i.e. the historical cost profit, before interest and tax, adjusted for the effects of price changes on DEPRECIATION, cost of sales, and, possibly, monetary working capital.

operational audit The review, often by an organization's own staff, of the performance of the organization, in both financial and non-financial terms, in order to assess efficiency and effectiveness.

operational variances Differences between the actual performance of an organization on particular criteria compared to the standard performance under the conditions actually prevailing. In contrast, a REVISION VARIANCE adjusts for differences between the expected and actual conditions.

opinion shopping Colloquial term for the practice of a company in testing out different audit firms to see if any would agree with a particular accounting policy proposed by the company.

Opinions of the Accounting Principles Board The main output of the former ACCOUNTING PRINCIPLES BOARD in the USA. Unless subsequently overridden, these documents still remain part of generally accepted accounting principles.

opportunity cost The benefit forgone by carrying out a particular activity. In the context of scarce resources, the opportunity cost of one activity is the inability then to undertake the best available alternative.

opportunity value Another way of saying DEPRIVAL VALUE.

option A right to purchase something at a particular price, in a particular period, and under particular conditions.

ordinary activities Under UK and INTERNATIONAL ACCOUNTING STANDARDS COMMITTEE rules, any activities of an enterprise carried out as part of its business and such related activities in furtherance of, incidental to, or arising from, these activities. This is a very wide definition which leaves very little to be included as EXTRAORDINARY ITEMS.

ordinary profit The profit of an enterprise from its ORDINARY ACTIVITIES.

ordinary resolution In UK law, a proposal by the shareholders of a company that can be passed by a simple majority, unlike an EXTRAORDINARY RESOLUTION or a SPECIAL RESOLUTION.

ordinary share UK expression for the main type of ownership capital of companies. The US equivalent is 'COMMON STOCK'. In a BALANCE SHEET, the amount of money contributed by shareholders is split into issued share capital (at NOMINAL VALUES) and SHARE PREMIUM (for the excess amounts).

A company will also have an AUTHORIZED SHARE CAPITAL, as specified in its MEMORANDUM OF ASSOCIATION. This is a maximum potential SHARE CAPITAL, which is disclosed as a note to the balance sheet.

The main alternative type of share capital is PREFERENCE SHARES, but these have been unpopular in the UK since 1965 due to a change in the tax system.

ordinary share capital The total nominal value of a company's ORDINARY SHARES.

ordinary shareholders' funds The SHARE CAPITAL and RESERVES of a company that relate to the owners of ORDINARY SHARES. This excludes PREFERENCE SHARE CAPITAL and MINORITY INTERESTS.

organizational slack The excess of the total resources available in an organization over those necessary for efficient operations.

origin of turnover In the context of SEGMENT REPORTING, the geographical area in which goods sold were produced, as opposed to the area where the customer is based.

original cost Another term for the HISTORICAL COST of an ASSET.

original entry, error of A mistake made in the context of DOUBLE-ENTRY BOOKKEEPING by recording the wrong amount in a BOOK OF ORIGINAL (or PRIME) ENTRY. This will lead to two incorrect and balancing entries, so it will not be discovered by drawing up a TRIAL BALANCE.

originated loans and receivables Financial assets created by the enterprise itself. For example, a bank creates an originated loan by lending to a customer. If the loan is then traded on by the bank, it is no longer originated by its new owner.

originating timing difference In the context of accounting for DEFERRED TAX, a timing difference arising in the accounting period under consideration.

OTC market Abbreviation for an OVER-THE-COUNTER MARKET.

other comprehensive income US expression for the elements of COMPREHENSIVE INCOME other than those recorded in the INCOME STATEMENT. Such elements include gains on revalued and unsold marketable securities.

out-of-the-money option A CONTRACT enabling the holder to purchase an item at a fixed price (a CALL OPTION), in those cases where that EXERCISE PRICE is above the current MARKET PRICE of the item.

output tax In the context of VALUE ADDED TAX, the total amount of the tax charged on the items sold by a trader.

outside director A US term for a NON-EXECUTIVE DIRECTOR.

outside shareholder A SHAREHOLDER in a subsidiary company other than its parent or other group companies.

overabsorbed overhead The amount by which the absorbed OVERHEAD COSTS exceed the costs actually incurred.

overcapitalization A state of affairs in which a company has more finance than is necessary for its operations. This is a bad thing because the providers of the finance require returns in the shape of DIVIDENDS or INTEREST.

overdraft An amount by which a bank's customer's account has gone into DEBIT, generally with the permission of the bank.

overhead Expenses of a business that cannot be traced to units of production or to processes that produce particular single products. The term 'INDIRECT COSTS' or, in the US, 'BURDEN' has the same meaning. Obvious examples of overheads include the computer used by the head office, the salaries of factory managers, and the property taxes on the company's buildings. There will be PRODUCTION OVERHEADS, ADMINISTRATION OVERHEADS, DISTRIBUTION OVERHEADS and possibly others.

overhead absorption The process of incorporating the OVERHEAD costs of an organization into the costs of various products or COST CENTRES.

overhead absorption rate The pre-determined rate at which OVERHEAD costs are charged to amounts of production. The rate can be measured in terms of units, direct labour hours, machine hours, and so on.

overhead analysis sheet A document, internal to an organization, on which are shown the calculations involved in the charging out of OVERHEAD costs to COST CENTRES.

overhead cost *See* OVERHEAD.

overhead cost absorbed/recovered The amount of the OVERHEAD cost charged to production for a period. It is calculated by multiplying the budgeted ABSORPTION RATE by the actual production of the period.

overhead efficiency (or productivity) variance The VARIABLE OVERHEAD ABSORPTION RATE per hour multiplied by the difference between the actual hours taken for production and the standard hours.

overhead total variance The difference between the OVERHEAD costs incurred in a period and the ABSORBED OVERHEAD.

overhead volume variance The FIXED OVERHEAD COSTS recovery rate multiplied by the difference between the actual volume of production and the budgeted volume.

overseas company Synonym for FOREIGN SUBSIDIARY.

over-the-counter market A market for shares, particularly to be found in the USA, outside an established stock exchange. The 'counter' in question was originally that of a bank.

over-the-counter securities Shares or other securities traded on an OVER-THE-COUNTER MARKET.

overtime Work done, generally by non-managerial staff, in excess of normal daily or weekly hours. Often the wage rate for such work is higher than for normal hours.

overtrading A state of affairs in which an enterprise is in danger of running out of cash because it has expanded too rapidly.

owners' equity One of the US terms for SHAREHOLDERS' FUNDS.

own shares A company's own shares bought back and held by the company. Until the Companies Act 1981, it was not possible for a UK company to purchase back its own ORDINARY SHARES from its shareholders. That rule was designed to protect CREDITORS. However, many countries did allow this; in the USA, own shares may be held by a company and are called 'treasury stock'. The UK joined the others, partly in order to allow private companies to buy out 'troublesome minorities' of their shareholders who could not find buyers.

In the UK, own shares are generally shown as assets. Under INTERNATIONAL ACCOUNTING STANDARDS COMMITTEE and US rules, they are shown as deductions from EQUITY.

Pacioli, Luca Fra Luca Pacioli is the most famous man in the history of accounting. He lived between about 1445 and about 1513. He was professor of mathematics at various Italian universities, and was a Franciscan friar (hence the 'Fra' for *frater*, i.e. brother). He was a friend of popes, princes and artists, including Leonardo da Vinci who drew the famous 'proportions of man' as an illustration for one of Pacioli's books.

His is the earliest surviving major treatise containing a description of DOUBLE-ENTRY BOOKKEEPING. It may be found in a book published in Venice in 1494, *Summa de Arithmetica, Geometria, Proportioni et Proportionalità*. This work had immense influence on the spread of double entry, as it was gradually adapted into several languages. Pacioli was certainly not the inventor of double entry (by about 200 years) but his book did much to popularize it.

P & L account Abbreviation for the PROFIT AND LOSS ACCOUNT.

P/E ratio Abbreviation for the PRICE/EARNINGS RATIO.

paid-in capital US term for SHARE CAPITAL plus SHARE PREMIUM, i.e. it is the amount paid to a company by its shareholders when they bought shares from it.

paid-in surplus One of the US expressions for part of the amounts of money paid by investors when they purchased a company's shares. Most shares in the USA have a PAR VALUE, which is a sort of label. Usually, shares are issued at above par value, in which case the capital paid in is divided into SHARE CAPITAL (at par) and PAID-IN SURPLUS (the excess above par). For most purposes, paid-in surplus is treated exactly as if it were 'share capital'. In the UK, the equivalent term is SHARE PREMIUM.

paid-up share capital UK term for the total of the share capital, valued at NOMINAL VALUE, that has been paid for by the shareholders.

paper profit A colloquial and vague term which might mean a profit not yet turned into cash or one that *could* not be turned into cash.

parent company Generally, a company that controls another undertaking (its subsidiary). The normal financial reporting treatment is to prepare CONSOLI-DATED FINANCIAL STATEMENTS for the group containing the parent and the subsidiaries.

parent undertaking An undertaking (a word wider than company) that controls another.

pari passu Latin term meaning, approximately, 'at an equal rate'. It can be used to describe two types of SECURITY that rank equally with each other in terms of DIVIDENDS or other rights.

partial tax allocation Accounting for DEFERRED TAX on the basis that deferred tax assets and liabilities should only be recognized when they are expected to crystallize in the foreseeable future. This was the UK requirement until FINANCIAL REPORTING STANDARD 19 was issued in 2000.

participating interest A UK legal term for a long-term interest in another undertaking for the purpose of securing a contribution to the investor. A holding of 20 per cent or more of shares is presumed to give rise to such an interest. The holding of a participating interest is one of the features of the existence of an ASSOCIATE.

participating preference share A type of PREFERENCE SHARE that entitles the holder not only to a fixed dividend but also to an extra dividend when the ordinary shareholders have received a DIVIDEND equal to or above a particular amount.

participative budgeting The process of formulating a BUDGET in those cases where the managers take part in setting the budgeted levels of their own performance.

participator In the context of UK tax regulations, a person having an interest in the CAPITAL or INCOME of a company, such as a SHAREHOLDER.

partly paid shares Shares on which not all of the NOMINAL VALUE (and any associated premium) has been paid. This may be because the shares are being issued in several calls and not all of them have yet occurred, or because the calls have not yet been fully answered.

partner One of the members (owners) of a PARTNERSHIP.

partnership A business arrangement whereby several persons pool their capital and skills, and share the risks and profits. Normally, most or all of the partners are directly involved in the management of the business, unlike many companies where most shareholders are not part of management. In the UK and the USA, except for LIMITED LIABILITY PARTNERSHIPS, PARTNERS are fully liable (do not have LIMITED LIABILITY) for the debts of the business, which is partly why they all wish to be involved in the management. Also, in the USA and the UK except for Scotland, partnerships are not legal entities; one would have to take the partners, not the partnership, to court. In continental Europe, there are several different forms of partnership, and many do have legal personality.

partnership accounts The books of account and the FINANCIAL STATEMENTS of partnerships. In the UK and the USA, PARTNERSHIPS are not generally required to appoint AUDITORS or to publish their FINANCIAL STATEMENTS. However, similar accounting practices to those of companies tend to be used. In place of shareholders' capital balances, there are capital and current accounts of the partners.

partnership agreement/deed A legal document recording the rights and duties of the partners in a PARTNERSHIP.

par value The normal US expression for the face value of a share, that helps to distinguish it from other types of share of the same company. The term is also used in the UK, where 'nominal value' is an equivalent expression. Share capital is recorded 'at par', although the issue price, after the company is formed, is usually in excess of par, because the MARKET PRICE for existing shares will usually be higher. The excess amounts over par are called SHARE PREMIUM.

passed dividend A DIVIDEND which a company has not paid.

past service cost An increase, in an accounting period, of an EMPLOYEE BENEFIT OBLIGATION for service in prior periods from improvements to employee benefits. The context is accounting for DEFINED BENEFIT EMPLOYEE OBLIGA-TIONS. Suppose that Company A takes over Company B, whose pension arrange-ments are more generous than Company A's. Company A may decide to improve its benefits to be in line with Company B's. This is a PAST SERVICE COST. Not all such costs are immediately treated as an expense. For example, under INTER-NATIONAL ACCOUNTING STANDARDS, past service cost for existing employees is spread over the average remaining life of employees in the pension scheme.

patent A legal entitlement, granted by the State, giving the holder the exclusive right of exploitation of an invention for a specified period.

pathfinder prospectus A forerunner to a full PROSPECTUS, published by a company to assess the potential for an issue of shares.

payables US term for CREDITORS.

pay and file In the context of the UK's CORPORATION TAX, a procedure of the 1990s for the payment of the tax.

pay as you earn A UK scheme whereby, as part of the income tax system, employers regularly deduct from the wages and salaries of employees the appropriate amount of tax such that, by the end of the tax year, the appropriate total of tax has been paid for the employee by the employer to the INLAND REVENUE.

pay as you go In the context of PENSIONS, a colloquial term for a method whereby an employer does not set up a fund to pay, or a provision to record, its PENSION OBLIGATIONS but pays the pension entitlements as they fall due as though they were current expenses.

pay-back method A popular technique for appraising the likely success of projects, or for choosing between projects. It involves the analysis of their expected future net cash inflows, followed by a calculation of how many years it will take for the original capital investment to be recovered. It seems that it is popular because it is simple to use and, perhaps more importantly, simple to explain to non-financial managers.

It may give a reasonable answer when choosing between projects which have similar expected patterns of cash flows and similar initial investments. However, several criticisms may be made about the more general use of it. First, the method ignores the NET CASH FLOWS that arise after the PAY-BACK PERIOD; the quicker pay-back project may actually be far less profitable in total. Second, the method ignores the TIME VALUE OF MONEY, i.e. it ignores the fact that money received in two years' time is less valuable than an equal amount received in one year's time.

More sophisticated methods of investment appraisal, such as the NET PRESENT VALUE method, adjust for both the above problems by discounting all the expected future income flows. However, these methods are not popular with businesspeople, presumably because they are more difficult to understand, and involve many more judgements. The pay-back method is often used in conjunction with others.

PAYE Abbreviation for PAY AS YOU EARN.

payments in advance Another term for PREPAYMENTS.

payment on account A partial payment for goods and services delivered or to be delivered or for the settlement of another form of LIABILITY.

pay-out ratio Another term for DIVIDEND COVER.

payroll accounting The BOOKKEEPING and CONTROL activities of an organization concerning its wages and salaries.

payroll tax A tax on an enterprise calculated by reference to its payroll costs.

PCG Abbreviation for the PLAN COMPTABLE GÉNÉRAL of France.

peer review The review by one firm of auditors of the work of another.

pension A postponed employee benefit paid by a former employer (or the State) to an employee after retirement.

pension costs The expenses charged in a PROFIT AND LOSS ACCOUNT relating to PENSIONS. These will include such items as elements of ACTUARIAL GAINS AND LOSSES.

pension fund ASSETS set aside for the eventual payment of PENSION OBLIGATIONS. The term is generally used when the assets have been irrevocably set aside by an employer, and handed over to TRUSTEES or to a financial institution.

pension liabilities/provision The amount shown in a BALANCE SHEET representing future payments to pensioners. The amount will be calculated after netting the PENSION FUND against the PENSION OBLIGATION.

pension obligation The future expected payments to pensioners as a result of rights built up by service already rendered. The OBLIGATION takes account of expected salary increases, and the total obligation is discounted to take account of the TIME VALUE OF MONEY.

pension plan The US and INTERNATIONAL ACCOUNTING STANDARDS COMMITTEE term for PENSION SCHEME.

pension scheme An arrangement for providing post-retirement income to employees. Several types exist, including State schemes, occupational schemes (arranged by employers) or private schemes. Schemes may involve an associated PENSION FUND.

PEP Abbreviation for a personal equity plan, a type of UK tax-efficient savings scheme.

percentage-of-completion method In the context of accounting for contracts, a method whereby revenues are recognized continuously by stage of completion of a contract rather than waiting till its end. For contracts whose outcome can be reliably estimated, the method is required under UK and INTERNATIONAL ACCOUNTING STANDARDS COMMITTEE rules.

perfect market A market with no transaction costs, with homogeneous products, with many buyers and sellers, and with perfect information.

performance Another way of saying PROFIT or NET INCOME, or the relationship between REVENUES and EXPENSES.

performance bond A GUARANTEE given by a selling company (or its bankers) to a customer that goods of a certain type and quality will be delivered.

performance measures Various ways in which the success of an enterprise or parts of it can be assessed for a period. *See*, for example, PROFITABILITY.

period (or periodicity) concept The idea that FINANCIAL STATEMENTS for an enterprise should be produced regularly (e.g. annually or quarterly), irrespective of whether production cycles have finished. This enables comparisons over time and between enterprises, but creates many of the problems of financial reporting because estimates and valuations need to be made since many activities are still in progress at a period end.

period costs Expenditures that are incurred on a time basis, such as rent or insurance, and therefore are not generally identifiable with any particular assets or production. They are treated as expenses of the periods to which they relate. For COST ACCOUNTING purposes, they are FIXED COSTS.

periodic stocktaking (or periodic inventory) The practice of counting and then valuing INVENTORY at particular times (e.g. at the accounting year end). The alternative is CONTINUOUS INVENTORY.

period of account The length of time for which an enterprise prepares its FINANCIAL STATEMENTS.

perks Benefits (or perquisites) given to employees beyond normal remuneration, and generally not in current CASH.

permanent difference In the context of some systems of accounting for DEFERRED TAX, a non-reversing difference between a financial reporting EXPENSE/REVENUE and the equivalent for tax purposes. For example, if entertainment expenses are not deductible for tax purposes, they cause a permanent excess of financial reporting expense over tax expense.

permanent diminution in value UK legal term for the circumstances in which FIXED ASSETS must be revalued downwards, with a related charge against profit. The word 'permanent' is unclear. The concept has been subsumed into IMPAIRMENT.

perpetual annuity An ANNUITY which lasts for ever.

perpetual debt A DEBENTURE or other loan with no repayment date.

perpetual inventory The process of recording all additions to, and usages of, INVENTORY such that the balance of inventory is always shown.

perpetual succession A legal term denoting the continuation of an entity despite any changes of ownership. For example, a COMPANY has perpetual succession but a PARTNERSHIP does not. The latter has to be discontinued (or re-arranged) when a partner leaves.

personal accounts Those ACCOUNTS in a bookkeeping system that relate to persons, such as DEBTORS and CREDITORS, rather than to items such as PROPERTY or EXPENSES.

personal allowance In the context of the UK's system of INCOME TAX, an amount deducted from GROSS INCOME in the calculation of TAXABLE INCOME. The amount was originally designed to take account of a person's need for food, clothing and shelter before the person had any ability to pay tax.

personal ledger The set of ACCOUNTS in a bookkeeping system that deal with persons, such as DEBTORS and CREDITORS.

personal pension scheme An arrangement, generally run by a financial institution such as a life assurance company, whereby individuals can pay a part of their salaries or business profits into a fund that will later repay a PENSION.

personal representative As a legal term, an EXECUTOR or ADMINISTRATOR.

personalty ASSETS such as cash or investments as opposed to REALTY, i.e. land and buildings.

PERT Abbreviation for programme evaluation and review technique (*see* CRITICAL-PATH ANALYSIS).

petroleum revenue tax A UK tax on a company's NET INCOME from oil exploration, calculated on a field by field basis.

petty cash Amounts of coin and notes kept by an organization for the payment of small items of expense.

petty cash book A document used to record all movements of PETTY CASH. Generally, it is run as an IMPREST ACCOUNT.

physical capital maintenance The idea that the profit of an enterprise must be calculated after taking into account the need to keep physical assets at the same level of productive potential. *See* CAPITAL MAINTENANCE CONCEPT.

physical inventory (physical stock check) Synonym for PERIODIC STOCK-TAKING.

physical life The period over which a FIXED ASSET could provide services. This may be longer than the asset's useful economic life which is calculated on the basis of the expected use of the asset by its present owner.

placing The sale of SHARES in a company by a financial institution without advertisement to the public.

plan assets ASSETS held by a legally separate entity (a fund) that are to be used only to settle EMPLOYEE BENEFIT OBLIGATIONS of an enterprise. Such assets are therefore not available to the enterprise's own creditors and cannot be returned to the enterprise. It is common in the UK and the USA for companies to establish PENSION FUNDS which contain such assets. The company's LIABILITY for employee benefits is shown as the obligation less the PLAN ASSETS in the fund.

plan comptable général An 'accounting plan' is the fundamental set of instructions for accounting practices in a number of European countries (such as France, Belgium and Spain) and in some developing countries. In France, the *plan comptable général* contains a standard decimalized CHART OF ACCOUNTS and instructions relating to the presentation of uniform published FINANCIAL STATEMENTS.

planning horizon The most distant point in the future for which quantified plans could reasonably be prepared. The actual planning period may be less than this.

planning period The period into the future for which quantified plans have been prepared.

planning variance Synonym for REVISION VARIANCE.

plant and equipment An enterprise's TANGIBLE FIXED ASSETS other than land and buildings. This includes PLANT AND MACHINERY, but also vehicles and fixtures and fittings.

plant and machinery The term used, but not defined, in the Companies Act for certain types of TANGIBLE FIXED ASSETS. The natural meaning of the words can therefore be used, given that other headings in the Act are 'Land and buildings', and 'Fixtures, fittings, tools and equipment'.

plant register A document recording an enterprise's PLANT AND EQUIPMENT, including its dates and costs of purchase, and amounts of DEPRECIATION.

PLC or plc Abbreviation for PUBLIC LIMITED COMPANY.

ploughed-back profits Another way of saying RETAINED EARNINGS/PROFITS.

point of sale The location and time of a sale/purchase.

poison pill An arrangement whereby the management of a company trying to resist a TAKEOVER BID ensures that a successful takeover would cause a serious loss or other disadvantage to the company under its new management.

political and charitable contributions Donations made to political or charitable organizations. When given by companies, they must be disclosed in the DIRECTORS' REPORT if above a certain amount.

political costs In the context of FINANCIAL REPORTING, the potential adverse consequences, particularly for a large company, of disclosures such as large profits.

political credit risk The risk, caused by foreign governments, that a foreign borrower will not be able to repay loans to an enterprise.

poll tax A tax per head (poll) rather than one charged on a tax base such as INCOME or SALES. Such a tax is widely regarded as unfair, and therefore as politically unacceptable.

pooling of interests US term for MERGER ACCOUNTING.

portable pension A PENSION that can move with a person from one employment or business to another.

portfolio The set of holdings of financial ASSETS, such as SHARES or loans, owned by a person or institution.

portfolio investment A holding in SHARES with the purpose of generating income or capital gain rather than to exercise influence or control over the INVESTEE.

portfolio theory The set of ideas concerned with how an investor can select the most appropriate PORTFOLIO. It is assumed that investors are averse to taking risks and need to be compensated for taking them by higher expected returns. Different investors will want a different mix of risks and returns. *See* CAPITAL ASSET PRICING MODEL.

positive accounting theory A body of ideas and research designed to explain the behaviour of accountants and the effects of accounting on share prices. The research is empirical rather than normative in style. It does not seek to improve accounting but to understand it.

positive consolidation difference *See* GOODWILL.

positive goodwill GOODWILL rather than NEGATIVE GOODWILL.

post balance sheet events Events that occur between the BALANCE SHEET date and the date when the FINANCIAL STATEMENTS are authorized for issue. Two types of events are generally identified:

(a) those that provide evidence of conditions that existed at the balance sheet date (*adjusting events*); and
(b) those that are indicative of conditions that arose after the balance sheet date (*non-adjusting events*).

Adjusting events should lead to a change to the ASSETS and LIABILITIES recognized in the balance sheet. An example of such an event is the discovery of better information about the status of a DEBTOR at the balance sheet date.

Non-adjusting events should not lead to a change to the figures in the balance sheet, but might require disclosures. An example of such an event would be the destruction by fire of some FIXED ASSETS after the balance sheet date.

post-completion audit A review of a CAPITAL INVESTMENT project after it has finished. This involves the comparison of actual results with those anticipated.

post-date To postpone the effectiveness of a document by writing in a date after the current date.

post-employment benefit plans Contractual or constructive arrangements under which an enterprise provides POST-EMPLOYMENT BENEFITS for employees.

post-employment benefits Employee benefits which are payable to employees by an enterprise after the completion of employment. Such benefits could include PENSIONS and medical benefits.

post-retirement benefits *See* POST-EMPLOYMENT BENEFITS.

post-retirement medical benefits A type of POST-EMPLOYMENT BENEFIT whereby an enterprise contracts to pay an employee's medical costs after retirement. This is common in the USA and leads to the appearance of large liabilities on the BALANCE SHEETS of many US companies.

potentially exempt transfer In the context of the UK's INHERITANCE TAX, a gift made during the lifetime of a donor which will be exempt from the tax as long as the donor lives for seven years after the donation.

potential ordinary share A contract that may entitle its holder to ORDINARY SHARES, depending on future circumstances. Such shares are taken into account in the calculations of some versions of EARNINGS PER SHARE.

Practice Notes Supplements to AUDITING STANDARDS issued in the UK and Ireland by the Auditing Practices Board.

pre-acquisition profits Profits of a SUBSIDIARY that had been earned before it was purchased by its present parent company. Thus, undistributed pre-acquisition profits are not seen as RESERVES of that group in CONSOLIDATED FINANCIAL STATEMENTS. Group reserves are calculated as the undistributed profits of the parent company, plus the group's share of undistributed post-acquisition profits of the consolidated companies. The term could also refer to the profits of the subsidiary in the year of acquisition up to the date of acquisition.

pre-acquisition reserves The cumulative undistributed PRE-ACQUISITION PROFITS of an enterprise.

preceding-year basis In the context of UK taxation of income or profits, the assessment of taxable income for a year on the basis of the earnings of the preceding year. This is not now generally the basis in the UK.

pre-closing trial balance A TRIAL BALANCE as drawn up before the adjusting entries at the end of a period for such items as closing inventory.

predetermined overhead rate An OVERHEAD ABSORPTION RATE as calculated before the overhead costs are incurred. This is the normal state of affairs, and BUDGETS can be used for the calculations.

predictive ability In the context of FINANCIAL REPORTING, the degree to which a DISCLOSURE will help the users of FINANCIAL STATEMENTS of an enterprise to estimate correctly its future profits or cash flows.

pre-emption rights A legal entitlement of existing SHAREHOLDERS to be offered any new SHARES to be issued by their company before anyone else is offered them.

preference dividend A DIVIDEND paid to holders of PREFERENCE SHARES.

preference shares Shares normally having preference over ORDINARY SHARES for dividend payments and for the return of capital if a company is wound up, i.e. ordinary dividends cannot be paid in a particular year until the preference dividend, which is usually a fixed percentage, has been paid. Further, it is usual for preference shares to be 'cumulative', i.e. for any unpaid dividends to cumulate into future years and to remain preferential to any ordinary dividend.

The disadvantage for preference shareholders is that, if a company is successful, the ordinary dividend will be expected to rise over the years, whereas the preference dividend will not.

Tax changes in the UK in 1965 made preference shares much less attractive than loans, because the interest on the latter is tax-deductible for companies, whereas dividends are not. Thus, preference share capital has become quite rare.

preference share capital The total of the share capital, at NOMINAL VALUE, contributed by holders of PREFERENCE SHARES.

preferential creditor A CREDITOR who owns a PREFERENTIAL DEBT.

preferential debt An amount owed by an enterprise that must legally be paid ahead of other debts if the enterprise cannot pay all its debts. Generally, amounts owed to the tax authorities are examples of preferential debts.

preferred stock US term for PREFERENCE SHARES.

preliminary announcement The publication of a LISTED COMPANY's summary profit figures before the full FINANCIAL STATEMENTS are published. Such announcements are compulsory for companies listed on the London Stock Exchange.

preliminary expenses The expenses caused by the setting up of a company, such as those relating to the issue of SHARES or the preparation of legal documents, are not allowed to be capitalized (shown as ASSETS) in either the UK or the USA. They must thus be treated as expenses immediately.

In some other countries, such as several continental European countries, these expenses can be capitalized as assets and gradually amortized.

premium A payment in excess of some stated level. *See*, for example, SHARE PREMIUM.

prepaid expenses *See* PREPAYMENTS.

prepayments Amounts recorded in a BALANCE SHEET which show that certain payments have been made in advance, perhaps for rents, property taxes or insurance premiums. Conventional accounting uses the ACCRUAL BASIS OF ACCOUNTING which is that only the expenses that *relate* to a period should be charged against profit for that period. Thus, prepayments will have been paid in the period leading up to the balance sheet, but will not be treated as EXPENSES until a subsequent period. Technically, instead of the DEBIT being treated as an expense, it is treated as an ASSET.

The parallel treatment for expenses paid late gives rise to 'ACCRUED EXPENSES' on the balance sheet.

presentation Those aspects of financial reporting related to the arrangement of the figures on the face of FINANCIAL STATEMENTS.

present value The future net cash inflows expected from an ASSET or a proposed project, 'discounted' to reflect the fact that money is more valuable if received now rather than later. For the valuation of an asset, it might be more normal to refer to the method as the 'ECONOMIC VALUE'; this makes an appearance as a possible valuation under unusual circumstances under some systems of INFLATION ACCOUNTING. When choosing between investment projects, these concepts are normally considered under the heading of NET PRESENT VALUE, abbreviated as NPV.

pre-tax profit The profit of an enterprise for a period before the deduction of the TAX EXPENSE.

price/earnings (P/E) ratio The ratio at any moment compares the market price of an ORDINARY SHARE in the company with the EARNINGS PER SHARE (abbreviated to EPS) of that company, based on the most recently available year's figure for the profit after interest, tax, MINORITY INTEREST and PREFERENCE DIVIDEND. The P/E ratio has become exceptionally important as a rapid means of summing up the way in which investors view a particular company.

A high P/E means that the company is expected to perform well in the future. Investors must deem it to be worth paying a large multiple of the earnings for the share, because of their high expectations. However, this does not help one to decide which share to buy; it merely shows one which shares are well thought of: they are, of course, more expensive. For large stock exchanges, such as those of London and New York, there is considerable evidence that available information is rapidly taken into account in share prices (this is called the EFFICIENT MARKET HYPOTHESIS). Thus, there should be no share that is obvious 'good value': good shares will command good prices.

price index An INDEX related to the price of a particular good or basket of goods. *See*, for example, the RETAIL PRICE INDEX.

price level accounting *See* CURRENT PURCHASING POWER ACCOUNTING.

price risk The risk of change in value of a FINANCIAL INSTRUMENT. Such a risk can be divided into three categories: (a) CURRENCY RISK, (b) INTEREST RATE RISK, and (c) MARKET RISK. Information on these risks should be disclosed in notes to the FINANCIAL STATEMENTS.

price-sensitive information Information that, if publicly available, would change the price of the company's SHARE.

price variance The actual quantity of units of a material purchased or used multiplied by the difference between the actual price paid for a unit and the standard price budgeted for.

pricing The setting by an enterprise of the prices for its goods to be sold.

primary auditor In the context of a group of companies, the AUDITOR of the PARENT COMPANY.

primary earnings per share A former US measure of EARNINGS PER SHARE.

primary financial instruments Those instruments such as CREDITORS, DEBTORS and SHARES that are not DERIVATIVE FINANCIAL INSTRUMENTS.

primary financial statements Where a company publishes more than one set of FINANCIAL STATEMENTS, those that comply with the full requirements of the Companies Act.

primary market The market for the sale and purchase of new issues of shares, as opposed to the SECONDARY MARKET for their exchange.

prime cost Another term for DIRECT COSTS, including direct labour, direct materials and other direct expenses.

prime documents Documents, such as invoices, which are the initial causes of entries in a BOOKKEEPING system.

prime rate A US term for the rate of interest charged by banks to top grade borrowers.

principal This term has two meanings of relevance here: the sum of a loan on which interest is paid, and the person who gives authority to an agent to act on the former's behalf.

principal budget factor In the context of BUDGETARY CONTROL, a limiting factor constraining the achievement of higher levels of performance.

principal private residence In the context of the UK's CAPITAL GAINS TAX, a person's main private dwelling house. Gains and losses on the disposal of this are exempt for the tax.

priority-based budgeting A system of BUDGETS whereby proposed changes from the previous period can be ranked because the proposals are accompanied by numerical analyses of their expected results.

prior-period adjustment *See* PRIOR-YEAR ADJUSTMENT.

prior-year adjustment The adjustment of an enterprise's opening BALANCE SHEET. This may be needed if the enterprise discovers an error of material size in its FINANCIAL STATEMENTS of previous years, or if there is a change in accounting policies due to new laws, standards or circumstances. It is UK practice under FINANCIAL REPORTING STANDARD 3, to adjust the balance sheet of the previous year (as presented as a CORRESPONDING AMOUNT this year) to take account of such events. This is because any changes that result are deemed not to be economic events of the current year, and thus not to be suitable items for a PROFIT AND LOSS ACCOUNT.

private company A company not allowed to create a market in its securities. In the case of the UK, *see* PRIVATE LIMITED COMPANY. Similar forms exist throughout the EU and elsewhere.

private ledger A LEDGER as part of a DOUBLE-ENTRY BOOKKEEPING system whose contents are kept secret from the normal BOOKKEEPERS. The system can be kept in balance by substituting for all the detail of the private ledger with a CONTROL ACCOUNT.

private limited company As registered under UK company law, a private company is one that is not allowed to sell its shares or loan stock on an open market. Such companies have 'limited' or an abbreviation of it as part of their names, as opposed to 'public limited company' for PUBLIC COMPANIES. The vast majority of UK companies are private companies.

The company law relating to private companies is slightly less onerous than that for public companies. For example, private companies under certain size limits are exempted from some annual publication requirements; and private companies have a slightly less restrictive definition of DISTRIBUTABLE PROFITS.

privatization The process of selling a government-owned entity into the private sector.

probable In the context of FINANCIAL REPORTING, a term that may mean 'more likely than not' or may imply some greater degree of likelihood. The word appears often, for example, in the definition of an ASSET.

probate value The valuation of an asset as included in the estate of a deceased person. The valuation should take account of restrictions on the use of an asset, and the need for fairly quick sale.

process costing A method of COST ACCOUNTING commonly found when production is carried out continuously in a series of processes, as in a chemical plant. Costs are charged to the processes rather than to jobs.

product costs Costs of an organization that have been identified with particular units of product. Thus, they include DIRECT COSTS and appropriate elements of OVERHEAD COSTS.

production budget The BUDGET as set for the production aspects of an organization. This will include details of the standard production volumes and costs.

production cost The total of all the costs (perhaps expressed per unit of production) that are associated with production, including direct costs and manufacturing OVERHEAD.

production cost centre In the context of COST ACCOUNTING, a part of an organization (a COST CENTRE) which is engaged directly in production.

production cost variance The difference between the actual cost of production and the standard cost.

production overhead The costs of production that cannot be directly associated with units of production, i.e. the MANUFACTURING COSTS other than DIRECT COSTS. The terms 'FACTORY OVERHEAD' or 'MANUFACTURING OVERHEAD' can also be used.

production–volume ratio *See* CONTRIBUTION MARGIN RATIO.

productivity variance *See* OVERHEAD EFFICIENCY VARIANCE.

professional indemnity insurance Insurance taken out by professional firms (e.g. auditors) against losses arising from negligence or other malpractice.

profit In accounting terms, the excess of the REVENUES over the EXPENSES of the period. The revenues and expenses are those that *relate* to the period, rather than necessarily those that were received or paid in cash in the period. That is, the ACCRUAL BASIS OF ACCOUNTING is followed. Another way of thinking of profit is that it is the increase in wealth of an enterprise over a period, after transactions with the owners have been adjusted for.

profitability Not the same as the PROFIT of a business. A profit of a particular size may be impressive for a corner grocery shop, but unimpressive for a large multinational company. Measures of profitability try to put the profit into the context of the size of the business. Thus, profitability is normally a measure of the return on the CAPITAL invested in the business. One possible ratio of profitability is of net profit before interest and tax *to* the total long-term finance of the business. Another ratio is the net profit after interest and tax *to* the SHAREHOLDERS' EQUITY.

Such ratios become useful when one company can be compared to another or to the average for its industry, or when one company's ratio can be seen in the context of the ratios for previous years. In all cases, it is important to try to compare ratios that have been defined consistently.

profitability index Another way of carrying out CAPITAL INVESTMENT APPRAISAL using DISCOUNTED CASH FLOWS. Projects are ranked in terms of their ratio of PRESENT VALUES of cash flows to the initial investment needed.

profit and loss account The UK term for the statement that summarizes the difference between the REVENUES and EXPENSES of a period. Such statements may be drawn up frequently for the managers of a business, but a full audited statement is normally only published for each accounting year. The equivalent US expression is 'income statement'.

Publication of PROFIT AND LOSS ACCOUNTS was first made compulsory for companies in the UK by the Companies Act, 1929. There is now a choice of formats among the four set out in the Companies Act 1985. It is normal for UK companies to choose a 'vertical' or 'statement' format, rather than a two-sided or 'account' format. For private companies below a certain size there are some exemptions from publication requirements.

profit and loss account reserve The legal UK term for RETAINED EARNINGS.

profit and loss appropriation account An account in which the profit for a period is allocated to various purposes, e.g. the payment of dividends. In the UK, the PROFIT AND LOSS ACCOUNT includes this appropriation.

profit centre A part of an organization to which REVENUES and COSTS can be traced for COST ACCOUNTING purposes.

profit forecast As a technical term, a published forecast of profit by the directors of a company. This is required, along with a report by accountants, in the case of a company issuing shares for the first time.

profit margin The difference between sales and production costs (gross margin) or all costs (net margin), or the difference expressed as a RATIO of sales.

profit-related pay A former UK arrangement whereby certain profit-related elements of an employee's remuneration were tax free.

profits available for distribution Those undistributed profits of a company that are legally available to be distributed (e.g. as DIVIDENDS) to the SHARE-HOLDERS. The general rule in the UK is that these comprise accumulated REAL-IZED PROFITS less accumulated realized losses. A group cannot have such profits because only legal entities (e.g. the parent) can make distributions.

profit-sharing ratio In the context of a PARTNERSHIP, the ratio in which its profits and losses are to be shared among the partners.

profit-sharing scheme An arrangement, under the auspices of UK tax law, whereby shares are allocated to employees but held in a trust.

profit variance The difference between the actual profit for a period and the budgeted profit.

profit–volume chart A graph showing profit on the vertical axis and volume on the horizontal.

profit–volume ratio *See* CONTRIBUTION MARGIN RATIO.

pro forma financial statements In the context of FINANCIAL REPORTING, a supplementary set of FINANCIAL STATEMENTS drawn up on a different basis from the PRIMARY FINANCIAL STATEMENTS. In other contexts, the term could mean financial statements for future periods drawn up under budgeted assumptions.

pro forma invoice A draft of an invoice sent to a customer to give information rather than as a request for payment.

programme evaluation and review technique *See* CRITICAL-PATH ANALYSIS.

program trading The practice of using a computer program to determine when securities should be bought and sold.

progressive tax A tax whose marginal rate exceeds its average rate. A tax that is progressive to income takes a larger proportion of a taxpayer's tax base as the taxpayer's income rises. The INCOME TAXES in most countries are progressive.

progress payment *See* PAYMENT ON ACCOUNT.

projected unit credit method An ACTUARIAL VALUATION METHOD used to calculate an enterprise's DEFINED BENEFIT EMPLOYEE OBLIGATIONS. This method sees each period as giving rise to an additional unit of benefit entitlement and measures each unit separately to build up the final obligation. This is the method required by INTERNATIONAL ACCOUNTING STANDARDS COMMITTEE and US ACCOUNTING STANDARDS.

project finance Money provided for a particular project, possibly with the loans secured only on the returns and assets of the project itself.

promissory note A document recording an unconditional promise to pay a certain amount at a certain time to a certain person or to the bearer of the note.

proper accounting records A former UK legal term for records that enable the directors to ascertain their financial position at any moment and enable satisfactory FINANCIAL STATEMENTS to be drawn up.

property As a US term, this can mean ASSETS in general or TANGIBLE FIXED ASSETS. As a UK term, it usually has the narrower meaning of land and buildings.

property, plant and equipment The US term for TANGIBLE FIXED ASSETS.

property tax Any tax based on the value or other amount of land and buildings owned or used by the taxpayer. In the UK, BUSINESS RATES is such a tax.

proportional consolidation A technique used in some countries as part of the preparation of CONSOLIDATED FINANCIAL STATEMENTS for a group of companies. It brings into the consolidated financial statements the group's share of all the ASSETS, LIABILITIES, REVENUES and EXPENSES of the partly owned company. The method is rare in the UK and USA, but is used by companies in France (and to some extent in several other countries) for dealing with investments in companies that are held on a JOINT VENTURE basis with one or more other investing companies.

proportional tax A tax whose marginal rate is equal to its average rate. In such a tax, the proportion of a taxpayer's TAX BASE that is taken in tax stays the same as the tax base (or, sometimes, as the taxpayer's income even if that is not the tax base) rises.

proportionate consolidation See PROPORTIONAL CONSOLIDATION.

proposed dividend A DIVIDEND announced by the directors of a company as intended to be paid. In the UK, a proposed final dividend needs to be approved at the ANNUAL GENERAL MEETING of the SHAREHOLDERS. It then becomes a DECLARED DIVIDEND. In the UK, proposed dividends are accrued in FINANCIAL STATEMENTS. However, under US or INTERNATIONAL ACCOUNTING STANDARDS COMMITTEE rules, they are not, on the ground that (at least for dividends on ORDINARY SHARES) there is no obligation to pay them at the balance sheet date.

proprietary company A type of PRIVATE COMPANY found in certain countries, such as Australia.

proprietary view One way of looking at an enterprise (or particularly at a group of enterprises) whereby it is seen from the perspective of the SHAREHOLDERS (especially a parent company's shareholders) rather than from the managers' point of view (ENTITY VIEW).

pro rata consolidation *See* PROPORTIONAL CONSOLIDATION.

prospective application Use of a new accounting policy only for those events and transactions occurring after the date of the change to the new policy. This is obviously simpler than re-calculating the effects of all past transactions as though the new policy had been in force. However, it does lead to a mixture of treatments in the same FINANCIAL STATEMENTS. Depending on the reason for the change in policy, ACCOUNTING STANDARDS sometimes require RETROSPECTIVE APPLICATION instead.

prospectus A document published by a company and used by potential investors that precedes the issue of shares to the public. It outlines the financial position and prospects of the company, and gives details of the senior executives. Assistance with the preparation of the document will usually have been sought from merchant bankers/investment bankers, and independent accountants will report on its reasonableness. A summary of previous years' financial results will also be included.

provision Unfortunately, this important term has two distinct meanings: (a) an allowance (or value adjustment) against the value of an ASSET, and (b) a liability of uncertain timing or amount. A company may thus have provisions for (a) DEPRECIATION or BAD DEBTS, or (b) taxation or pensions or law suits that are expected to go against the company. In US terminology, 'allowance' is often used instead of 'provision' for the first of these meanings. All these provisions, when they were set up or added to, lead to a reduction in the reported profit figure. When the law suit is lost or the doubtful debt goes bad, the provision will be reduced, and (assuming that the provision was adequate) no further charge against profit will be needed.

However, usage is loose. For example, some US accountants talk about a 'bad debt reserve'; and in some continental European countries there may be very large 'provisions for contingencies' that Anglo-Saxon practice would treat as RESERVES.

See, also, CONTINGENT LIABILITY.

provision for bad debts An allowance against the recorded value of DEBTORS. The net amount is shown in a BALANCE SHEET. The provision can be 'specific' against a particular suspected defaulter or 'general' based on experience. The double entry for setting up or increasing the provision is an EXPENSE.

provision for depreciation An allowance against the BOOK VALUE of an ASSET with a limited useful life to record the reduction in that life in a period. The double entry for setting up or increasing the provision is a DEPRECIATION expense.

proxy A person authorized to act for another, e.g. to cast a SHAREHOLDER's vote at an ANNUAL GENERAL MEETING.

PRT Abbreviation for the PETROLEUM REVENUE TAX.

prudence A concept to be found in the accounting practices of nearly all countries. As the term suggests, it implies being cautious in the valuation of ASSETS or the measurement of PROFIT. It means taking the lowest reasonable estimate of the value of assets; anticipating losses but never anticipating profits (*see* REALIZATION CONVENTION).

In ACCOUNTING STANDARDS and company law, 'prudence' may be found as a compulsory, fundamental principle. However, the word conservatism is also in use, sometimes meaning a slightly stricter version of prudence. An example of prudence is the use of the 'LOWER OF COST AND MARKET' rule for the valuation of STOCKS (inventories).

Given that prudence is a bias in financial reporting, its importance has been down-graded over the decades. It is now seen as a component of RELIABILITY.

Pty Abbreviation for PROPRIETARY COMPANY.

Public Accounts Commission A committee of members of the UK's House of Commons that examines the FINANCIAL STATEMENTS of the NATIONAL AUDIT OFFICE and appoints its auditor.

publication of financial statements In the UK, making FINANCIAL STATE-MENTS available to the SHAREHOLDERS and the public. This is required for LIMITED COMPANIES. The statements are made available to the shareholders by being sent to them, and to the public by being filed with the REGISTRAR OF COMPANIES. In some countries, the idea of publication might be restricted in meaning to the public, given that the shareholders are the owners of the company. In several continental European countries, publication means displaying the statements in newspapers or gazettes, e.g. the BALO in France.

public company A company whose shares are allowed to be traded on a public market. In the UK, this means a PUBLIC LIMITED COMPANY. There are equivalent legal forms throughout the EU and elsewhere. However, the term is often used informally to mean a company that actually is listed on a stock exchange.

public issue/offering The issue of new securities by means of advertisement to the public. Compare, for example, RIGHTS ISSUE and PLACING.

publicity costs A possible heading for costs in a PROFIT AND LOSS ACCOUNT. It would include advertising costs and the expenses of related staff.

public limited company A company whose securities (shares and loan stock) may be publicly traded. In the UK, the legal form of such a company is set out in the COMPANIES ACTS. The company must have 'public limited company' (or plc) as part of its name. There are equivalents to this form in other European countries (*see* COMPANY), but in the USA the nearest equivalent is a corporation that is registered with the SECURITIES AND EXCHANGE COMMISSION.

There are about 10,000 companies in the plc form, about 2,000 of which are listed on the London Stock Exchange. Public companies have to obey slightly stricter rules than private companies. For example, there are no exemptions from the publication requirements of the Companies Acts, as apply to smaller private companies. Also, there is a slightly more restrictive definition of DISTRIBUTABLE PROFITS.

public sector accounting Accounting and reporting by all levels of government, including any government agencies that are not required to account as though they were in the private sector.

published accounts *See* PUBLICATION OF FINANCIAL STATEMENTS.

purchase accounting US term for ACQUISITION ACCOUNTING, the most common method of accounting for BUSINESS COMBINATIONS.

purchase consideration A legal term for something of value given as part of entering into a CONTRACT with a seller.

purchased goodwill The excess of the price paid for a business (whether or not the business is itself an entity) over the FAIR VALUES of the NET ASSETS purchased. In the case of the purchase of an entity, goodwill on CONSOLIDATION arises. Non-purchased goodwill can be called INTERNALLY GENERATED GOODWILL.

purchase method Another name for purchase accounting (*see* ACQUISITION ACCOUNTING).

purchase requisition An internal form completed in an organization requesting the purchasing department to make a purchase of specified items.

purchases budget An organization's detailed numerical plan (BUDGET) concerning the volumes and costs of purchases.

purchases day book A chronological listing of the purchases on CREDIT of an enterprise. This is a BOOK OF ORIGINAL ENTRY in a BOOKKEEPING system. It leads to credit entries to the accounts of individual suppliers (creditors) and combined DEBIT entries to the purchases account.

purchases journal Another term for PURCHASES DAY BOOK.

purchases ledger Another term for CREDITORS' LEDGER or bought ledger.

purchases ledger control account *See* CREDITORS' LEDGER CONTROL ACCOUNT.

purchases returns *See* RETURNS OUTWARDS.

purchase tax A type of tax levied on certain sales in proportion to the value of those sales. The seller collects the tax and pays it to the tax authorities. Unlike VALUE ADDED TAX, no deduction is allowed for tax paid on the seller's inputs.

purchasing power loss or gain A loss or gain due to holding MONETARY ITEMS in times of inflation. For example, as price levels rise, so an enterprise could be seen to make a gain on a borrowing that is fixed in monetary terms. *See* MONETARY WORKING CAPITAL ADJUSTMENT.

purchasing power parity theorem The theory that the EXCHANGE RATE between one country's currency and another's moves in proportion to the differential movements in their price levels, i.e. a comparatively high inflation country will have a depreciating currency. This theory seems to hold in the long run.

pure research In the context of accounting for RESEARCH AND DEVELOPMENT COSTS, experimental or theoretical work designed primarily to obtain scientific knowledge for its own sake rather than for a specific application.

push down accounting US term for incorporating into the FINANCIAL STATEMENTS of subsidiaries or other investees the adjustments (e.g. to FAIR VALUE) made in the preparation of CONSOLIDATED FINANCIAL STATEMENTS. This is generally not done in the EU, but it is in the USA, where subsidiaries' statements are not generally published.

put option A contract giving the holder the right to sell something at a specified price on a particular date or dates.

pyramid of ratios *See* RATIO PYRAMID.

Q

qualified audit report An AUDIT REPORT that states that (in UK terms) the FINANCIAL STATEMENTS give a TRUE AND FAIR VIEW *except for*, or *subject to*, certain qualifying remarks. The qualifications may concern the infringement of COMPANY LAW or ACCOUNTING STANDARDS. If there are sufficiently serious problems, the AUDITORS may withhold their opinion (perhaps due to major uncertainties) or may give an adverse opinion. The term does not refer to the qualifications of the auditors, although the UK COMPANIES ACT and the SECURITIES AND EXCHANGE COMMISSION in the USA do indeed require financial statements of certain companies to be audited by independent qualified accountants.

qualifying degree Those academic degrees that allow entry to training programmes or exemption from some examinations of professional accountancy bodies. *See* RELEVANT DEGREES.

qualifying distribution A former UK term for a payment to a SHAREHOLDER which was relevant for ADVANCE CORPORATION TAX.

qualifying loss In the context of UK taxation of business profits, a trading loss calculated according to tax regulations.

qualitative characteristics of accounting information Those qualities identified in a CONCEPTUAL FRAMEWORK that impart usefulness to FINANCIAL STATEMENTS. In particular, RELEVANCE and RELIABILITY are stressed.

quality assurance The processes in an organization whereby it tries to ensure that its products are fit for their purposes and of good quality.

quantitative budgets Generally, detailed numerical plans (BUDGETS) but of the non-financial aspects of an organization, such as hours worked or units of production.

quarter days Fixed days in the year when, traditionally, payments were made and contracts started. For example, in England and Wales (but not Scotland) these are 25 March (Lady Day), 24 June (Midsummer), 29 September (Michaelmas) and 25 December (Christmas). The INCOME TAX and CORPORATION TAX years in the UK derive from 25 March, as affected by calendar and other changes.

quarterly report In the context of financial reporting by companies registered with the SECURITIES AND EXCHANGE COMMISSION of the USA, a condensed set of FINANCIAL STATEMENTS required within ninety days of the end of a quarter.

quasi-subsidiary UK expression (in FINANCIAL REPORTING STANDARD 5) for an UNDERTAKING which should be treated as a SUBSIDIARY for the purposes of financial reporting because it is controlled for benefit by another company, even though it is not legally a subsidiary.

quick assets An inexact term, generally meaning those CURRENT ASSETS of an enterprise that are CASH or expected to turn into cash fairly quickly. This usually excludes INVENTORIES.

quick ratio A company's quick ratio (or 'acid test') is a measure of its LIQUIDITY. The ratio is normally measured by comparing the CURRENT ASSETS less INVENTORIES of a company to its CURRENT LIABILITIES. An alternative measure (of all current assets to all current liabilities) is called the CURRENT RATIO.

quick-succession relief In the context of the UK's INHERITANCE TAX, a tax reduction that is available when an inheritor dies within five years of a donor.

quorum The minimum number of people necessary to make valid decisions at a meeting, e.g. an ANNUAL GENERAL MEETING.

quoted company An alternative expression for LISTED COMPANY, i.e. a company whose name appears on the list of a stock exchange. Such companies must be public limited companies in the UK, or registered with the SECURITIES AND EXCHANGE COMMISSION in the USA.

quoted investments Shares or other securities of companies listed on a stock exchange.

R

R & D Abbreviation for research and development. *See* RESEARCH AND DEVELOPMENT COSTS.

random-walk hypothesis The suggestion that share prices move like molecules in Brownian motion, i.e. executing a random-walk whereby the next move cannot be predicted from past movements.

ratchet effect A tendency for variables (e.g. prices or wages) to move easily one way but not the other.

rate of exchange The RATIO at which one item (e.g. a unit of currency) is exchanged for another.

rate of interest The rate at which the return of interest is paid on an amount borrowed. The rate of interest is the price at which money is borrowed.

rate of return A measure of the profitability of a business; it normally compares the annual profit of the business with the amount of capital invested in it. The rate of return may be measured before tax or after tax; it is important to be clear which one is concerned with. Such a measure will normally be used to compare one company with another. Thus, it is also important to define the profit figure and the capital or asset base carefully.

rating In the context of the assessment of the quality of the loans issued by a company or other institution, the grading given by a credit RATING AGENCY.

rating agency A commercial organization specializing in the grading of corporate and other DEBT on the basis of its CREDITWORTHINESS.

ratio The expression of one number in terms of another. *See* RATIO ANALYSIS.

ratio analysis An activity of investment analysts, financial journalists, textbook writers and examination setters involving the comparison of a company with its past or with other companies, by setting one piece of financial data in the context of another. For example, comparisons would be obviously meaningless if one looked at the absolute levels of profit for two companies of different sizes. However, they may be valuable when the profits of the two companies can be set in the context of their TOTAL ASSETS or capital figures. This would lead to a comparison of PROFITABILITY ratios.

Similarly, there are GEARING ratios that measure the proportion of debt finance, and liquidity ratios that measure the size of CURRENT ASSETS in the context of the debts of a company. There is also the frequently used PRICE/EARNINGS RATIO, which sets the market price of an ordinary/common share in the context of its part of the annual earnings of the company.

Like most useful simplifications, ratio analysis contains great dangers. First, it is important to ensure that there is consistency of definition from year to year and from company to company. When international comparisons are being made, ratio analysis is especially dangerous, because there are major differences in the methods used for valuing assets and measuring profits.

Another danger is that 'ideal' ratios may be thought to exist. Let us take a LIQUIDITY RATIO as an example. One can find textbooks that suggest that the CURRENT RATIO (i.e. current assets/CURRENT LIABILITIES) should be above 2/1. However, it is nonsense to regard this as a general rule. For some companies in some industries (e.g. heavy engineering), this level might be dangerously low; for other companies (e.g. supermarket chains) it would suggest exceptional inefficiency in the use of resources.

ratio covenant A clause in a contract whereby an institution raising finance promises to comply with certain conditions expressed in the form of a RATIO. For example, a borrower might promise not to exceed a specified GEARING RATIO.

ratio pyramid The splitting up of a RATIO into subsidiary ratios. For example, a profit/assets ratio could be split into profit/sales and sales/assets, and so on. This could be presented as a pyramid with the first ratio at the top.

raw materials stock (inventory) At a point in time, an organization's amount of materials that have not been worked on but remain in their state as purchased.

real account An old term for an ACCOUNT in a BOOKKEEPING system which relates to various types of property, as opposed to a personal account (e.g. for a DEBTOR) or a nominal account, e.g. for an EXPENSE.

real estate US term for land and buildings.

real gain In the context of accounting or economics, an amount that has been corrected for inflation. Thus a 'real gain' is one that has been reduced to the extent that it is due merely to the change in the value of money. *See* INFLATION ACCOUNTING.

realizable assets An inexact term for ASSETS that could be sold fairly easily.

realizable profit A gain that could be made by selling an ASSET. A profit is realizable, but unrealized, if productive activity or price rises mean that assets could be sold for more than they were previously recorded at in an enterprise's accounts. Conventional HISTORICAL COST ACCOUNTING ignores realizable profits until they become objective and easily measurable by being realized, basically by sale. This is partly due to traditional CONSERVATISM, and partly to the greater simplicity and auditability of objective, realized amounts.

However, the problem that results from this 'REALIZATION CONVENTION' is that the profits recorded for any year are a very incomplete indication of what happened in that year. To take a simple example, suppose that an asset is bought as an investment, and that it is sold after ten years. In the first nine years no gains will be recorded, but in the tenth year the full gain will be treated as profit even if the asset had actually lost value during the tenth year.

realizable value The price that could be obtained on sale of an ASSET. Generally, accountants measure the NET REALIZABLE VALUE.

realization convention A well-established principle of conventional accounting, that gains or profits should only be recognized when they have been objectively realized by a sale being agreed. This is consistent with the all-pervasive concept of PRUDENCE, which anticipates losses but not profits. However, accounting rules and practice have been shifting towards treating gains on certain items (e.g. marketable securities) as realized even before sale.

realized gain If used to mean one type of REALIZED PROFIT, a profit coming from the sale of an ASSET other than in the normal course of trading, i.e. one could restrict the word 'gain' to sales of such assets as buildings rather than inventory. On the other hand, the word 'gain' could be used synonomously with profit.

realized profit (*or* loss) Profits that have been objectively verified by the evidence of a sale or some other event (*see* REALIZATION CONVENTION). Conventional accounting rests heavily upon the PRUDENCE and objectivity that this allows. COMPANY LAW in the UK requires that only realized profits may be recorded in the PROFIT AND LOSS ACCOUNT. However, 'realized' is to be interpreted in the context of 'principles generally accepted' for accounting purposes. Thus, the rules of ACCOUNTING STANDARDS will normally determine what is deemed to be realized.

Also, UK company law requires that dividend distributions must not exceed accumulated realized profits less accumulated realized losses. Thus, profits and dividends cannot result from a plot of land that has been growing in value over many years, until the land is sold.

real ledger An old-fashioned term which, in the context of DOUBLE-ENTRY BOOKKEEPING, means a book containing the accounts relating to tangible items such as buildings, as opposed to DEBTORS, CREDITORS, EXPENSES, etc. (*See*, also, NOMINAL LEDGER and PERSONAL LEDGER.)

real property *See* REALTY.

real rate of interest The RATE OF INTEREST adjusted for inflation. The higher the inflation, the higher the real rate of interest needs to be in order to take account of the falling value of money.

real terms accounting Forms of INFLATION ACCOUNTING that separate out the effects of general price movements (inflation) from those of the specific price movements relating to an enterprise.

realty Legal term for immovable property such as land and buildings.

rebate A DISCOUNT or a partial return of a payment.

recapitalization Re-arranging a company's financing by changing the balance of its DEBT compared to its SHARE CAPITAL.

receipts and payments account A summary of cash amounts coming in or going out in a period. For certain unincorporated enterprises, particularly those of a not-for-profit nature, conventional accounting, based on the ACCRUAL BASIS OF ACCOUNTING, may appear unnecessarily complicated.

As an example of the differences between this and conventional accounting, to consider the purchase of a new photocopying machine that is expected to last for ten years. Accountants would normally charge an amount of DEPRECIATION each year for the using up of the machine. However, a RECEIPTS AND PAYMENTS ACCOUNT would merely show the amount paid for the machine in the year that it was paid.

Non-profit organizations that are obliged to or wish to retain the accrual basis still produce INCOME STATEMENTS (US) or, in the UK, INCOME AND EXPENDITURE ACCOUNTS. These arrive at SURPLUSES or DEFICITS, rather than PROFITS or LOSSES.

receipts and payments basis Another term for a cash basis rather than an ACCRUAL BASIS OF ACCOUNTING. The term might be used in the context of the way in which certain items are calculated for tax purposes.

receivables The US expression for amounts of money due to a business from customers. This is often known as ACCOUNTS RECEIVABLE, but also there may be NOTES RECEIVABLE. The UK term is 'DEBTORS'.

receiver A person appointed to carry out RECEIVERSHIP.

receivership A state of affairs in which a company's ASSETS are being sold in order to repay a DEBT to a lender who holds a legal CHARGE over them.

recognition The process of including an item in a BALANCE SHEET or PROFIT AND LOSS ACCOUNT. An item should only be included if it meets the definition of an ELEMENT OF THE FINANCIAL STATEMENTS and it also meets certain recognition criteria. For example, an item might fit the definition of an ASSET, but to be recognized in a balance sheet it must also be probable that benefits will flow to the enterprise and the item must have a cost or value that can be measured reliably. Certain items, such as RESEARCH costs, may well be assets but they do not pass the recognition criteria, so they are treated as expenses.

recognized gain (or loss) A gain (or loss) recorded in an enterprise's FINANCIAL STATEMENTS. Compare to REALIZED PROFIT.

Recognized Professional Body A body recognized by the SECURITIES AND INVESTMENT BOARD in the UK as one whose members may carry out investment business, in cases (such as accountancy firms) where this is not their main business.

Recognized Qualifying Body An ACCOUNTANCY BODY recognized in the UK by the Secretary of State for Trade and Industry as one providing suitable qualifications for AUDITORS.

Recognized Supervisory Body An ACCOUNTANCY BODY recognized in the UK by the Secretary of State for Trade and Industry for the purposes of the supervision of REGISTERED AUDITORS.

Recommendations on Accounting Principles Documents issued from 1942 to 1969 by the INSTITUTE OF CHARTERED ACCOUNTANTS IN ENGLAND AND WALES in order to guide its members on appropriate financial reporting practices for companies. They have been superseded by ACCOUNTING STANDARDS.

recommended dividend *See* PROPOSED DIVIDEND.

reconciliation As an accounting term, the numerical explanation of how one set of numbers leads to another, e.g. there may be BANK RECONCILIATION STATEMENTS or reconciliations of the movement of FIXED ASSETS over a year.

recoverable advance corporation tax Formerly, amounts of ADVANCE CORPORATION TAX paid that could be used to reduce payments of tax in future.

recoverable amount The higher of the FAIR VALUE (or, under INTERNATIONAL ACCOUNTING STANDARDS COMMITTEE rules, the NET SELLING PRICE) of an

ASSET and the discounted expected future net cash receipts from it. The recoverable amount is used in some measures of IMPAIRMENT.

recovered overhead Synonym for ABSORBED OVERHEAD.

recovery rate Synonym for ABSORPTION RATE.

redeemable shares Shares that are allowed to be bought back by the company that originally issued them. In the UK, most shares are not redeemable, whereas most LOAN STOCKS or DEBENTURES are. However, there is legal provision for shares to be made redeemable, and this is more normally used for PREFERENCE SHARES.

The irredeemable nature of most UK shares is designed to protect creditors, by ensuring that a company cannot pay capital back to shareholders unless it is wound up, when all other claims would take priority. Thus, when UK shares are allowed to be redeemed, the conditions are strict, and amounts have to be transferred from DISTRIBUTABLE RESERVES to UNDISTRIBUTABLE RESERVES (called CAPITAL REDEMPTION RESERVES).

redemption The buying back of SECURITIES by their issuer.

redemption date The date on which a SECURITY is to be bought back by its issuer.

redemption premium An amount in excess of the NOMINAL VALUE of a SECURITY payable by its issuer on its REDEMPTION.

redemption yield A measure of the return to a holder of a SECURITY, after taking account of the amount receivable on REDEMPTION.

reducing-balance depreciation A technique for calculating the DEPRECIATION charge, usually for machines, whereby the annual charge reduces over the years of an ASSET's life. A fixed percentage depreciation is charged each year on the cost (first year) or the undepreciated cost (subsequent years). This technique is also known as declining-balance depreciation.

reduction of capital A reduction in the ISSUED SHARE CAPITAL of a company. This process is strictly regulated by law but, under certain circumstances, companies can buy back, or otherwise cancel, SHARES.

registered auditor An AUDITOR (a person or firm) approved to carry out audits under the COMPANIES ACT.

registered capital *See* AUTHORIZED SHARE CAPITAL.

registered company In the USA, a company registered with the SECURITIES AND EXCHANGE COMMISSION.

registered office The official address of a company for legal purposes.

registered trader In the context of the UK's VALUE ADDED TAX, a person who has registered to pay the tax. All traders with a turnover above a certain size must register.

register of charges A book (or other document) required by law to be kept by a UK company to record charges over its ASSETS.

register of directors and secretaries A book (or other document) required by law to be kept by a UK company to record details of its DIRECTORS and COMPANY SECRETARY.

register of directors' interests A book (or other document) required by law to be kept by a UK company to record details of the holdings of its DIRECTORS in SHARES or other SECURITIES of the company.

register of interests in shares A book (or other document) required by law to be kept by a UK PUBLIC LIMITED COMPANY to record details of any holding by one person of 3 per cent or more of any class of its VOTING SHARE capital.

register of members A book (or other document) required by law to be kept by UK LIMITED COMPANIES to record details of all its SHAREHOLDERS.

Registrar of Companies A UK government official who is charged with the collection, organization and granting of public access to the ANNUAL REPORTS of companies.

registration for value added tax *See* REGISTERED TRADER.

registration statement A document required by the SECURITIES AND EXCHANGE COMMISSION of the USA as part of the procedures for a new issue of shares.

regressive tax A tax whose average rate is above its MARGINAL RATE. A regressive tax takes a smaller proportion of a taxpayer's TAX BASE as the taxpayer's tax base (or, sometimes, as the taxpayer's income even if that is not the tax base) rises.

regular way contract In the context of FINANCIAL INSTRUMENTS, a contract for purchase or sale of ASSETS within the normal conventions of the market place for the particular assets.

Regulation In the context of harmonization in the EU, a document drafted by the Commission and adopted by the Council of Ministers that has direct effect without needing to be turned into national laws.

Regulation S-K An important source of rules relating to disclosures required from companies registered with the SECURITIES AND EXCHANGE COMMISSION in the USA.

Regulation S-X An important source of rules relating to the preparation of FINANCIAL STATEMENTS for those companies registered with the SECURITIES AND EXCHANGE COMMISSION in the USA, e.g. the regulation requires the presentation of cash flow statements.

reinsurance An arrangement whereby one insurance company insures another for all or part of the latter's risk on particular policies.

related company A former UK legal term for a company in which another held an interest above 20 per cent.

related parties Enterprises or persons who have a relationship with the reporting entity. The exact definition will vary from country to country, but in the UK and the USA it includes SUBSIDIARIES and ASSOCIATES and relatives of the directors. Generally, parties are considered to be related if one party can control the other party or exercise significant influence over its financial and operating decisions.

related party transaction A transfer of resources or obligations between RELATED PARTIES. The details of a related party transaction must be disclosed in the NOTES TO THE FINANCIAL STATEMENTS. This is because such transactions may be made at non-market prices, so they might mislead the readers of FINANCIAL STATEMENTS.

relevance A quality of information whereby the economic decisions of users of FINANCIAL STATEMENTS are facilitated by helping them to evaluate past, present or future events, or to confirm, or correct, former evaluations. This is one of the key desirable qualities that financial reporting information should have. However, sometimes, an increase in relevance may lead to some reduction in another key quality: RELIABILITY. For example, rapid information is likely to be more relevant but may be less reliable if prepared in a hurry and without being checked. Similarly, the FAIR VALUE of an ASSET may be more relevant information than its HISTORICAL COST, but fair values rely on estimates which may reduce reliability. This suggests that some trade-off between relevance and reliability is often necessary.

relevant accounts In the context of the determination of the DISTRIBUTABLE

PROFIT of a UK company, the latest audited FINANCIAL STATEMENTS presented to the SHAREHOLDERS.

relevant cost A cost that would be affected by a particular decision, so that it is relevant for appraisal of the decision.

relevant degrees Academic degrees that allow entry into the training programmes or exemption from some parts of the examinations of various accountancy bodies. In some cases, the term 'QUALIFYING DEGREE' is used instead. Normally, such degrees contain FINANCIAL ACCOUNTING, MANAGEMENT ACCOUNTING, business finance, taxation, economics, law and statistics. Thus, some degrees that might be thought to be relevant for the work of an accountant, like a degree specializing in economics, will not be counted for this purpose.

relevant income A type of REVENUE that would be affected by a particular decision, so that it is relevant for appraisal of the decision.

relevant revenue *See* RELEVANT INCOME.

reliability A quality of information when it is free from material error and bias. This is one of the key desirable qualities that financial reporting information should have. However, efforts to increase reliability may reduce RELEVANCE.

remuneration committee A committee commonly found in UK PUBLIC LIMITED COMPANIES that considers the remuneration of a company's EXECUTIVE DIRECTORS. The establishment of such committees was recommended by the GREENBURY REPORT, which proposed that they should comprise NON-EXECUTIVE DIRECTORS only.

rent The return to the owners of land and buildings for granting rights of use to others. *See*, also, ECONOMIC RENT.

re-order level In the context of the control of INVENTORY, the quantity below which an order for replacement is triggered.

re-order quantity In the context of the control of INVENTORIES, the amount which is automatically re-ordered when the inventory falls below a specified level.

reorganization costs The costs of restructuring the finances or operations of a company or group of companies. The costs should not be recognized, under UK or INTERNATIONAL ACCOUNTING STANDARDS COMMITTEE rules, until they have been carried out or there is an OBLIGATION to carry them out. In the UK, they should be shown separately as an EXCEPTIONAL ITEM if they have a material effect on the nature and focus of operations.

repairs and maintenance Expenses of an enterprise designed to maintain productive ASSETS at their originally assessed standard of performance. If EXPENDITURES improve an asset they should be added to the BOOK VALUE of the asset rather than being treated as repairs and maintenance expense.

replacement cost The cost of replacing an ASSET; generally this term has the same meaning as CURRENT REPLACEMENT COST.

replacement cost accounting A system of preparing FINANCIAL STATEMENTS in which all ASSETS (and expenses relating to them, such as DEPRECIATION) are valued at CURRENT REPLACEMENT COSTS.

reportable segment A segment of an enterprise for which information is required to be disclosed. Segmentation can either be by line of business or by geographical market. Generally, a segment is reportable if its sales, profit or assets are at least 10 per cent of the total figures for the REPORTING ENTITY.

report and accounts UK term for annual FINANCIAL STATEMENTS and other contents of the ANNUAL REPORT.

reporting accountants A firm of accountants, possibly a company's AUDITORS, who provide a report on the information contained in a company's PROSPECTUS for a new issue of shares.

reporting currency The currency used in presenting FINANCIAL STATEMENTS. Normally, the reporting currency is that of the country where the enterprise is legally based. For a group of companies, the reporting currency for the CONSOLIDATED FINANCIAL STATEMENTS is usually the currency of the country where the PARENT COMPANY is legally based.

reporting entity/enterprise The enterprise or group of enterprises for which a set of FINANCIAL STATEMENTS are designed to show the FINANCIAL POSITION and results.

report of the auditor UK legal term for AUDIT REPORT.

representation letter *See* LETTER OF REPRESENTATION.

representative member In the context of the UK's system of VALUE ADDED TAX, the company in a group of companies that is responsible for the returns to Customs and Excise.

repurchase agreement A CONTRACT committing an enterprise to re-acquire an ASSET that it is selling. Such a contract would specify the repurchase price (often higher than the sale price) and other details.

repurchase of own debt The buying back by a company of its own DEBT before the MATURITY DATE.

required rate of return The RATE OF RETURN set by an organization as the threshold (or hurdle) rate for positive decisions for its CAPITAL INVESTMENT APPRAISAL.

requisition A form used inside an organization as a request for action by one department to another. *See*, for example, PURCHASE REQUISITION.

research In the context of accounting, such scientific or technical investigations up to the stage of their application to the production of new materials or products. *See* RESEARCH AND DEVELOPMENT COSTS.

research and development costs The EXPENDITURES of an enterprise in a period on research and development activities. There has been controversy about how to account for these. They are designed to bring benefit in future years, so it would seem unfair to charge all the costs to the PROFIT AND LOSS ACCOUNT this year (when there are no related REVENUES), and to recognize the revenues in a later year (when there are no related EXPENSES). Thus, there is an argument for using the MATCHING CONCEPT, and for treating the expenditure as an ASSET (capitalizing it), and only treating it as an expense in the future when the related revenues arrive.

Unfortunately, this goes against the principle of PRUDENCE because one can never be totally sure what (if any) the future revenues coming from present research and development will be.

In the UK, STATEMENT OF STANDARD ACCOUNTING PRACTICE 13 allows some DEVELOPMENT EXPENDITURE (but not research) to be capitalized under certain prudent conditions. Development expenditure may be distinguished because it has practical application to products or processes. Under INTERNATIONAL ACCOUNTING STANDARDS COMMITTEE rules, capitalization of such development costs is required. In the USA and Germany it is not allowed.

reservation of title A legal term for the keeping of ownership of goods sold by a seller until the buyer has paid. In contract law in the UK, this is achieved by a ROMALPA CLAUSE.

reserve An amount of PROFIT or other gain of an enterprise not yet distributed to its owners. Reserves should be distinguished from PROVISIONS. The latter are charged in the calculation of profit, and represent reductions in the value of ASSETS or the recognition of estimated LIABILITIES. Neither reserves nor provisions are amounts of CASH. A charge for the increase in a provision is an accounting expense, and setting up a reserve is an accounting allocation of UNDISTRIBUTED PROFIT or gains. Reserves belong to SHAREHOLDERS, and are part of a total of shareholders' equity, which also includes SHARE CAPITAL. This total is represented by all the assets of the business, less the liabilities owed to outsiders. The amount of reserves can be split into various headings, e.g. to denote that some parts are legally undistributable.

It should be noted that this terminology is used somewhat loosely by some accountants. For details of examples of PROVISIONS *see* the entry under that heading. In the USA, 'reserve' is sometimes used to cover some of the meanings of 'provision' in the UK.

reserve accounting The taking of items of gain or loss straight to RESERVES rather than passing them through the PROFIT AND LOSS ACCOUNT.

reserve arising on consolidation A former location on the BALANCE SHEET for NEGATIVE GOODWILL.

reserve recognition accounting In OIL AND GAS ACCOUNTING, the capitalization of discoveries of oil and gas based on their value rather than on the cost of discovering them.

residence In taxation law, the country in which a taxpayer is deemed to live.

residual equity The remaining interest in a company after all other claimants have been satisfied. Generally, this means the interest of the holders of ORDINARY SHARES.

residual income In the context of calculations inside a complex organization, the NET INCOME of a division after taking account of a notional interest expense for the resources used by it.

residual value The sale value of an ASSET at the end of its useful economic life. An estimate of this amount is deducted from the asset's cost in the calculation of DEPRECIATION under certain methods. The term 'SCRAP VALUE' is also used.

resolution A decision of a meeting of SHAREHOLDERS. *See*, for example, ORDINARY RESOLUTION.

responsibility accounting A system of control within an organization whereby individual managers at all levels are held responsible for specific costs and, perhaps, REVENUES.

responsibility centre A section of an organization for which an individual manager is held to account in terms of its COSTS or REVENUES.

restricted funds In the context of a charity, amounts of money that can only be applied for particular purposes. Such funds have to be accounted for separately.

restricted surplus A US expression for amounts of past PROFIT that are unavailable for distribution to SHAREHOLDERS. The UK equivalent would be 'undistributable reserves'.

restrictive covenant A clause in a CONTRACT whereby one party to the contract is stopped from certain actions.

restructuring A programme of activities whereby the management of an enterprise materially changes either the scope of its business or the manner in which the business is conducted.

retail inventory method A method for INVENTORY VALUATION used in retail stores in which all the inventories are counted and valued at retail marked prices, and then individually or in total the retail values are reduced to an estimate of cost by deducting the MARK-UP.

Retail Price Index A UK government-published monthly index of the prices of a typical basket of goods purchased by retail customers. It is one measure of inflation. The equivalent in the USA is the Consumer Price Index. For financial reporting purposes, such an index is used in CURRENT PURCHASING POWER ACCOUNTING.

retained earnings/profits Amounts of PROFIT that have not yet been paid out as DIVIDENDS. The context should make clear whether the term refers to the amounts earned in the period or to the cumulative amounts for all periods.

retention of title *See* RESERVATION OF TITLE.

retentions *See* RETAINED EARNINGS.

retirement benefit plans *See* EMPLOYEE BENEFITS.

retirement relief In the context of the UK's system of CAPITAL GAINS TAX, a reduction in the tax related to the disposal of certain business assets.

retrospective application Use of a new accounting policy for all past, present and future events and transactions as if the new accounting policy had always been in use. Such application is required for some types of changes in accounting policy. It enables an easier comparison of financial information over time. However, it involves more complex calculations than PROSPECTIVE APPLICATION.

return on assets A company's PROFIT before interest and tax for a period expressed as a percentage of its TOTAL ASSETS.

return on capital employed (ROCE) A company's PROFIT for a period expressed as a percentage of its resources used. The profit is generally that before interest and tax, and the resources used (capital employed) might be the NET ASSETS, or might be the TOTAL ASSETS less CURRENT LIABILITIES.

return on equity (ROE) A company's PROFIT after interest and tax for a period expressed as a percentage of the SHAREHOLDERS' FUNDS.

return on investment (ROI) Various measures of PROFITABILITY, such as RETURN ON CAPITAL EMPLOYED. These measures can be used for whole enterprises or for divisions of them.

return on ordinary owners' equity (ROOE) A company's EARNINGS expressed as a percentage of the SHAREHOLDERS' FUNDS relating to ordinary shareholders.

return on owners' equity *See* RETURN ON EQUITY.

return on plan assets Revenue derived from PLAN ASSETS (such as interest and dividends), plus REALIZED and UNREALIZED gains or losses on the plan assets.

returns inwards book In a BOOKKEEPING system, a BOOK OF ORIGINAL ENTRY in which RETURNS INWARDS are recorded. Such records lead to CREDIT entries in individual DEBTOR's accounts and to amounts that are eventually set off against sales.

returns inwards (sales returns) Goods formerly sold but now returned to an enterprise by its customers as unwanted or unsatisfactory.

returns on investments and servicing of finance One of the main headings in a CASH FLOW STATEMENT in the UK. It contains most types of receipts from INVESTMENTS and payments to providers of finance. Excluded are dividends received from investments accounted for by the EQUITY METHOD and payments of dividends on equity capital.

returns outwards Goods formerly purchased but now returned by an enterprise to suppliers as unwanted or unsatisfactory.

returns outwards book In a BOOKKEEPING system, a BOOK OF ORIGINAL ENTRY in which RETURNS OUTWARDS are recorded. Such records lead to DEBIT entries in individual CREDITOR's accounts and to amounts that are eventually set off against purchases.

revalorization of currency The reform of a country's currency by its government whereby one currency is replaced by another. This may be part of a process to halt HYPERINFLATION and continuous DEVALUATIONS of the currency.

revaluation The changing (generally upwards) of the value of an ASSET on a BALANCE SHEET. Conventional accounting uses HISTORICAL COST as the basis for the valuation of assets. However, in some countries, including the UK but not the USA, it is acceptable to revalue FIXED ASSETS. These revaluations, often on the basis of CURRENT REPLACEMENT COST, must be kept up to date. It is quite common for large UK companies to show land and buildings at revalued amounts in their balance sheets. Clearly, one purpose of this is to avoid a seriously misleading impression of their worth, when prices have risen substantially.

revaluation account In the context of PARTNERSHIP ACCOUNTS, an account used to record the counter entries when ASSETS and LIABILITIES are revalued to current values on the admission, death or retirement of a partner. The balance on the account is shared amongst the partners.

revaluation method One means of calculating DEPRECIATION for such ASSETS as loose tools. Instead of making estimates (of, for example, useful lives) relating to the individual assets, the total of such assets is valued at the beginning and at the end of the accounting period, and the difference (after adjusting for purchases) is the depreciation.

revaluation of currency The change (generally a rise) in the value of a currency as expressed in terms of another currency (or, formerly, of gold).

revaluation reserve The sum of UNREALIZED GAINS (that have not been taken to the PROFIT AND LOSS ACCOUNT) relating to FIXED ASSETS that have been revalued above their cost.

revenue Traditionally, a receipt of any period that relates to the ACCOUNTING PERIOD. An analogous definition applies to EXPENSES and payments. This is in accordance with the ACCRUAL BASIS OF ACCOUNTING. For example, if an insurance company receives cash in 2005 for a 2006 insurance premium, the REVENUE will be recognized in 2006, not in the year of receipt. Similarly, when sales are made to customers 'on account' or 'on credit', those sales are recognized immediately, rather than waiting until the cash arrives.

A more modern approach would concentrate on the BALANCE SHEET, and would define revenues as the gross inflow of economic benefits during a period that results in increases in EQUITY, other than increases relating to contributions from equity participants.

In the INTERNATIONAL ACCOUNTING STANDARDS COMMITTEE's framework the word 'revenue' is distinguished from GAINS. In the UK, revenues are included in gains.

revenue centre The analogy to a COST CENTRE for the purpose of collecting together an organization's REVENUES by section for the purposes of MANAGEMENT ACCOUNTING.

revenue expenditure An apparently self-contradictory term used in the UK for those COSTS which are charged currently to the PROFIT AND LOSS ACCOUNT rather than being capitalized. The opposite term is CAPITAL EXPENDITURE.

revenue recognition The process of treating items as revenues to be recorded in the current period's INCOME STATEMENT. According to the INTERNATIONAL ACCOUNTING STANDARDS COMMITTEE, revenue should be recognized when control of ASSETS has passed to another party and when the amount of revenue (and any costs to be incurred) can be measured reliably and will probably be received.

revenue reserve A former UK legal term for amounts of RETAINED PROFIT that are available for distribution as DIVIDENDS. Other reserves would be CAPITAL RESERVES.

revenue transaction A transaction leading to REVENUE EXPENDITURE.

reverse acquisition An acquisition whereby Enterprise A obtains ownership of the shares of Enterprise B but as part of the exchange transaction issues enough VOTING SHARES, as CONSIDERATION, that control of the combined enterprise passes to the owners of Enterprise B.

reverse premium In the context of LEASES, a cash payment made to encourage a LESSEE to take out a lease.

reverse takeover The purchase of a larger (or listed) company by a smaller (or unlisted) one.

reverse yield gap An excess of the interest rate on government bonds over the YIELD on EQUITIES.

reversing entries In a DOUBLE-ENTRY BOOKKEEPING system, entries made at the beginning of an ACCOUNTING PERIOD to correct for adjustments made when closing the BOOKS OF ACCOUNT at the end of the previous period.

reversionary bonus A sum added by a life assurance company to the amount payable on a life assurance policy.

Review Panel A committee (properly called the Financial Reporting Review Panel) which is part of the standard setting and enforcement machinery of the FINANCIAL REPORTING COUNCIL introduced in the UK in 1990. The Review Panel investigates suspected 'DEFECTIVE ACCOUNTS', in particular breaches of COMPANY LAW (including the failure of accounts to give a TRUE AND FAIR VIEW), which are referred to it. The Panel can then take companies to court under procedures introduced by the Companies Act 1989.

revision variance In the context of a STANDARD COSTING system, an adjustment to a basic standard to take account of changed circumstances. *See*, also, OPERATING VARIANCES.

rights issue The sale of additional shares by a company to its existing SHAREHOLDERS. The 'rights' to buy the shares, at slightly lower than the MARKET PRICE in order to ensure a full sale, are given out in proportion to the existing holdings. Thus, the existing group of shareholders may be largely preserved.

Since the sale is to existing shareholders, the advertisement and PROSPECTUS preparations need not be so expensive as for issues to the public. Thus, rights issues are cheaper and more popular than other means of selling new shares.

Rights issues should be distinguished from BONUS ISSUES (also called capitalization or scrip issues), where no money is paid to the company, but where existing shareholders receive a proportionate amount of free extra shares, and DISTRIBUTABLE PROFITS are relabelled as SHARE CAPITAL.

risk-based audit A type of AUDIT in which concentration of effort is placed on those areas of the audited organization that are judged to be most likely to contain error or fraud.

risk capital Finance (such as that in exchange for ORDINARY SHARES) supplied to a company that is expected to lead to a good return because it carries some risk of loss.

risk class A category of investments deemed to have similar risk to each other.

risk-free rate of return The interest rate to be received from an investment with no risk of CAPITAL LOSS or of non-payment of the INTEREST. Generally, the interest rate on government bonds of respected countries would approximate to this.

risk premium The excess of the RATE OF RETURN on an investment over the return on risk-free assets such as government bonds.

ROCE Abbreviation for RETURN ON CAPITAL EMPLOYED.

ROE Abbreviation for RETURN ON EQUITY.

ROI Abbreviation for RETURN ON INVESTMENT.

rolling budget A detailed numerical plan (a BUDGET) for an organization or section of it that is extended into the future by one budget period (e.g. a month) as each period passes.

rolling GAAP In the context of COVENANTS, the ACCOUNTING POLICIES of an enterprise at the current date. The reverse of this is FROZEN GAAP, under which such things as GEARING RATIOS would be measured using the rules in force when the covenant was drawn up.

roll-over relief A postponement of the taxation of the CAPITAL GAINS realized on the sale of those ASSETS that are replaced.

Romalpa clause A clause (named after a legal case of 1976) which might be inserted by a seller into a contract of sale in order to achieve RESERVATION OF TITLE.

ROOE Abbreviation for RETURN ON ORDINARY OWNERS' EQUITY.

rotation of directors The retirement of DIRECTORS of a company (generally one-third of them each year), as generally required by the ARTICLES OF ASSOCIATION of UK companies. Retiring directors can stand again for election.

royal charter A document whereby the Crown grants corporate status to an entity. Some companies used to be created by royal charter. The ACCOUNTANCY BODIES in the UK have such charters.

Royal Mail case Perhaps the most famous British legal case (of 1931) concerned with financial reporting. Among other things, it drew attention to the need to control SECRET RESERVES.

royalty A payment made by a user of ASSETS (such as minerals or intellectual property) to someone with rights over them.

RPI Abbreviation for a RETAIL PRICE INDEX.

running costs The recurring expenses relating to FIXED ASSETS. Such expenses include servicing and CONSUMABLE MATERIALS such as fuel.

S

SA Abbreviation for *société anonyme*, a French, Belgian, Luxembourg or Swiss PUBLIC COMPANY.

SAB Abbreviation for STAFF ACCOUNTING BULLETIN (in the USA).

safety stock *See* BUFFER STOCK.

salaried partner Generally a junior member of a PARTNERSHIP who receives a fixed remuneration rather than a share of profits.

sale and leaseback A method of raising funds by a company without immediately depleting resources or incurring LIABILITIES. If a company owns and uses FIXED ASSETS, it may find it advantageous, for tax or other reasons, to sell them to a financial institution (the LESSOR) which then leases them back to the company.

sale and repurchase agreement A legal arrangement whereby an ASSET is sold by an enterprise but can or must be bought back under fixed conditions. If the seller retains most of the risks and rewards, then the sale is deemed not to have taken place for financial reporting purposes.

sale by tender A method of issuing SECURITIES in which investors are asked to bid at prices above a specified minimum.

sale or return basis An arrangement whereby a seller agrees to take back goods from the buyer under certain conditions.

sales The figure for sales, recorded in the FINANCIAL STATEMENTS for a period, which includes all those sales agreed or delivered in the period, rather than those that are paid for in cash. The sales figure will be shown net of sales taxes, i.e. VALUE ADDED TAX in the UK.

In the UK, the word 'TURNOVER' is used in the financial statements, although 'sales' is generally used in the BOOKS OF ACCOUNT.

sales account The ACCOUNT in a BOOKKEEPING system that records all the SALES of an enterprise, whether for cash or on credit.

sales budget An organization's detailed numerical plan for the volume of SALES and other REVENUES, split into periods.

sales day book A chronological listing of the SALES on credit of an enterprise. In a BOOKKEEPING system, this is a BOOK OF ORIGINAL ENTRY that records all the invoices sent to customers. From it, entries are raised in the accounts of individual DEBTORS and, in total, to the SALES ACCOUNT. Despite its name, this book deals only with sales on credit; the cash sales are initially recorded in the CASH BOOK.

sales discount A reduction in the price of goods allowed by a seller to customers, generally those who pay cash.

sales forecast An estimate of sales based on experience and expectations of market conditions. The forecast may need to be adjusted to take account of production and other internal factors before the SALES BUDGET can be established.

sales invoice A document sent by a seller to a customer outlining details of a sale.

sales journal *See* SALES DAY BOOK.

sales ledger *See* DEBTORS' LEDGER. Despite its name, this ledger contains the collection of accounts of DEBTORS, i.e. only sales made on credit.

sales ledger control account *See* DEBTORS' LEDGER CONTROL ACCOUNT.

sales margin price variance The difference between the actual prices of goods sold and the standard prices, multiplied by the actual volume sold.

sales margin volume variance The difference between the actual and budgeted amount of goods sold in a period, valued at the standard PROFIT MARGIN.

sales mix The proportions of various products that make up the total units sold by an organization in a period.

sales price variance *See* SALES MARGIN PRICE VARIANCE.

sales returns *See* RETURNS INWARDS BOOK.

sales returns book *See* RETURNS INWARDS BOOK.

sales revenue *See* SALES.

sales tax General term for a tax levied at the POINT OF SALE of goods. Specific examples of such taxes are VALUE ADDED TAX and PURCHASE TAX.

sales volume The quantity (rather than the value) of units sold by an enterprise in a period.

sales volume variance *See* SALES MARGIN VOLUME VARIANCE.

salvage value *See* RESIDUAL VALUE.

samurai bond Informal term for a loan issued in yen in Japan by a foreign issuer.

Sandilands Report The report of 1975 by the UK government committee on INFLATION ACCOUNTING chaired by Sir Francis Sandilands. It recommended that a system of CURRENT COST ACCOUNTING be developed to take account of changing prices.

SARL Abbreviation for *société à responsabilité limitée*, a Belgian, French or Luxembourg PRIVATE COMPANY.

satisficing An economist's term for achieving a target level of profits (or of some other variable) rather than maximizing profits. This may avoid adverse reaction from SHAREHOLDERS and so allow managers to put their energies into other activities, e.g. maximizing their own benefits.

save-as-you-earn A government-sponsored arrangement in the UK whereby regular savings can be made in a tax-free environment.

savings and loan associations Approximate US equivalent of building societies.

schedule In the context of a COMPANIES ACT, an appendix containing detailed requirements. For example, many of the rules for UK financial reporting are contained in Schedule 4 to the Companies Act 1985.

schedules of tax *See* INCOME TAX SCHEDULES.

scheme of arrangement A compromise agreement, made in difficult financial circumstances, between a company and its CREDITORS or SHAREHOLDERS. It will generally involve the payment by the company of only a proportion of its DEBTS.

scrap The waste products left over after a production process, which may either be sold or re-processed.

scrap value *See* RESIDUAL VALUE.

scrip A UK term (derived from 'subscription') for the certificates evidencing the existence of securities.

scrip issue *See* BONUS SHARES.

SEAQ Abbreviation for Stock Exchange Automated Quotations system.

SEC Abbreviation for the SECURITIES AND EXCHANGE COMMISSION (of the USA).

secondary auditor In cases where a group of companies has more than one AUDITOR, an auditor other than that of the PARENT COMPANY.

secondary market A market for the sale and purchase of SECURITIES other than the primary market in them when they were first sold by the issuing company.

secret reserves Various means by which a company, particularly a financial institution, can make its true financial strength unclear in its FINANCIAL STATEMENTS. The purpose of this is to build up resources in case of future difficulty. If that future difficulty eventually emerges, it may be possible to hide it completely by merely absorbing it with the secret reserves. This event may avoid a dangerous loss of confidence in the bank or other company concerned.

Secret reserves may be created by unnecessarily recording diminutions in the value of ASSETS or by creating unnecessary PROVISIONS.

secured A term that can be applied to various forms of LIABILITY, such as CREDITORS or DEBENTURES, when the DEBTOR concerned has a legal charge over the creditor's ASSETS which can be brought into effect if the creditor defaults.

securities Those financial assets, such as shares or debentures, that are represented by documents stating the size of holdings.

Securities and Exchange Commission (SEC) US government agency set up in 1934 after the Wall Street crash of 1929. Its function is to control the issue and exchange of publicly traded shares. Companies with such shares must register with the SEC, and then obey a mass of detailed regulations about DISCLOSURE and AUDIT of financial information. An SEC-registered company in the USA is the nearest equivalent to a PUBLIC LIMITED COMPANY in the UK. In both countries, not all such companies are listed on a stock exchange.

The SEC issues its own rules for financial reporting, such as REGULATION S-X, which requires annual statements of changes in financial position and quarterly disclosure of sales and profit. Indeed, the only powerful requirements for disclosure and audit in the USA come from the SEC, directly or indirectly. The SEC requires its registrants to report using 'GENERALLY ACCEPTED ACCOUNTING PRINCIPLES' (GAAP), which include ACCOUNTING STANDARDS. The private body that now sets accounting standards – the FINANCIAL ACCOUNTING STANDARDS BOARD – is given 'substantial authoritative support' by the SEC. However, the SEC's interpretation of GAAP is a key issue, and its staff publish their views in STAFF ACCOUNTING BULLETINS.

The form that must be sent annually by REGISTERED COMPANIES to the SEC is called FORM 10-K. This contains much accounting and economic information that supplements the published FINANCIAL STATEMENTS. Form 10-K is available to the public. Foreign registrants who do not produce US GAAP statements must file FORM 20-F.

Securities and Futures Authority A UK self-regulatory organization that supervised brokers and dealers in securities. Its functions were transferred to the FINANCIAL SERVICES AUTHORITY.

Securities and Investment Board A body that was responsible to the Secretary of State for Trade and Industry for the regulation of the financial markets in the UK. The self-regulatory organizations in various fields reported to it. Its functions were transferred to the FINANCIAL SERVICES AUTHORITY in 2000/1.

securitization The transformation of FINANCIAL ASSETS into SECURITIES.

security Backing for a loan in the form of an ASSET that could be sold if a borrower defaulted. This is sometimes called 'COLLATERAL'. *See*, also, SECURITIES.

segmental reporting UK term for what the INTERNATIONAL ACCOUNTING STANDARDS COMMITTEE calls SEGMENT REPORTING.

segment assets Those ASSETS that are used by a segment in its operating activities and that either are directly attributable to the segment or can be reasonably allocated to the segment.

segment expense Expense resulting from the operating activities of a segment that is directly attributable to the segment or can be reasonably allocated to it.

segment reporting An analysis of SALES, PROFIT or ASSETS by line of business or by geographical area. This analysis is required to be disclosed for REPORTABLE SEGMENTS by certain enterprises.

segment result SEGMENT REVENUE less SEGMENT EXPENSE. Segment result is determined before any adjustments for MINORITY INTEREST.

segment revenue Revenue reported in the enterprise's INCOME STATEMENT that is directly attributable to a segment or can be reasonably allocated to it.

self-assessment In the context of systems of taxation, an arrangement whereby a taxpayer is initially responsible for filling-in the details of tax forms and many of the calculations which work towards the annual assessment of taxes due.

self-balancing ledgers Those ledgers (such as the NOMINAL LEDGER) within a DOUBLE-ENTRY BOOKKEEPING system that should balance because they are designed to have the same totals of DEBIT and CREDIT entries.

self-financing The use by an enterprise of its own PROFITS as a source of funds for expansion.

self-regulatory organizations Organizations authorized in the UK by the FINANCIAL SERVICES AUTHORITY to regulate sections of the financial markets.

selling costs Another term for DISTRIBUTION COSTS.

selling overhead In the context of COST ACCOUNTING, the DISTRIBUTION COSTS of an organization, such as advertising costs and the wages of sales staff.

selling price variance *See* SALES MARGIN PRICE VARIANCE.

semi-fixed cost A term with the same meaning as SEMI-VARIABLE COST.

semi-variable cost An item of cost containing both fixed and variable elements such as an organization's expense for using a utility that may contain an annual standing charge.

senior debt/security US term for FINANCIAL INSTRUMENTS that, in the event of default, have a higher claim on the ASSETS of the issuer than other DEBT.

sensitivity analysis Presenting calculations in such a way as to show how the conclusions would change as certain variables changed. This could be used, for example, in CAPITAL INVESTMENT APPRAISAL to see how projects would appear under different assumptions about DISCOUNT RATES.

separable asset An ASSET that could be sold by an enterprise without selling the whole business. It is not internationally agreed whether this is the same thing as an identifiable asset (*see* IDENTIFIABLE ASSETS AND LIABILITIES).

separable costs In the context of a joint production process, those costs incurred after the SPLIT-OFF POINT.

separate taxation of wife's earnings As a former part of the UK's system of INCOME TAX, an option to treat the earnings of a husband and wife separately. This is now not relevant because there is always separate taxation.

separation point *See* SPLIT-OFF POINT.

sequestration A legal process in which a court arranges for the assets of a person to be held while a dispute or a payment is settled.

Serious Fraud Office A government-funded body that investigates and, where appropriate, prosecutes major cases of commercial fraud.

SERPS Abbreviation for the UK's State Earnings-Related Pension Scheme.

service contract *See* EMPLOYMENT CONTRACT.

service cost centre A COST CENTRE within an organization that collects the costs of a SERVICE DEPARTMENT.

service department A section within an organization which provides services to production departments and for which costs are separately collected.

service potential The benefits expected from an ASSET as a result of using it to the end of its USEFUL ECONOMIC LIFE.

set-off *See* OFFSETTING.

settlement date The date that a FINANCIAL ASSET is delivered to the enterprise that purchased it.

settlement (of employee benefit obligations) The cancellation of all further OBLIGATIONS for the benefits provided under a DEFINED BENEFIT PLAN, e.g. this might occur when a lump-sum cash payment is made to pensioners in exchange for their rights to receive specified post-employment benefits.

settlement value The amounts expected to be paid to satisfy a LIABILITY in the normal course of business.

set-up time The time taken to prepare a machine or process for normal operations.

Seventh Directive A DIRECTIVE on COMPANY LAW of the EU concerning the CONSOLIDATED FINANCIAL STATEMENTS of groups headed by a LIMITED COMPANY. The Directive was adopted by the Council of Ministers in 1983 and led to a degree of harmonization in group accounting.

severe long-term restrictions A legal phrase used to describe those constraints on the control over the ASSETS of a SUBSIDIARY that are so severe that it should not be consolidated.

SFA Abbreviation for the SECURITIES AND FUTURES AUTHORITY (of the UK).

SFAC Abbreviation for STATEMENTS OF FINANCIAL ACCOUNTING CONCEPTS (in the USA).

SFAS Abbreviation for STATEMENTS OF FINANCIAL ACCOUNTING STANDARDS (in the USA).

SFO Abbreviation for the SERIOUS FRAUD OFFICE (of the UK).

shadow director A person who, while not formally being a DIRECTOR of a company, nevertheless has influence over the company like that of a director. For certain legal purposes (e.g. WRONGFUL TRADING), a shadow director is treated as a director.

shadow price The increase in the value of a business (i.e. the PROFIT) that would be forgone if the business had one unit fewer of a scarce resource.

shallow discount bond A BOND issued at a discount of not more than 10 per cent.

share A part of the ownership of a company. SHAREHOLDERS jointly own a company. In the case of most companies, the shareholders have LIMITED LIABILITY for the company's DEBTS. Thus, they are content to delegate the management of the company to boards of directors.

Most of the SHARE CAPITAL of a company will normally have been provided by the holders of ORDINARY SHARES (UK)/COMMON STOCK (US). These shareholders can generally exercise their votes at the company's ANNUAL GENERAL MEETING, when DIVIDEND decisions and much other business is done. They also share in the prosperity of the company because the dividends and the share value may be expected to rise over the years.

Shares are recorded in FINANCIAL STATEMENTS at their par or NOMINAL VALUE, which distinguishes one type of share from another. Amounts paid in by shareholders who bought shares from the company at above par value are shown as SHARE PREMIUM (UK)/PAID-IN SURPLUS (US).

Shares are normally not redeemable by the company that issued them. However, most of the business of stock exchanges is done in the secondary (i.e. second-hand) market for such securities. *See*, also, BONUS SHARES, PREFERENCE SHARES and RIGHTS ISSUES.

share capital The number of a company's shares multiplied by the NOMINAL VALUE. *See* AUTHORIZED SHARE CAPITAL and ISSUED SHARE CAPITAL.

share certificate A document evidencing the existence and ownership of a SHARE.

shareholder A member (or part-owner) of a COMPANY LIMITED BY SHARES. A more common term in the USA is 'stockholder'.

shareholders' equity One of the US terms for SHAREHOLDERS' FUNDS.

shareholders' funds The total of the shareholders' interests in a company. This will include the original SHARE CAPITAL, amounts contributed in excess of the NOMINAL VALUE of shares (i.e. SHARE PREMIUM), RETAINED PROFITS and other RESERVES. In the USA, this total is sometimes called stockholders' (or shareholders' or shareowners') equity. The shareholders' funds will equal the NET ASSETS or net worth of the company.

share option A contract enabling the holder to buy a share in a company at a specified price during a specified period.

shareowners' equity One of the US terms for SHAREHOLDERS' FUNDS.

share premium Amounts paid into a company (by SHAREHOLDERS when they purchased shares from the company) in excess of the NOMINAL VALUE of the shares. Share premium may be treated for most purposes exactly as if it were SHARE CAPITAL. Both are included in SHAREHOLDERS' EQUITY. One US equivalent is 'paid-in surplus'.

share premium account The UK heading shown in a BALANCE SHEET for a company's amount of SHARE PREMIUM.

share price indices A measure of the average price of a set of shares of listed companies, expressed as a percentage of the average at a base date. For example, the most widely used index on the London Stock Exchange is the Financial Times Stock Exchange (FTSE) Index of 100 leading shares, calculated as a value-weighted arithmetic mean. Another index, the Financial Times Ordinary Share Index, is based on 30 shares.

In New York, there is the Dow Jones Industrial Average and Standard and Poor's 500. In Hong Kong, there is the Hang Seng index; in Frankfurt the DAX; and in Paris the CAC.

share register *See* REGISTER OF MEMBERS.

share split *See* STOCK SPLIT.

share transfer form (or deed) A document that must be signed by a seller of shares in order to enable the sale.

share warrant A document giving its owner the right to purchase a specified number of particular shares at a specified price and during a specified period.

shell company A legal entity with little activity and few ASSETS which could be bought cheaply by another enterprise as a vehicle for its own activities.

short-dated security A security which is approaching its MATURITY DATE. At this stage in its life, the MARKET VALUE will be close to the FACE VALUE.

short-form audit report US term for the standard AUDIT REPORT as attached to FINANCIAL STATEMENTS filed with the SECURITIES AND EXCHANGE COMMISSION. This is as opposed to a LONG-FORM REPORT which would be more detailed and addressed to a company's management.

short lease In the context of LEASES on property in the UK, a lease with less than fifty years to run.

short position A state of affairs in which a trader in securities has agreed to sell an amount of a particular security in excess of the amount owned plus that agreed to be bought. The trader will be expecting the price of the security to fall.

short seller A seller of securities that are not yet owned by the seller.

short-term employee benefits According to the INTERNATIONAL ACCOUNTING STANDARDS COMMITTEE, EMPLOYEE BENEFITS which are to be wholly paid within one year after the end of the period in which the employees rendered the service that gave rise to the benefits.

short-term interest rates The rates of interest charged on short-term loans. 'Short-term' is a vague expression, possibly meaning less than one year.

shrinkage A decrease in the amount of an organization's INVENTORIES caused by the processes of production.

SIB Abbreviation for the SECURITIES AND INVESTMENT BOARD (of the UK).

SIC Abbreviation for the STANDING INTERPRETATIONS COMMITTEE of the INTERNATIONAL ACCOUNTING STANDARDS COMMITTEE.

sight draft A BILL OF EXCHANGE which is payable without a notice period.

significant influence The ability to participate in the financial and operating policy decisions of an enterprise which stops short of control or joint control over those policies. *See* ASSOCIATED COMPANY.

simple interest Interest calculated by reference to the original amount of a loan, without taking account of a return for any interest unpaid by the borrower. Compare to COMPOUND INTEREST.

simplified financial statements Reduced versions of the FINANCIAL STATE-MENTS of a company filed for legal purposes. The simplified statements are designed for less sophisticated users rather than for financial analysts, fund managers, etc.

single capacity system In the context of trading in securities, the separation of the task of BROKERS who act as agents for investors from that of jobbers who deal on their own account and with brokers.

single-entry bookkeeping A system of BOOKKEEPING in which a transaction gives rise to one entry only. For example, when a business makes a sale, the entry would record only the resulting increase in cash or in DEBTORS.

sinking fund A fund of money (or investments) designed to accumulate over time in order to pay a DEBT or EXPENSE at a particular future date. The sinking fund will increase with receipts of interest or with periodic receipts from the parties that set up the fund.

sinking fund reserve A RESERVE which is raised in line with a SINKING FUND in order to signal that an amount equal to its contents is not distributable.

sleeping partner A PARTNER who is not active in the running of the partnership but has contributed capital.

small companies rate A lower rate of tax in the UK's system of CORPORATION TAX designed to achieve SMALL COMPANIES RELIEF.

small companies relief A means of lowering the CORPORATION TAX liabilities of small companies by subjecting their taxable profits to a lower tax rate than that for other companies. However, the definition of 'small company' for this purpose rests upon falling below a particular definition of small *profits*. A large company with small profits would therefore benefit from the relief.

The lower tax rate applies to companies with profits below one threshold, and the normal tax rate to companies with profits above a second (higher) threshold. In-between, a system of tapering relief moves the average rate from the low rate to the normal rate. The profits of most UK companies fall below the higher threshold, so most companies benefit in some way from the relief.

small company For the purposes of the COMPANIES ACT (as opposed to tax law), a PRIVATE LIMITED COMPANY falling below two of three criteria for the year and the preceding year. One criterion is that the average number of employees should not exceed fifty. The other criteria are expressed in terms of TURNOVER and BALANCE SHEET TOTAL of ASSETS, and they are raised from time to time.

Small companies may file abbreviated accounts with the REGISTRAR OF COM-

PANIES, and may reduce the DISCLOSURES in the ANNUAL REPORT to SHARE-HOLDERS.

A bank or insurance company or a company in a group containing a PUBLIC COMPANY is not allowed to take advantage of the exemptions.

small group A GROUP of companies that in total would meet the criteria to be a SMALL COMPANY. The size criteria for TURNOVER and TOTAL ASSETS are measured after CONSOLIDATION ADJUSTMENTS (i.e. net) but slightly larger thresholds are available in gross terms.

smoothing *See* INCOME SMOOTHING.

social audit A review of the effects of an organization on society in general. This term would include an ENVIRONMENTAL AUDIT.

socially responsible investment *See* ETHICAL INVESTMENT.

social responsibility reporting Publishing statements concerning the costs and benefits relating to the impact of an organization on society. Relevant issues include pollution, energy consumption and charitable donations.

sociedad anónima A Spanish PUBLIC COMPANY, abbreviated to SA.

societas europea The name (in Latin) of a EU PUBLIC COMPANY as proposed by the Commission of the European Communities.

société anonyme A French, Belgian, Luxembourg or Swiss PUBLIC COMPANY, abbreviated to SA.

société à responsabilité limitée A French, Belgian, Luxembourg or Swiss PRIVATE COMPANY, abbreviated to Sarl.

soft currency A currency that tends to depreciate in value compared to other currencies.

sole practitioner An accountant or other professional who operates without partners.

sole proprietor A person who runs an unincorporated business or professional practice without partners. In a professional context, this would be a sole practitioner.

sole trader A person who runs an unincorporated commercial enterprise without PARTNERS.

solicitors' accounts Accounting records prepared under a professional set of requirements called Solicitors' Account Rules, which in particular specify that clients' moneys must be separated from the firm's money.

Solomons Reports Two reports authored by the late Professor David Solomons on education and training of accountants in the UK (*Prospectus for a Profession*, 1974) and on a CONCEPTUAL FRAMEWORK for the UK (*Guidelines for Financial Reporting Standards*, 1989).

solvency The ability of a business (or person) to pay bills or accounts as they fall due. The likely ability of a business to do this can be measured by examining its LIQUIDITY.

SOP Abbreviation for STATEMENTS OF POSITION (in the US).

SORP Abbreviation for STATEMENTS OF RECOMMENDED PRACTICE (in the UK).

source and application of funds statements Statements which show by category the sources and applications of funds of an enterprise. Such statements were once required as part of the FINANCIAL STATEMENTS of companies in the UK. They are also known as 'funds flow statements'. The definition of 'funds' was not clear, and these statements have now been superseded by CASH FLOW STATEMENTS.

source document A document which contains the initial record of a transaction.

sovereign risk The risk to an overseas project or investment caused by the possibility that the government of the country in which it is located might expropriate the ASSETS.

SpA Abbreviation for *società per azioni*, an Italian PUBLIC COMPANY.

special category companies Banking and insurance companies that are exempted from certain accounting requirements of the COMPANIES ACT.

Special Commissioners A body of UK civil servants who are expert in tax law and hear appeals against TAX ASSESSMENTS, particularly in cases that concern questions of law rather than matters of fact. The latter might be addressed instead by GENERAL COMMISSIONERS.

specialized journal A JOURNAL dealing with a single type of frequently occurring transactions, e.g. SALES.

special resolution A proposal at a meeting of SHAREHOLDERS of a company that requires a three-quarters majority to be passed.

specific duty An EXCISE DUTY based on weight, size or units rather than on value.

specific identification In the context of the determination of the cost of INVENTORIES, the keeping of records for, and the use of, the costs of individual items of inventory, rather than the use of some flow assumption such as FIRST-IN, FIRST-OUT.

specific order costing *See* JOB COSTING.

split depreciation The splitting of the DEPRECIATION charge on a revalued FIXED ASSET into an element based on the HISTORICAL COST of the asset (charged to the PROFIT AND LOSS ACCOUNT) and an element relating to the REVALUATION (taken to RESERVES). This practice is not now allowed under UK INTERNATIONAL ACCOUNTING STANDARDS COMMITTEE rules.

split-off point In the context of PROCESS COSTING, the stage of the production process after which JOINT PRODUCTS become separately identifiable.

split-rate system A type of CORPORATION TAX which has a lower rate for DISTRIBUTED PROFIT than for RETAINED PROFIT. Such a system has been used from time to time in Austria and Germany, for example.

spoilage Material lost as part of a production process. Normal amounts of this are included in the cost of production.

spot market A market for the immediate delivery of COMMODITIES, currencies or other items.

spot price The price payable for immediate delivery of something, as opposed to a forward price.

spot rate The RATE OF EXCHANGE of a currency at the date of a transaction, as opposed to a FORWARD RATE.

spread The difference between a selling price and a buying price of a particular item (e.g. a SHARE) in a market.

spreadsheet A table of columns and rows of numbers representing, over time periods, such items as an enterprise's costs' or sales figures. A computer program can up-date or manipulate the numbers for planning purposes.

square mile In the context of business in the UK, the City of London.

square position A state of affairs in which a trader had agreed to sell more of a unit than he or she owned or had agreed to buy (or vice versa) but where the difference has now been covered or hedged. *See* HEDGING.

SSAP Abbreviation for a STATEMENT OF STANDARD ACCOUNTING PRACTICE (in the UK).

stabilized accounts The adjustment of the numbers in FINANCIAL STATE-MENTS on to a basis of the price of gold or of general purchasing power.

Staff Accounting Bulletin A document published by the SECURITIES AND EXCHANGE COMMISSION of the USA in which is explained the views of its accounting staff on the correct interpretation of elements of GENERALLY ACCEPTED ACCOUNTING PRINCIPLES.

stag A speculator on a stock exchange who buys newly issued securities in advance at a fixed price, hoping that there will be a shortage of them so that they can be rapidly sold when the price rises. *See*, also, BEAR and BULL.

stakeholders Persons with an interest in an organization, such as its owners, employees and creditors.

stamp duty A tax levied on the sale of certain items, such as shares or land, as evidenced by a stamp on a document relating to the transaction.

standard A pre-determined level in a STANDARD COSTING system. The word can be applied as an adjective to many variables, e.g. price, time, wage rates, materials usage, mix of sales.

standard cost allowance The level of VARIABLE COSTS (e.g. DIRECT LABOUR) allowed, given the actual volume of production.

standard costing A system of record-keeping and control within an organiz-ation whereby the operations are divided into jobs or processes for which standard costs are determined in advance and then compared to actual costs. Differences (variances) can then be investigated.

standard hour An amount of production that can be achieved in an hour at normal levels of efficiency.

standardization In the context of FINANCIAL REPORTING, the process of reducing the variation between the accounting of different enterprises.

standard rate In the context of the UK's system of VALUE ADDED TAX, the rate of tax applied to a large majority of goods and services. *See*, also, BASIC RATE OF INCOME TAX.

standard setting The process of preparing and publishing ACCOUNTING STANDARDS.

standard spending assessment The amount that the UK central government determines should be spent by a local government authority.

Standing Interpretations Committee A sub-committee, set up in 1997, by the INTERNATIONAL ACCOUNTING STANDARDS COMMITTEE. Its task is to publish interpretations of existing international accounting standards in cases where certain of their requirements have been misinterpreted or interpreted variously.

start-up costs Costs of an enterprise caused when setting up a machine or process. Such costs are generally added to the other costs of the ASSET. However, the term can also be used to mean the legal and other costs of setting up a company. These costs must be treated as expenses under UK and INTERNATIONAL ACCOUNTING STANDARDS COMMITTEE rules but can be capitalized in some continental European countries.

stated value In the US, the NOMINAL VALUE of a share or, where there is none, a value decided by the directors as that to be used in the accounts for SHARE CAPITAL.

statement of affairs A presentation of the LIABILITIES and the BREAK-UP VALUES of the ASSETS of a person in BANKRUPTCY or a company being wound up.

statement of changes in financial position US term for SOURCE AND APPLICATION OF FUNDS STATEMENTS.

statement of financial activities The main accounting statement of a charity in the UK. It shows the incoming resources and the expended resources for a period, and provides a reconciliation of all movements in the charity's funds.

statement of financial position One of the US terms for a BALANCE SHEET.

statement of movements in equity The INTERNATIONAL ACCOUNTING STANDARDS COMMITTEE term for a compulsory major statement which explains all gains and losses and other items that have caused an enterprise's EQUITY to change in the year, but optionally excluding transactions (such as dividend payments) with an enterprise's owners.

Statement of Principles UK term for a CONCEPTUAL FRAMEWORK, as published by the ACCOUNTING STANDARDS BOARD in 1999.

statement of source and application of funds *See* SOURCE AND APPLICATION OF FUNDS STATEMENTS.

statement of total recognized gains and losses A major FINANCIAL STATEMENT required from UK companies from 1993. It includes gains and losses that are not recorded in the PROFIT AND LOSS ACCOUNT, such as those on foreign currency translation of the statements of FOREIGN SUBSIDIARIES and on the REVALUATION of FIXED ASSETS. The common abbreviation is STRGL.

Statements of Auditing Standards Documents issued by the AUDITING PRACTICES BOARD for the guidance of auditors in their auditing of FINANCIAL STATEMENTS and other work.

Statements of Financial Accounting Concepts Documents issued by the FINANCIAL ACCOUNTING STANDARDS BOARD in the USA that form component parts of its CONCEPTUAL FRAMEWORK.

Statements of Financial Accounting Standards The US term for ACCOUNTING STANDARDS as set by the FINANCIAL ACCOUNTING STANDARDS BOARD since its foundation in 1973. These are the technical rules of RECOGNITION, MEASUREMENT and DISCLOSURE for FINANCIAL STATEMENTS. The abbreviations FAS and SFAS are found.

Statements of Position An element of US GENERALLY ACCEPTED ACCOUNT-ING PRINCIPLES, but with a lower status than ACCOUNTING STANDARDS. State-ments of Position (generally abbreviated to SOP) are issued by the AMERICAN INSTITUTE OF CERTIFIED PUBLIC ACCOUNTANTS.

Statements of Recommended Practice UK documents (abbreviated to SORP) with less authority than ACCOUNTING STANDARDS. They are designed to deal with particular industries or with specialist technical problems, and are drafted by an industry or special interest group.

Statements of Standard Accounting Practice The UK term for those ACCOUNTING STANDARDS issued up to 1990 by the former ACCOUNTING STAN-DARDS COMMITTEE. These standards (abbreviated to SSAP) are still in force unless subsequently overridden.

Statements on Auditing Documents issued by the INSTITUTE OF CHARTERED ACCOUNTANTS IN ENGLAND AND WALES that are gradually being superseded by STATEMENTS OF AUDITING STANDARDS.

state plan In the context of EMPLOYEE BENEFITS, a plan run by a government.

static budget See FIXED BUDGET.

statutes A term that can mean Acts of Parliament or the ARTICLES OF ASSOCI-ATION of a company, or their equivalents in countries other than the UK.

statutory accounts FINANCIAL STATEMENTS as required by law to be prepared by companies in the UK.

statutory audit AUDIT as required by COMPANY LAW in the UK for the FINANCIAL STATEMENTS of LIMITED COMPANIES (except for SMALL COMPANIES and DORMANT COMPANIES and some other organizations. This must be performed by a REGISTERED AUDITOR.

statutory books The various books (such as the REGISTER OF MEMBERS and the REGISTER OF DIRECTORS AND SECRETARIES) that must by law be maintained by a UK company.

statutory company A company incorporated by Act of Parliament rather than in the normal way by registration under the COMPANIES ACT.

statutory declaration A written announcement in a specified form, required by law for certain purposes, such as the commencement of business by a PUBLIC LIMITED COMPANY.

statutory instrument In the UK, detailed regulations prepared by government departments and giving effect to sections of an Act of Parliament.

stepped (or step-function) cost A cost that increases as volume in an organization increases but in discrete rather than continuous form. This would be caused where particular resources come in large and indivisible units.

stewardship The original purpose of ACCOUNTING; also called 'accountability'. Kings or lords who were away at war or for other purposes would leave their estates in the hands of a steward. The steward would keep an account of the payments and receipts of the estate so that he could be discharged of responsibility when the owner returned. The steward would 'render an account' to the owner, who might have been illiterate and had thus to hear it ('AUDIT' derives from the Latin for 'he hears').

Today, SHAREHOLDERS are the owners of companies, and DIRECTORS are their apppointees, who look after the ASSETS in their absence. Thus, the annual FINANCIAL STATEMENTS need to be checked by independent experts (the AUDITORS) and sent to the shareholders. Thus it may be seen whether the directors have been proper stewards.

In recent years, the financial statements have come to be seen as the provision of information useful for taking decisions about whether to buy or sell a company's securities. This requires forward-looking information, whereas stewardship is essentially backward-looking. This conflict has led to difficulties in setting rules for, and in interpreting, financial statements. For example, it could be claimed that HISTORICAL COST ACCOUNTING was more useful for stewardship than for financial decision-making.

stock US term for securities of various kinds, e.g. common stock or preference stock (equivalent to ORDINARY and PREFERENCE SHARES in UK terminology). However, the word 'share' is also understood in the USA, so that 'stockholder' and 'shareholder' are interchangeable.

In the UK this meaning survives, particularly in the expressions 'stock exchange' and 'loan stock'.

A source of great confusion in Anglo-American conversation is the UK use of the word 'STOCKS' for what are called INVENTORIES in the USA.

stock appreciation relief A UK tax relief that operated between 1973 and 1984. It was designed to allow for the fact that reported profits included gains on the holding of inventories/STOCKS that were merely due to price increases.

stock budget A detailed numerical plan (a BUDGET) concerning the volumes and values of an organization's STOCKS throughout a budget period.

stock control All those elements of a system inside an organization concerned with the management of STOCKS. This includes ascertaining and then maintaining the optimum holdings so as to avoid stock shortages but not to waste resources. *See*, for example, ECONOMIC ORDER QUANTITY and RE-ORDER LEVEL.

stock dividend US term to describe the issue of free extra shares to existing SHAREHOLDERS, combined with the capitalization of retained earnings. A stock dividend is an extra issue of up to about 25 per cent of the number of existing shares. A STOCK SPLIT is an extra issue of over about 20 per cent. The two issues are accounted for differently.

The UK equivalent expressions are BONUS/CAPITALIZATION/SCRIP ISSUES.

stock exchange An organized and regulated market for the new issue and subsequent exchange of securities of companies and other organizations.

stock exchange indices *See* SHARE PRICE INDICES.

stockholder A US term for SHAREHOLDER.

stockholders' equity One of the US expressions for the total stake in a company owned by the stockholders, including their invested capital and retained earnings. A more detailed entry may be found under SHAREHOLDERS' FUNDS, which is the expression generally found in the UK.

stock-in-trade *See* STOCKS.

stock market Another term for STOCK EXCHANGE.

stock option A CONTRACT giving the holder the right to buy a specified number of SHARES in a company at a set price during a specified period. In principle, this term means the same thing as SHARE OPTION, but in the UK it tends to be used to refer to options held by DIRECTORS or other employees of a company.

stock out A state of affairs in which an organization runs out of a material necessary for its operations.

stockowners' equity One of the US expressions for SHAREHOLDERS' FUNDS.

stock record A document kept inside an organization to record all movements of particular STOCKS.

stock relief *See* STOCK APPRECIATION RELIEF.

stocks As used in the UK, this word means the RAW MATERIALS, WORK IN PROGRESS and FINISHED GOODS of a business. Unfortunately, in the USA the word 'inventories' is used instead, and 'stocks' means SHARES there.

The valuation of stock (inventories) is a very important exercise for a business. The figure usually forms an important part of the CURRENT ASSETS total on a BALANCE SHEET, and it is a vital part of the calculation of PROFIT. The GROSS PROFIT of a business is the sales *less* the cost of sales. The cost of sales is the purchases of goods, adjusted for the change in the level of stocks during the period, plus any other manufacturing costs.

The normal valuation method is to use 'the lower of cost and market value'. The use of cost is a normal method of accounting for all assets, under the HISTORICAL COST ACCOUNTING convention. However, because stocks are current assets and may soon be sold, their market value will also be relevant. The principle of PRUDENCE causes accountants to reduce the value of stocks below cost in those fairly unusual cases where MARKET VALUE has fallen below cost. 'Market value' in the UK means NET REALIZABLE VALUE.

'Cost' includes all the expenses associated with the purchase of stocks, plus those costs of bringing them to their existing condition and location; this includes PRODUCTION OVERHEADS. For most stocks, it is either impossible or impracticable to know the precise units of raw material, etc. that are being used up in production or that remain at the year end. Thus, it is normal for accountants to make assumptions about the flow of such stocks. Such assumptions include: first in, first out (FIFO), last in, first out (LIFO) and average cost (AVCO). In the UK, FIFO and AVCO are normal, whereas LIFO is not allowed for taxation purposes and is discouraged by STATEMENT OF STANDARD ACCOUNTING PRACTICE 9. In the USA, LIFO is allowed for tax purposes. It usually reduces income, so it is popular; more details are given under the entries for FIFO and LIFO.

stock split US term for the subdivision of shares.

stocktake The process, particularly as performed at an enterprise's accounting year end, whereby the various STOCKS of the enterprise are counted and valued in order to establish the CLOSING STOCK.

stock turnover The number of times in a year that the total of STOCKS in an enterprise is turned over by being sold. This is measured by dividing the cost of sales (or, if that is not available, the sales) by the CLOSING STOCK or by the average stock for the year.

stock valuation The determination of the value of an enterprise's CLOSING STOCK for its BALANCE SHEET. After the stock is counted, it is generally valued at the LOWER OF COST AND MARKET.

stock watering US term for the excessive issuing of new shares in a company such that it may not be possible to maintain dividends or to pay back SHARE CAPITAL in full on a LIQUIDATION.

stores requisition A form used within an organization that requires, and then records, the issue of particular amounts of particular materials from an organization's stores to be used up and charged to a job or process.

stores returns note A form used within an organization that records the return of materials from a part of the organization to the store. It cancels an EXPENDITURE charged to a particular job or process.

straight-line depreciation A system of calculating the annual DEPRECIATION expense of a FIXED ASSET. This method charges equal annual instalments against profit over the useful life of the asset. In total, the cost of the asset less any estimated RESIDUAL VALUE is depreciated. This method is simple to use and thus very popular.

strategic investment appraisal A form of CAPITAL INVESTMENT APPRAISAL that considers matters beyond the financial, including the long-term strategic effects of a decision.

strategic management accounting A type of MANAGEMENT ACCOUNTING which takes account of factors external to the firm, e.g. competitors' costs. Consequently, it should assist in pricing strategy and other such decisions.

strategic planning Making decisions on the long-term goals of an organization and the policies that are likely to achieve them. This will include making forecasts of the organization's strengths and weaknesses and its future environment.

STRGL Abbreviation for the STATEMENT OF TOTAL RECOGNIZED GAINS AND LOSSES.

strike price The price at which an OPTION can be exercised by its holder.

'subject to' opinion A type of audit opinion (*see* QUALIFIED AUDIT REPORT).

subordinated debt A loan that ranks below others in the queue for repayment in the case that the borrower has to be wound up.

subscribed share capital *See* ISSUED SHARE CAPITAL.

subsidiary Generally, an enterprise, controlled by another (the PARENT COMPANY). *See* CONSOLIDATED FINANCIAL STATEMENTS.

subsidiary undertaking UK legal term for a SUBSIDIARY that may or may not itself be a company.

substance over form The presentation in FINANCIAL STATEMENTS of the economic or commercial substance of a particular transaction, rather than the superficial legal or technical form of it. This is one of the necessary qualitative characteristics of accounting information, according to a CONCEPTUAL FRAMEWORK.

substantive tests Tests, as part of an AUDIT, designed to gather evidence about actual transactions and balances rather than to test a system.

successful efforts method In the context of accounting for oil and gas exploration costs, the capitalization of only those costs related to successful work.

summary accounts *See* SUMMARY FINANCIAL STATEMENT.

summary financial statement UK legal term for a type of abbreviated FINANCIAL STATEMENTS and DIRECTORS' REPORT that may, under certain conditions, be sent to the SHAREHOLDERS of a LISTED COMPANY instead of the full statements.

sum-of-the-digits method A method of calculating a declining charge of DEPRECIATION for a FIXED ASSET. The useful economic life of the asset is estimated in years, and the digits of each year are then added together. For example, if the life is expected to be five years, then the sum of digits is $5 + 4 + 3 + 2 + 1 = 15$. In the first year, the depreciation expense is set as $5/15$ of the net cost; in the second year, $4/15$, and so on.

sum-of-the-years-digits *See* SUM-OF-THE-DIGITS METHOD.

sundry expenses Items of small expense which are not otherwise classified but are added together as 'miscellaneous' under this heading.

sunk costs Costs already incurred and therefore irrelevant when making financial decisions.

superannuation Literally, the condition of being too old, but generally meaning a PENSION for retired employees.

superannuation fund *See* PENSION FUND.

super profits An economist's term for the excess of the actual profit of an enterprise over that 'normal profit' which would be sufficient to persuade enterprises to continue in operation in the industry.

supervisory board A board of NON-EXECUTIVE DIRECTORS of a company who appoint and oversee the members of the company's executive or administrative board. Such a two-tier structure is compulsory for PUBLIC COMPANIES in Germany and The Netherlands. *See*, also, CORPORATE GOVERNANCE.

supplementary financial statements FINANCIAL STATEMENTS presented by an enterprise in addition to those required by law or other regulations.

surplus For a non-commercial organization, an excess of REVENUES over EXPENSES for a period.

surplus advance corporation tax That amount of the former ADVANCE CORPORATION TAX that was in excess of what could be set off against a company's CORPORATION TAX liability.

surplus franked investment income Formerly, the amount by which a company's FRANKED INVESTMENT INCOME exceeded its FRANKED PAYMENTS. This could be carried forward in order to reduce payments of ADVANCE CORPORATION TAX.

surrender value The amount receivable by a policyholder from a life assurance company on the cancellation of a policy before the end of its term.

suspense account A temporary ACCOUNT in a BOOKKEEPING system designed to record a BALANCE that will be put into another account later, e.g. when the source of an error has been found.

swap An exchange of one FINANCIAL INSTRUMENT for another. For example, one currency is exchanged for another, or an amount of spot currency is exchanged for an amount of forward currency or a fixed-interest loan is exchanged for a FLOATING RATE LOAN.

SWOT analysis Decision making by analysing the Strengths, Weaknesses, Opportunities and Threats of an organization.

syndicated loan A large loan made by a lead bank and then spread to other financial institutions.

systematic risk *See* MARKET RISK.

systems-based audit An AUDIT carried out after an analysis of the INTERNAL CONTROL SYSTEM of the organization being audited, followed by concentrating the SUBSTANTIVE TESTS on areas of perceived weakness.

T

10-K *See* FORM 10-K.

10-Q *See* FORM 10-Q.

20-F *See* FORM 20-F.

Table A A model set of ARTICLES OF ASSOCIATION, to be found in the UK COMPANIES ACT. The Articles of a company are the rules that govern the relationships among SHAREHOLDERS, and between shareholders and the company and its DIRECTORS. A company in the process of formation may adopt or amend Table A for its own purposes.

T-account *See* ACCOUNT.

take-over bid An offer to a company's SHAREHOLDERS to acquire at least enough of the company's VOTING SHARES to enable a CONTROLLING INTEREST in it. The directors of the TARGET COMPANY may advise shareholders against accepting the bid, whereupon it becomes a HOSTILE TAKE-OVER BID. Alternatively, it may be an AGREED BID.

Takeover Panel A committee which oversees the operations of the CITY CODE ON TAKEOVERS AND MERGERS.

tally sticks Accounting devices comprising sticks of wood with notches representing transactions. The sticks are split so that two parties to the transaction can have the same record. This method was used for some purposes by the UK Exchequer until the beginning of the nineteenth century. It was the burning of old tally sticks that led to the destruction by fire of the Houses of Parliament in 1834.

tangible assets Assets with physical existence, such as property, plant or equipment. Tangible assets may be contrasted with investments and with INTANGIBLE ASSETS, such as patents, licences, trademarks or goodwill.

tangible fixed assets Those TANGIBLE ASSETS intended by the directors of an enterprise for continuing use in the business. This would apply to most tangible assets except INVENTORIES. The US term for this would be property, plant and equipment.

tapering relief *See* SMALL COMPANIES RELIEF.

taper relief In the context of the UK's system of CAPITAL GAINS TAX, a proportionate reduction in the amount of gains on an asset that are charged to tax, depending on how long the asset had been held by the taxpayer.

tap stock A UK term for those government fixed interest securities that are released slowly 'on tap' because they remain unsold after an issue.

target company The object of a TAKEOVER BID.

target costing The establishment of a planned limit to the costs of production of a product by beginning with a prediction of the maximum selling price that would be competitive and working back to the maximum costs.

tax A compulsory levy made by a public authority for which nothing is received directly in return. Taxes come in many forms. Some examples of these are shown in Figure 3 (p. 284).

taxable income For a business, the annual NET INCOME, as adjusted from accounting rules to tax rules. In the UK, there are numerous adjustments from accounting net profit to taxable income. For example, accounting DEPRECIATION is added back, and CAPITAL ALLOWANCES are granted instead. Dividend income from other companies is deducted, but certain legal fees and entertainment expenses are added back.

taxable supply In the context of the UK's system of VALUE ADDED TAX, goods and services received by a registered taxpayer that are relevant for the tax, i.e. other than EXEMPT SUPPLIES.

taxable temporary difference A TEMPORARY DIFFERENCE that will result in taxable amounts in future periods when the CARRYING AMOUNT of an ASSET or LIABILITY is recovered or settled. The context is the calculation of DEFERRED TAX. A taxable temporary difference generally gives rise to the recognition of a DEFERRED TAX LIABILITY. The opposite of a taxable temporary difference is a DEDUCTIBLE TEMPORARY DIFFERENCE.

tax allocation US term for splitting up the TAX EXPENSE of a business into appropriate accounting periods (*see* DEFERRED TAX), or the splitting up of tax expense into various headings in an INCOME STATEMENT.

tax allowance A deduction from a taxpayer's TOTAL INCOME allowed in the calculation of TAXABLE INCOME.

tax assessment The presentation of the calculation of a taxpayer's liability for tax for a period. An assessment may be drawn up entirely by the tax authorities or, under self-assessment, mainly by the taxpayer.

tax avoidance The manipulation by a taxpayer of his or her affairs, within the letter of the law, in order to reduce tax liabilities. *See*, also, TAX EVASION.

tax base That which is liable to taxation. Examples are income, wealth or expenditure.

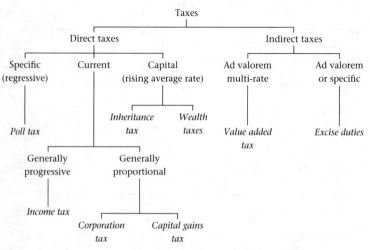

Source: S. James and C. Nobes, *The Economics of Taxation*, Prentice Hall, 2000.

tax base of an asset or liability The amount attributed to that ASSET OR LIABILITY in the records of the taxation authorities. Given the many differences that there might be between tax valuation rules and financial reporting rules, the tax base of an asset or liability could differ substantially from its CARRYING VALUE for financial reporting. This would give rise to a TEMPORARY DIFFERENCE which might lead to accounting for DEFERRED TAX.

tax bracket An informal term for a range of income (or other TAX BASE) for which the same MARGINAL RATE OF TAX applies.

tax code In the context of the UK's system of INCOME TAX, a summarization into one alphanumeric code of the allowances of a taxpayer for the tax year. This allows an employer continuously to deduct the correct amount of tax from the wage or salary under the PAY AS YOU EARN system.

Tax Commissioners *See* GENERAL COMMISSIONERS and SPECIAL COMMISSIONERS.

tax credit A credit against tax. For example, in the UK CORPORATION TAX system, DIVIDENDS to SHAREHOLDERS are accompanied by a tax credit which is set against shareholders' tax liabilities. The term can also be used in the context of a NEGATIVE INCOME TAX.

tax deductible Allowed by the tax regulations to be treated as an EXPENSE in the calculation of TAXABLE INCOME or profits.

tax evasion The illegal manipulation by a taxpayer of his or her affairs, or of information given to the tax authorities, in order to reduce tax LIABILITIES. *See*, also, TAX AVOIDANCE.

tax expenditure A fiscal advantage conferred on a group of taxpayers, or in respect of a particular activity, by reducing tax liability rather than by the payment of a cash subsidy.

tax expense The total included in the determination of NET PROFIT or loss for the period for CURRENT TAX and DEFERRED TAX. The tax expense is the figure seen in an enterprise's PROFIT AND LOSS ACCOUNT, but it is most unlikely to be the tax paid in the year. Even the current tax (the tax relating to the year) may be paid after the year end; and the deferred tax rests on accounting calculations which look forward for several years.

tax harmonization The process of reducing the degree of difference between the TAX BASES and the other aspects of tax systems of different states, e.g. those within the EU.

tax havens Countries or areas where tax rates are substantially lower than those to which a taxpayer would be subject elsewhere.

tax holiday A period during which a tax jurisdiction allows a taxpayer (particularly a company) to pay no tax or reduced tax as an incentive for moving to that jurisdiction or for complying in some other way with the wishes of the authorities in the jurisdiction.

tax invoice In the context of the UK's system of VALUE ADDED TAX (VAT), an invoice drawn up by a REGISTERED TRADER that shows such details as the amount of VAT charged on supplies and the trader's VAT registration number.

tax loss The loss for a period as calculated according to tax regulations.

tax loss carryforward An amount of tax losses that has not been set against TAXABLE INCOME and is allowed by the tax regulations to be carried forward for use in future tax years.

tax period The period covered by a tax return. In the context of VALUE ADDED TAX, this is three months. *See*, also, FISCAL YEAR.

tax planning The arrangement of one's affairs (intended to be legal) so as to maximize after-tax returns.

tax point For VALUE ADDED TAX purposes, the date on which the tax is chargeable on a supply of goods or services.

tax rebate A repayment by the tax authorities to a taxpayer of tax overpaid.

tax return In the context of INCOME TAX or CORPORATION TAX, an annual form sent to the tax authorities by a taxpayer upon which the taxpayer provides details of the sources and amounts of income, other gains and relevant expenses for the year.

tax schedules *See* INCOME TAX SCHEDULES.

tax shield A partial protection of income from tax caused by having related expenses that are tax-deductible.

tax tables In the context of the UK's system of INCOME TAX, numerical tables issued by the Inland Revenue to employers to enable them to calculate the correct amounts of tax to deduct from employees' wages and salaries under the PAY AS YOU EARN system.

tax treaty *See* DOUBLE TAXATION AGREEMENT.

tax year *See* FISCAL YEAR.

teeming and lading The misappropriation by an employee of cash amounts received in a business from customers, followed by covering this up by using later receipts as though they applied to the earlier customer.

temporal method The main method of FOREIGN CURRENCY TRANSLATION used in the USA between 1975 and 1981 under STATEMENT OF FINANCIAL ACCOUNTING STANDARDS 8. It is now only to be used there when a subsidiary is in a hyperinflationary environment or closely held by the parent. The method involves the translation of balances and transactions at RATES OF EXCHANGE relating to the times of their valuation. For example, a twenty-year-old cost of a building would be translated at the historical rate but cash would be translated at the closing rate.

The method is also used by some German groups.

temporal principle In the context of FOREIGN CURRENCY TRANSLATION, the idea that transactions and balances should be translated at rates suitable to their valuation basis. The TEMPORAL METHOD is the application of this principle to HISTORICAL COST ACCOUNTING.

temporary difference A difference between the tax basis of an ASSET or LIABILITY and its accounting CARRYING VALUE. ACCOUNTING STANDARDS of the INTERNATIONAL ACCOUNTING STANDARDS COMMITTEE and the USA now require DEFERRED TAX to be accounted for on these temporary differences. The UK rule still bases deferred taxation on TIMING DIFFERENCES.

temporary diminution in value An undefined term in the UK COMPANIES ACT to describe a fall in value of a FIXED ASSET that is not expected to reverse in the foreseeable future. Such falls should be recognized in BALANCE SHEETS, with a related loss being recorded. In practice, this idea has now been absorbed into the more detailed rules on IMPAIRMENT.

term deposit A deposit held in a financial institution for a specified period.

terminal bonus An additional variable amount paid to an insured person (or to the estate of the insured) on the maturity of the policy (or on the death of the insured). The size of the bonus depends on the value of the policy and on the success of the investments of the life assurance company.

terminal value The value to which an investment will accumulate at a specified rate of interest, assuming that the interest is allowed to compound rather than being paid out.

termination benefits EMPLOYEE BENEFITS payable because an enterprise terminates an employee's employment before the normal retirement date or because the employee accepts voluntary redundancy in exchange for the benefits.

TESSA Abbreviation for the Tax Exempt Special Savings scheme of the UK.

testator A person who has made a valid will.

thin capitalization The financing of a company by means of a large amount of DEBT and a small amount of SHARE CAPITAL. The tax authorities may object to a very thin capitalization because the interest payments on the debt are tax-deductible.

thrifts US colloquial term for SAVINGS AND LOAN ASSOCIATIONS.

throughput accounting A system of a MANAGEMENT ACCOUNTING which concentrates on short-term decisions in the context of a particular CONSTRAINT or bottleneck in production. The objective is to maximize the return per unit of the scarce resource.

times covered Ratios that measure the security of a company's future DIVIDENDS, INTEREST payments or PROFITS. The 'times covered' or 'dividend cover' normally refers to the number of times that the company's most recent total annual dividends could have been paid out of its annual EARNINGS available for that purpose.

The 'TIMES INTEREST EARNED' ratio compares the most recent annual interest expense of a company with its NET PROFIT before interest and tax, which is available for such interest payments.

times interest earned The number of times that an enterprise's profit before interest and tax for a period could pay the interest expense for the period. This is a measure of how protected the company is from liquidity problems.

time value of money The idea that, irrespective of any fall in value due to inflation, money now is worth more to its holder than money later. Consequently, amounts of money to be received or paid in the future should be discounted to establish their PRESENT VALUES.

timing differences Differences, in any period, between TAXABLE INCOME and accounting income which will reverse in a future period. For example, in the UK, CAPITAL ALLOWANCES often enable plant and machinery to be charged for tax purposes over a shorter period than that used for DEPRECIATION in FINANCIAL STATEMENTS. In this case, although the total expense for tax and accounting purposes will eventually be the same, there will be originating, and then reversing, timing differences. Such ORIGINATING TIMING DIFFERENCES lead to the need to account for DEFERRED TAX. Compare to TEMPORARY DIFFERENCES.

tombstone In the context of the financial press, a notice advertising the success of a financial institution in issuing securities for a company.

total assets The total of all the types of ASSETS of an enterprise that are shown in its BALANCE SHEET.

total capital A somewhat vague term, possibly meaning SHAREHOLDERS' FUNDS or perhaps that amount plus LONG-TERM LIABILITIES or plus all liabilities.

total capital and liabilities Either the total of long-term financing (i.e. SHAREHOLDERS' FUNDS plus LONG-TERM LIABILITIES) or that plus all other liabilities.

total cost of production The sum of an organization's FIXED COSTS and VARIABLE COSTS of production for a period.

total income For tax purposes, a taxpayer's income for a tax year from all sources before various deductions and allowances that lead to TAXABLE INCOME.

total quality management An all-embracing and integrated system of planning and control in an organization designed to ensure customer satisfaction. The system includes the setting of clear goals, the continuous measurement of quality, and the establishment of means to involve employees in ensuring business improvements.

total profits For tax purposes, a company's TOTAL PROFITS including CHARGEABLE GAINS.

trade credit The total of the short-term funds that are, in effect, provided to an enterprise because suppliers have not yet been paid.

trade creditors Suppliers of goods or services to the business, who are not paid immediately at the time of purchase. At a BALANCE SHEET date, outstanding amounts owed to them are shown in the UK as 'TRADE CREDITORS' as part of CURRENT LIABILITIES. The US term for this is 'accounts payable'.

trade date In the context of FINANCIAL INSTRUMENTS, the date on which an enterprise becomes committed to purchase a FINANCIAL ASSET.

trade debtors Customers of an enterprise who have not yet paid for their purchases. At the BALANCE SHEET date, the total of the outstanding amounts, less any PROVISION FOR BAD DEBTS, is shown in the UK as 'TRADE DEBTORS' as part of CURRENT ASSETS. The US term for this is 'accounts receivable'.

trade discount A reduction in the price of goods or services allowed to a customer who is not generally the final customer for the product.

trade marks Names or designs that a business has a right to use in connection with its products. Trade marks are examples of INTANGIBLE ASSETS. Accountants will put a value on these for BALANCE SHEET purposes only if that 'value' can be verified because the trade mark was bought or was created using separately identifiable EXPENSES. Thus, the value of a trade mark will be recorded at its cost, with appropriate AMORTIZATION and IMPAIRMENT.

trading account A name sometimes given to the first part of a PROFIT AND LOSS ACCOUNT in which the COST OF SALES is netted against the sales to show GROSS PROFIT.

trading asset or liability When referring to securities, those intended by an enterprise to be bought and sold.

trading financial assets FINANCIAL ASSETS acquired or held in order to give PROFIT from short-term changes in price.

trading profit A term with no precise meaning but perhaps equivalent to OPERATING PROFIT.

tranche A significant part of an investment (or loan) that is being sold (or paid off) in instalments. The word derives from the French for 'slice'.

transaction costs INCREMENTAL COSTS directly attributable to the acquisition or disposal of an ASSET.

transaction date Generally, the date on which control of an ASSET passes from a seller to a buyer. However, there are legal complexities here, and the term could also mean the date on which an OFFER FOR SALE is accepted.

transaction exposure The risk that an enterprise may suffer loss on its trans-actions because of EXCHANGE RATE movements. For example, a purchase denomi-nated in a foreign currency and not paid for immediately involves the risk of loss because the foreign currency may rise in value compared to the enterprise's reporting currency.

transfer deed *See* SHARE TRANSFER FORM.

transfer pricing The notional or real price charged by one part of a company (or group of companies) to another part when goods or services are transferred. In the context of multinational organizations, the manipulation of transfer prices is designed to enable PROFIT to be moved from high tax to low tax countries.

translation *See* FOREIGN CURRENCY TRANSLATION.

translation exposure *See* ACCOUNTING EXPOSURE.

treasurer A term, sometimes used in NOT-FOR-PROFIT ORGANIZATIONS in the UK but more widely in the USA, meaning the person responsible for an organization's MONETARY ASSETS and LIABILITIES.

Treasury bill A BILL OF EXCHANGE issued by the government.

treasury shares EQUITY INSTRUMENTS bought back and held by the issuing enterprise (or its subsidiaries). Such shares are called 'own shares' in the UK, and might be called 'treasury stock' in the USA. The shares are held 'in the corporate treasury'. The term 'treasury stock' is confusing to a UK reader because it might appear to refer to government bonds. In the UK, such shares are shown as ASSETS in the BALANCE SHEET; but under INTERNATIONAL ACCOUNTING STANDARDS or US rules as deductions from EQUITY.

treasury stock US expression for a company's shares that have been bought back by the company and not cancelled. *See* TREASURY SHARES.

trend analysis In the context of the financial appraisal of a company, the use of moving averages and other statistics to examine performance over a period in order to predict future performance.

trial balance Part of the exercise of producing FINANCIAL STATEMENTS from the records in a DOUBLE-ENTRY BOOKKEEPING system. The trial balance marshals all the DEBIT and CREDIT BALANCES on the various accounts on to one page. If this does not balance immediately, then errors must be investigated. Once balance is achieved then some of the individual items are used to prepare the INCOME STATEMENT, and the remaining items are shown on the BALANCE SHEET.

true and fair view The overriding legal requirement for the presentation of FINANCIAL STATEMENTS of companies in the UK, the rest of the EU and most of the Commonwealth. It is difficult to tie down an exact meaning to the expression, and it would ultimately have to be interpreted in a court of law. However, most laws demand *a* true and fair view, rather than *the* true and fair view, and it is clear that the instruction has to be interpreted in the context of normal accounting practice at the time of the financial statements. One interpretation of the phrase could be that it means 'in accordance with the facts, and not misleading'.

In the UK, the law requires that extra information must be disclosed if this is necessary to give a true and fair view. In exceptional cases, detailed provisions of the law must be departed from if this is the only way of giving a true and fair view. In such cases, there must be disclosure of the reasons and effects of the departures.

Trueblood Report A report of 1971 in the USA, chaired by Robert Trueblood, and recommending that a CONCEPTUAL FRAMEWORK should be developed.

truncation Removal (rather than rounding) of some of the final digits of a number.

trust A legal arrangement whereby an organization or a set of ASSETS is placed in the custody of a group of persons (trustees) who pledge to look after the organization/assets in the interest of other parties or of the public in general. For example, a deceased rich person might have placed assets in trust for a young daughter. The trustees are then required to administer the assets in the daughter's interest. As another example, the INTERNATIONAL ACCOUNTING STANDARDS

COMMITTEE is ultimately responsible to a group of trustees who have agreed to operate in the public interest.

Another US meaning of the term 'trust' is a cartel of companies in one industry that operate together.

trust deed A legal document that creates and sets out the arrangements of a TRUST.

trustee One of a group of persons who holds assets on behalf of others. *See* TRUST.

trustee in bankruptcy A person who operates on behalf of the CREDITORS of a BANKRUPT person.

trustee investments Types of investments that are approved by law in the UK as suitable for the investment by the TRUSTEES of the funds held by certain types of TRUSTS.

turnover The UK legal expression used in a PROFIT AND LOSS ACCOUNT for the SALES revenue of an ACCOUNTING PERIOD. This is shown net of VALUE ADDED TAX. The term in the USA might be taken to mean the turnover of staff members in a period.

two-tier board structure The governance of a company by means of a SUPERVISORY BOARD and a MANAGEMENT BOARD.

UCITS *See* UNDERTAKINGS FOR COLLECTIVE INVESTMENTS IN TRANSFERABLE SECURITIES.

UEC Abbreviation for the *Union Européenne des Experts Comptables Economiques et Financiers*, a representative body of European accountants absorbed into the FÉDÉRATION DES EXPERTS COMPTABLES EUROPÉENS in 1986.

UITF Abbreviation for the URGENT ISSUES TASK FORCE

ultimate holding company In the context of a group of companies involving several layers of PARENT COMPANIES and subsidiaries, the top company in the structure.

ultra vires Latin expression for 'beyond the powers'. An action of a company or a director is *ultra vires* if it is beyond the legal powers of the company (as set out in the MEMORANDUM OF ASSOCIATION) or of the director (as set out in the ARTICLES OF ASSOCIATION or in the COMPANIES ACTS). Such actions may, for example, lead to contracts being void.

unadjusted trial balance A list (TRIAL BALANCE) of the balances in a BOOK-KEEPING system before adjustment at a period end for various items such as closing inventory/STOCK.

unallotted shares The shares of a company that have been issued but not yet allocated to particular shareholders.

unappropriated profits Those profits of an enterprise for the current and previous periods that have neither been distributed to the owners nor set aside in some other way as specific RESERVES.

uncalled share capital Amounts of the ISSUED SHARE CAPITAL of a company for which the shareholders have not yet been asked to pay.

unconsolidated subsidiary A SUBSIDIARY that has been omitted in the preparation of CONSOLIDATED FINANCIAL STATEMENTS, e.g. because there are severe long-term restrictions that hinder the exercise of the rights of control of the parent. Such a subsidiary would be shown in a CONSOLIDATED BALANCE SHEET as an investment.

uncontrollable costs In MANAGEMENT ACCOUNTING, those costs of an organization that are regarded as not within the control of the managers at the particular level of the organization being considered.

undated stock Securities that denote DEBT with fixed interest payments but no REDEMPTION DATE.

underabsorbed overhead In the context of ABSORPTION COSTING, the excess of the actual overhead cost of an organization for a period over the amount charged to production.

underapplied overhead US term for UNDERABSORBED OVERHEAD.

undercapitalization The state of affairs in which a company has insufficient funds for its scale of operations, generally because it has expanded too quickly.

understandability In the context of the desirable qualitative characteristics of financial information, being comprehensible to users with a reasonable knowledge of business and a willingness to study the information. *See*, also, CONCEPTUAL FRAMEWORK.

undertaking A wide UK legal term for an enterprise, including a COMPANY, PARTNERSHIP or UNINCORPORATED ASSOCIATION that carries on business with a view to profit.

undertakings for collective investments in transferable securities UNIT TRUSTS and similar funds, securities which can be sold in any country in the EU.

underwriter A person (or institution) who agrees to take on risks in exchange for a COMMISSION. So, in an insurance context, an underwriter would be the person who accepts, after analysis, certain insurance risks. In the context of an issue of shares, an underwriter guarantees to take all or a proportion of unsold shares.

underwriting The activities of an UNDERWRITER.

underwriting expenses Costs incurred when a company engages a financial institution to act as UNDERWRITER for a new issue of shares.

undistributable profit An amount of profit or other gains that is not legally available for distribution to the shareholders as DIVIDENDS. The term could refer to amounts earned this year or to a cumulative amount, although the term 'undistributed reserves' would be clearer for the latter.

undistributable reserves Amounts notionally allocated out of profits or other gains that are not legally available for distribution to the shareholders as dividends. Such reserves include those on the revaluation of assets. The US term is 'restricted surplus'.

undistributed profit An amount of profit or other gains that has not yet been paid out to the shareholders. The term could refer to amounts earned this year or to a cumulative amount, although the term 'undistributed reserves' would be clearer for the latter.

undistributed reserves Amount of profit for the current and previous period that have not yet been paid out to the shareholders. The US term is 'retained earnings'.

unearned finance income In the context of a FINANCE LEASE, the difference between (a) the minimum lease payments plus any UNGUARANTEED RESIDUAL VALUE, and (b) that amount discounted at the interest rate implicit in the lease.

unearned income In the context of the UK's system of INCOME TAX, a former category of income that derived from investments rather than from employment, trade or profession.

unexpired cost A literal explanation of the amount of an ASSET as shown on an HISTORICAL COST ACCOUNTING balance sheet. It is the depreciated historical cost, written down value or net book value not yet charged to the PROFIT AND LOSS ACCOUNT.

unfavourable variance In the context of COST ACCOUNTING, an adverse difference between an actual amount and a budgeted or standard amount for a period.

unfranked investment income Income of a company, such as interest received, that has been paid out of the income of another company but not subjected to CORPORATION TAX. The unfranked income includes any income tax deducted at source, which is reclaimable by the company.

unguaranteed residual value In the context of LEASE accounting, the element of the RESIDUAL VALUE of a leased ASSET whose realization is not assured.

uniform accounting policies In the preparation of CONSOLIDATED FINAN-CIAL STATEMENTS, the use of the same ACCOUNTING POLICIES for all the enterprises in the group. This may entail the adjustment of the policies of some of the subsidiaries (or even of the parent) from those used in their own individual FINANCIAL STATEMENTS.

uniform business rate *See* BUSINESS RATES.

uniform costing The use, by several companies in the same industry, of the same COST ACCOUNTING system. This may be done in order to aid inter-firm comparisons of efficiency.

uniformity The use of the same rules of RECOGNITION and MEASUREMENT and, particularly, of financial statement PRESENTATION from one company to another. Improvements in uniformity are encouraged by the setting of ACCOUNTING STANDARDS. One reason for this is to improve comparability between the financial statements of different companies.

The word 'consistency' tends to be used, instead, to mean the use by any individual company of the same accounting methods year by year. This is required by COMPANY LAW.

unincorporated association An association of persons that is not a CORPORATION.

unissued share capital That part of a company's AUTHORIZED SHARE CAPITAL that has not been issued to the SHAREHOLDERS.

unitary taxation The taxation of corporate profits by a tax authority on the basis of a corporation's worldwide income rather than merely on its income in the country of the tax authority.

unitholder A person who owns an interest in a UNIT TRUST.

uniting of interests INTERNATIONAL ACCOUNTING STANDARDS term for MERGER ACCOUNTING (UK) or pooling of interests (USA).

unit of account The monetary unit in which transactions are recorded.

unit price The amount paid/received on the sale of one item of product.

units of production method of depreciation A method of DEPRECIATION that allocates the cost of an ASSET over its useful economic life in proportion to the units that it produces in a period.

unit trust A financial institution whose main aim is to use the money provided by its investors in order to own and manage profitably a PORTFOLIO of investments in other stocks and shares. Unlike INVESTMENT TRUSTS, unit trusts are 'open-ended funds' in that investors will be constantly contributing and with-drawing cash by buying and selling units in the trust. The equivalent US term is 'mutual fund'.

unlimited company A legal entity in the form of a company whose SHARE-HOLDERS do not have LIMITED LIABILITY for the DEBTS of the company. Such companies are fairly rare, but they do have the advantage that some provisions of COMPANY LAW do not apply, including the requirement to publish FINANCIAL STATEMENTS.

unlimited liability A LIABILITY for DEBTS that is not limited to capital already contributed by an investor to an organization but extends to the investor's personal assets.

unlisted company A company that has none of its securities listed on a recognized stock exchange.

unlisted securities Securities, such as SHARES or BONDS, that are not listed on a recognized stock exchange.

unlisted securities market A former second-tier market for SHARES in the UK.

unpaid cheque A cheque that has been returned by a bank to the payee because money cannot be transferred from the DRAWER, perhaps because of insufficient funds.

unpresented cheques Cheques properly completed by a DRAWER and in the possession of the payee but not yet deposited with a bank.

unquoted company Synonym for UNLISTED COMPANY.

unrealizable gains Apparent increases in the value of ASSETS that could not be turned into REALIZED PROFIT for various reasons.

unrealized gains Increases in the value of ASSETS that have not yet become REALIZED PROFIT because, for example, the assets have not been sold.

unrealized profit (*or* loss) *See* UNREALIZED GAINS. There is no international agreement about the relationship of the word 'PROFIT' to the word 'GAIN'.

unregistered company In the USA, a company not registered with the SECURITIES AND EXCHANGE COMMISSION.

unrestricted income funds In the context of a charity, amounts of money available for trustees to apply for the general purposes of the charity as set out in its governing document.

unsecured loan stock DEBT securities for which no ASSETS have been specifi-cally identified as those to be sold if the borrower cannot repay the loan.

upside potential Colloquial term for the possibilities of gain.

upstream transactions Sales (or other transactions) from an investee to an investor, e.g. sales from an ASSOCIATE to its investor or to other parts of the investor's group. Profits on such transactions are generally eliminated (unless REALIZED to third parties) wholly for group companies but proportionally for associates and JOINT VENTURES.

Urgent Issues Task Force (UITF) A sub-committee of the ACCOUNTING STANDARDS BOARD which is part of the standard setting machinery introduced in the UK in 1990. The UITF seeks consensuses on detailed areas of accounting issues which are already covered by law or ACCOUNTING STANDARDS. Abstracts of the consensuses are then published, and legal counsel's opinion is that companies generally have to comply with them in order for accounts to give a TRUE AND FAIR VIEW.

usage variance *See* DIRECT MATERIALS USAGE VARIANCE.

useful economic life The period over which a depreciable ASSET is expected to be used by an enterprise. Sometimes, the life is measured in terms of the number of production or similar units expected from the asset.

useful life *See* USEFUL ECONOMIC LIFE.

USM Abbreviation for the former Unlisted Securities Market in the UK.

V

value added The value of the sales of an enterprise for a period minus the cost of goods and services bought.

value added statements Supplementary FINANCIAL STATEMENTS prepared by a few companies that rearrange, and may add to, the information provided in a PROFIT AND LOSS ACCOUNT. The statement begins with a calculation of a measure of total output: sales, changes in STOCKS (inventories), other incomes, and FIXED ASSETS created by the business for its own use. Then the statements show deductions from this: amounts paid to suppliers of goods and services, amounts paid to employees, DEPRECIATION, INTEREST, taxation and DIVIDENDS.

value added tax A multi-stage sales tax paid by suppliers but borne, at least partly, by consumers in terms of higher prices. Each time that goods or services move from one supplier to the next, or to the final customer, the tax is levied. However, in general, the tax to be paid by a supplier to the tax authorities can be reduced by the tax suffered by the supplier in his capacity as a purchaser.
   Such a tax is in operation throughout the EU. In the UK, a few goods are EXEMPT SUPPLIES and others are ZERO-RATED SUPPLIES.

value driver A feature of a product (including a service) which improves its worth for the consumer and therefore the producer.

value for money audit An investigation of the efficiency of use of its resources by an organization whose main aim is not profit. The accountability of some such bodies is very poor; they may have no owners, multiple objectives and no clear measure of success.

value in use The PRESENT VALUE of the estimated future NET CASH FLOWS expected from an ASSET, including that from its disposal at the end of its useful life. The value in use is the normal value (under UK or INTERNATIONAL ACCOUNTING STANDARDS rules) to be substituted for the previous CARRYING VALUE when an asset suffers IMPAIRMENT. The rules require reduction to RECOVERABLE AMOUNT, which is the higher of value in use and selling price, but the former is generally higher because otherwise the asset would have been sold.

value to the business/owner *See* DEPRIVAL VALUE.

variable cost   Costs that vary in proportion to the volume of production. Normally, raw materials and direct labour input will be variable costs. Some OVERHEAD costs, that cannot be directly ascribed to particular units of production or processes may, nevertheless, still be variable with total production.

Variable costs are sometimes called MARGINAL COSTS by accountants. The opposite of these are fixed costs, that do not vary in the short term over the range of production levels being considered.

variable costing *See* MARGINAL COSTING.

variable cost ratio   The total of an organization's VARIABLE COSTS for a period divided by its sales.

variable overhead   INDIRECT COSTS that vary with the volume of operations. In addition to those related to production, such costs would include commission paid to salesmen.

variable production overheads   INDIRECT COSTS of production that vary with the volume of production. Such overheads might include indirect materials and indirect labour.

variable-rate note/stock   A DEBT security, including one issued by the government, on which the interest rate changes in line with market interest rates.

variance analysis   The investigation of the detailed operations of an organization by its management by means of a review of VARIANCES.

variances   In the context of COST ACCOUNTING, differences between actual amounts of COSTS, REVENUES, production levels, etc. for a period, and the plans for those amounts set down in BUDGETS.

VAT   Abbreviation for VALUE ADDED TAX.

VAT group   A set of related companies that have applied (successfully) to the UK Customs and Excise to be treated as a single taxpayer for the purposes of VALUE ADDED TAX.

vendor placing   An arrangement whereby a company issues some of its own shares in order to acquire a business, but where an agreement has already been made to allow the vendor of the business to turn those shares into cash by placing them with particular investors.

venture capital Finance supplied to a new business or to one being restructured, particularly in those cases where the risks and rewards are likely to be high.

venturer In the context of a JOINT VENTURE, one of the parties that has joint control over that venture.

verification In an AUDIT, a substantive test of the existence, ownership and valuation of an enterprise's ASSETS and LIABILITIES.

vertical equity In the context of taxation, the principle that a taxpayer in different circumstances should be taxed differently.

vertical form The presentation of a FINANCIAL STATEMENT by showing a column of figures rather than by showing all the DEBIT BALANCES together and then all the CREDIT BALANCES, as in horizontal form. For an example, *see* BALANCE SHEET FORMATS.

vertical integration The control by one organization of operations involving several stages of production. For example, in the oil industry, a group would be vertically integrated if it owned exploration, production and distribution companies.

vested employee benefits EMPLOYEE BENEFITS that are not conditional on future employment. It is normal for benefits to be vested by the time an employee retires.

VFM Abbreviation for VALUE FOR MONEY audit.

virement The permission to use an amount of underspending related to one heading of expenditure in order to cover overspending on another.

volume variances Differences in actual costs or revenues compared to budgeted amounts caused by the level of activity being different from that budgeted for.

voluntary arrangement An agreement between a company in financial difficulties and its CREDITORS whereby the latter accept reduced or delayed payments.

voluntary liquidation/winding-up *See* CREDITORS' VOLUNTARY LIQUIDATION and MEMBERS' VOLUNTARY LIQUIDATION.

voluntary registration In the context of the UK's system of VALUE ADDED TAX, registration by a trader for the purposes of the tax even though the trader has a lower turnover than would require registration. This would be done in order to reclaim tax on inputs.

vostro account An account (literally, from Italian, 'your' account) held by a bank on behalf of another.

votes (on account) In the context of UK government finances, amounts of money granted by Parliament in order to continue spending in a fiscal year before final authorization of the totals for the year.

voting rights The rights attached to VOTING SHARES.

voting shares Shares in a company that give the holders the right to vote at meetings of the SHAREHOLDERS, such as the ANNUAL GENERAL MEETING. Usually, ORDINARY SHARES have votes but PREFERENCE SHARES do not.

voucher A document, such as an invoice or a receipt note, that provides evidence of a transaction.

vouching One of the substantive tests in an AUDIT whereby documentary evidence is examined for its correctness and then traced to accounting records.

Vredeling Directive A proposal for a DIRECTIVE concerning the harmonization in the EU of employee information and consultation.

WACC Abbreviation for WEIGHTED AVERAGE COST OF CAPITAL.

wages The payments made by an organization to its employees who are paid weekly.

wages costs *See* LABOUR COSTS.

waiting time The period during which an operator of a machine is available but cannot work because of shortage of materials or because of repairs or re-tooling of the machine.

walk-through test An AUDIT procedure whereby sample transactions are followed in detail through an organization's ACCOUNTING SYSTEM.

Wall Street A colloquial term for the financial markets in New York City.

war loan A UK government bond, originally issued to finance wartime expenditures, that pays a fixed interest and has no REDEMPTION DATE.

warrant A contract that gives the right to purchase ORDINARY SHARES. This is an example of a FINANCIAL INSTRUMENT.

warranty A promise made by a supplier of goods and services to rectify any defects in them within a stated period after delivery. The supplier then has an OBLIGATION which should be recognized by setting up a PROVISION for repairs.

waste In the context of COST ACCOUNTING, discarded material that has no value.

wasting asset An ASSET with a limited useful economic life, particularly in cases where there is a non-renewable resource such as a gold mine.

watered stock *See* STOCK WATERING.

WDA Abbreviation for WRITING DOWN ALLOWANCE.

WDV Abbreviation for WRITTEN DOWN VALUE.

wealth tax A tax on a measure of the wealth of taxpayers at a date. For example, an annual wealth tax operated in France in the 1980s.

wear and tear The diminution in the useful economic life of a TANGIBLE FIXED ASSET as a result of physical use or damage. This is recognized for accounting purposes by DEPRECIATION.

weighted average cost method A method of determining the cost of STOCKS (inventories) that are on hand at the end of an accounting period, in those normal cases where it is either difficult or impossible to determine exactly which units remain. If a business buys and uses many types of raw materials, it may be hard to tell which units have been used and which remain, and thus difficult to calculate the exact costs. Thus, it is normal to make flow assumptions such as first in, first out (FIFO) or last in, first out (LIFO) or AVERAGE COST.

'Weighted average cost' values units used and units remaining at the average cost of the purchases, weighted by volume. The average may be worked out each time there is another purchase, or at pre-determined intervals.

weighted average cost of capital The average return that has to be paid by an organization on its finance (including shares and debt securities issued, as well as bank loans) weighted by the proportions that the various elements comprise in the TOTAL CAPITAL.

weighted average number of ordinary shares The number of ORDINARY SHARES at the beginning of a period, adjusted for shares cancelled, bought back or issued during the period multiplied by a time-weighting factor. This number is used as the denominator in the calculation of basic EARNINGS PER SHARE.

Wheat Report A report of 1972 in the USA that led to the establishment of the FINANCIAL ACCOUNTING STANDARDS BOARD.

wholesale price index A PRICE INDEX relating to the prices of goods bought by retail organizations from wholesalers.

wholly owned subsidiary A SUBSIDIARY all of whose shares (or other owner-ship interests) are owned by its parent. In this case there is no MINORITY INTEREST.

windfall gains and losses Gains and losses that were not expected by a person or an organization.

winding-up The legal procedures for the termination (or LIQUIDATION) of a company.

winding-up petition A request to a court of law for compulsory LIQUIDATION of a company.

window-dressing The manipulation of figures in FINANCIAL STATEMENTS in order to make them appear better (or perhaps worse) than they otherwise would be. *See*, also, CREATIVE ACCOUNTING.

WIP Abbreviation for WORK IN PROGRESS.

withholding tax A tax whereby a payer (of, for example, DIVIDENDS) deducts at source an amount of tax on behalf of the recipient. The payer is responsible for handing the tax to the tax authorities. The recipient of the net amount can reclaim the withholding tax under certain circumstances.

working capital The difference between CURRENT ASSETS and CURRENT LIABILITIES. This total is also known as NET CURRENT ASSETS, under which entry there are more details.

working capital ratio The CURRENT ASSETS of an enterprise expressed as a ratio or percentage of its CURRENT LIABILITIES.

work in process US term for WORK IN PROGRESS.

work in progress Partially manufactured goods, on their way from being raw materials to being finished products. Such goods are included in STOCKS (inventories) and are usually valued at the various costs involved in their production.

WP Abbreviation for *Wirtschaftsprüfer*, a German auditor.

write down As a verb, to reduce the recorded value of an ASSET.

write off As a noun, a one-off diminution in the recorded value of an ASSET, perhaps to zero. As a verb, the process of writing off.

writing down allowances Annual DEPRECIATION expenses of FIXED ASSETS for tax purposes in the UK. The allowances form part of the CAPITAL ALLOWANCE system.

written down value The amount at which ASSETS are usually held in BOOKS OF ACCOUNT and in FINANCIAL STATEMENTS. This is the HISTORICAL COST (or other revalued amount) less an allowance for wearing out or other reduction in useful life, called ACCUMULATED DEPRECIATION. The expression 'net book value' has the same meaning.
  The same expression may also be used for the amount of an asset that has not

yet been allowed as DEPRECIATION for tax purposes; this would be the 'tax written down value'.

wrongful trading UK legal term for the continuation of trading by a company when its directors should have concluded that it could not avoid insolvent liquidation.

X

XBRL Abbreviation for Extensible Business Reporting Language, a data sub-set for business reporting in the context of the internet and other electronic means of communication. It was launched in 2000.

Y

yankee bond A bond issued by a non-US company in a USA market.

Yellow Book Colloquial name for a book of instructions concerning the requirements for admission to, and continuing membership of, the official list of quoted companies on the London Stock Exchange. It was formerly issued by the Exchange but is now under the control of the FINANCIAL SERVICES AUTHORITY.

yield The earnings yield or the dividend yield of an ORDINARY SHARE is the latest annual EARNINGS or dividend as a proportion of the market price of the share.

yield curve The line on a graph which describes the relationship between the YIELD of a security and the number of years to its MATURITY DATE.

yield gap An excess of the YIELD on EQUITIES over the interest rate on government bonds.

yield to maturity *See* GROSS REDEMPTION YIELD.

YK Abbreviation for a Yugen Kaisha, a Japanese PRIVATE COMPANY.

ZBB Abbreviation for ZERO-BASE BUDGETING.

zero-base budgeting A system of budgeting originally developed in the USA for enterprises facing rapid changes in technology and sales. The system involves a more radical starting from scratch each year than the traditional system of BUDGET does. Managers must justify their activities as though they were being started for the first time.

zero coupon bond A contract requiring the repayment of its FACE VALUE to the holder by the issuer but with no interest payments. The bond would have been issued at a DISCOUNT of its face value.

zero-rated goods and services In the context of the UK's VALUE ADDED TAX, goods and services on which no tax is levied on sale.

zero-rated supplies In the context of the UK's VALUE ADDED TAX, inputs of goods and services on which no tax was levied but for which tax as inputs can be reclaimed by a REGISTERED TRADER who purchases them. For contrast, *see* EXEMPT SUPPLIES.

Z-score A measure of the likelihood of a business becoming insolvent. It uses a combination of commonly used RATIOS. The combination is calculated by studying the ratios of businesses that have failed in the past.